Bitch

Bitch is a bitch of a word. It used to be a straightforward insult, but today – after so many variations and efforts to reject or reclaim the word – it's not always entirely clear what it means. Bitch is a chameleon. There are good bitches and bad bitches; sexy bitches and psycho bitches; boss bitches and even perfect bitches. This eye-opening deep-dive account takes us on a journey spanning a millennium, from its humble beginnings as a word for a female dog through to its myriad meanings today, proving that sometimes you *can* teach an old dog new tricks. It traces the colorful history and ever-changing meaning of this powerful and controversial word, and its relevance within broader issues of feminism, gender, race, and sexuality. Despite centuries of censorship and attempts to ban it, bitch has stood the test of time. You may wonder: is the word going away anytime soon? Bitch, please.

Karen Stollznow is a linguist and the author of *On the Offensive*, *Missed Conceptions*, *God Bless America*, and *Language Myths, Mysteries, and Magic*. She writes for *Psychology Today*, *Scientific American Mind*, and *The Conversation* and has appeared on the History Channel's *History's Greatest Mysteries* and Netflix's *The Unexplained Files*. Karen is currently a researcher at Griffith University and a host of Monster Talk, an award-winning science-based podcast.

"A single word can tell us a lot. Karen Stollznow's fascinating exploration of the word bitch provides valuable insights on social history, language, gender, race, politics, and entertainment."

"Karen Stollznow provides a well-researched, scholarly, feminist, and often confronting discussion of the word bitch which has shape-shifted, chameleon-like, over many centuries. Drawing on an impressive array of sources from dictionaries and scholarly texts to social media, she analyses its use in many languages, contexts, and ethnic and social groups, as well as the issue of its attempted reclamation along with similar misogynist slurs."

"A sparkling and sophisticated examination of one of my favorite vulgarities – and one of the English language's most fraught. I had been waiting for a detailed, book-length account of this word, whose long life is more colorful and fascinating than I even knew. Karen Stollznow was the perfect person to write it!"

Bitch

The Journey of a Word

Karen Stollznow

Griffith University, Queensland

Shaftesbury Road, Cambridge CB2 8EA, United Kingdom

One Liberty Plaza, 20th Floor, New York, NY 10006, USA

477 Williamstown Road, Port Melbourne, VIC 3207, Australia

314–321, 3rd Floor, Plot 3, Splendor Forum, Jasola District Centre,
New Delhi – 110025, India

103 Penang Road, #05–06/07, Visioncrest Commercial, Singapore 238467

Cambridge University Press is part of Cambridge University Press & Assessment,
a department of the University of Cambridge.

We share the University's mission to contribute to society through the pursuit of
education, learning and research at the highest international levels of excellence.

www.cambridge.org
Information on this title: www.cambridge.org/9781009392327

DOI: 10.1017/9781009392358

First published 2024

A catalogue record for this publication is available from the British Library.

*A Cataloging-in-Publication data record for this book is available from the Library
of Congress*

ISBN 978-1-009-39232-7 Hardback
ISBN 978-1-009-39236-5 Paperback

Contents

Acknowledgments

I'd like to thank unnamed people who have, over the years, demonstrated to me the scope and power of this fascinating and complicated word.

With sincere thanks to Rebecca Taylor, Isabel Collins, and the amazing team at Cambridge University Press for believing in this quirky concept and for daring to publish this book with such an esteemed publisher. My heartfelt gratitude goes to Mark Newbrook and Karen Woodman for their insightful feedback and helpful suggestions.

Much love and appreciation to my son Blade, husband Matthew, mother Gaye, and various friends and family for their unwavering support and encouragement throughout the research and writing of this book.

Introduction

A Bitchin' Word

A few years ago, I was called a bitch in the workplace. It was during a meeting when I respectfully disagreed with a coworker, and then offered my own ideas and suggestions. In response, he shook his head and mumbled under his breath.

"Bitch."

"Excuse me?" I asked.

"Nothing," he replied meekly.

Everyone else in the room stared at the floor.

I was shocked. Then I felt hurt, which was quickly followed by anger. Calling someone a bitch in the workplace is unprofessional. It's unacceptable. It's sexist. No one else called him out on his behavior, so I did. To be honest, though, this wasn't the first time I'd been called a bitch, nor would it be the last. There are some who might say I'm the perfect person to write this book.

Most women don't like to openly admit to being called a bitch, because society has taught us that this is a shameful character flaw. But then I've never met a woman who *hasn't* been called a bitch, more times than she can remember, and for many different reasons. A woman is branded a bitch for being too assertive, too powerful, too opinionated, or too whatever. She might be a bitch if she's considered to be mean, spiteful, or a gossip. She's a bitch if she refuses to smile when a man orders her to do so, or when she rejects his sexual advances. (As we'll see, the word "bitch" often says more about the person using the word.) She is labeled a bitch when she's "hormonal," "emotional," or "difficult." Sometimes a woman is called a bitch – just because. Over time, bitch has become a generalized term of abuse for women. Sure, there are lots of slurs for men too, from *bastard* to *asshole*, but there's no true male counterpart for bitch.

When leveled against a woman, bitch is a mic drop.

And yet, bitch is so much more than a gendered slur. This is where things get confusing. Bitch is a linguistic chameleon. It began its life as a literal word for a female dog before it became an insult for women. But in a world of basic bitches and boss-ass bitches, perfect bitches and prison bitches, and both good bitches and bad bitches alike, what exactly does the word mean anymore? Bitch is a hardworking, multi-tasker that's happy to switch from noun to verb to adjective. It can jump from canine to human, and even from female to male. Bitch can shift from a person to a situation or a thing. To some, it's invariably an insult, to others, it's a compliment. Bitch is an eclectic word that can be friendly, funny, playful, or sexual. Bitch is used in a positive light when it's adopted by women to empower themselves. But it has a much darker side too; it can be misogynistic, abusive, and violent. Bitch is rich and complex in meaning, and with so many semantic nuances, we must always look to its context to understand what's intended.

Bitch is everywhere. It's found across the Anglosphere. It's also a near-universal word that's spoken the world over. Equivalents of bitch are found in numerous other cultures, countries, and languages, from Arabic to Zulu, and it's often borrowed straight from English. (For those who speak foreign languages, it can be fashionable to insult people in English.) Bitch is trendy, but it can also be taboo. Some people say it all the time, for others, the word never passes their lips. What's for certain is that everyone has a strong opinion about it. Bitch is a high-caliber word, and as with any weapon, it should be used with caution and awareness.

Bitch is a powerful word.

Some people think that the phonology of bitch, that is, the very sound of the word, lends itself to its potency. There's no doubt that it's a satisfying word to say, erupting with a furious *b*- followed by a forceful -*itch*, which is as close to spitting as you can get while still actually speaking. Author Charles Panati says, "Some theorize that its explosive sound made it ideal for firing off as a slur. The psycholinguistics of all curse words require that they carry maximal energy on minimal sound, a spiked waveform characteristic of consonants. This gives the word energetic punch, making it explosive."[1] While bitch might be fun to say, it can be much less fun to hear. The word can make the hair on the back of your neck bristle. Being called a bitch – in a bad way – is a personal affront, akin to having a glass of wine thrown in your face. It can mean many things, but it's first and foremost an insult. And it's been an insult for almost as long as it's been a word for a female dog.

Bitch is old; even older than fuck and cunt. In fact, the word has been around for over a millennium. For some historical background, bitch existed back in the Dark Ages; around the time the epic poem *Beowulf* was written, during the days of the Holy Roman Empire, and just before William of Normandy was crowned King of England following the Battle of Hastings. In terms of language, bitch dates back to Old English or Anglo-Saxon, the ancestor of the English we speak today.[2] Many words that existed back then didn't make it into our modern version of the language.[3] For example, Old English *ymbsittend* meant "near-sitting," or those people living nearby.[4] It makes an appearance in *Beowulf*, referring to Danish king Hrothgar's hostile neighbors, although *ymbsittend* is now a dead word. Some linguists estimate that as much as eighty percent of the vocabulary of Old English was lost by the end of the Middle English period, right around the time of the death of Chaucer. But bitch lived on, broadening from its original meaning to its many modern ones. Remarkably, bitch has stood the test of time. It's outlasted contemporaneous slurs for women like *shrew, scold, harlot,* and others favored by Shakespeare. Perhaps the enduring popularity of bitch lies in its capacity to continually shape-shift in order to keep up with the times.

The story of bitch is not as simple and straightforward as you might think. Its journey is full of unexpected twists and turns. Obviously, it's complicated and interesting enough to be the subject of an entire book. And within these pages, we explore bitch in all of its elaborate guises. We start by tracing its lineage. Bitch boasts an impressive pedigree. (Excuse the pun.) Over one thousand years ago, it was originally a word for a "female dog," and later, by extension, any female of the canine kind. As mentioned, bitch is an Old English word, but it was originally spelled as *bicce.* This spelling looks strange to modern eyes, although over time, the word morphed into the form that we recognize so well today. Bitch then expanded in meaning. It metamorphosed into a slur for a promiscuous or sensual woman, a metaphorical extension of the behavior of a "bitch in heat."[5] This grew into a generalized insult for women, and surprisingly, around the same time it also became an insult for men. Over the centuries, bitch branched off in many different directions. Most of these meanings have long since died out, some are still around today, while many more have been created along the way.

When people hear the word "bitch" nowadays, they don't usually think about dogs, unless they're breeders or veterinarians. Of all the meanings in the present day, the most salient sense of bitch is a "bad woman." She is frequently described as annoying, mean, malicious, difficult or, as the dictionaries put it so vaguely, she's an "unpleasant woman." Bitch has a long history of association with women, but the word's status as a gendered slur was solidified by the emergence of feminism. Bitch became a backlash against women seeking equal rights and opportunities in society. But in response, there was pushback when feminists committed an act of rebellion, righteously reclaiming the hateful word as an empowering one, much the same way that *queer* and *gay* have been reappropriated by the LGBTQ+

community. Taking control of the word and turning the definition on its head, bitch got a feminist facelift, becoming a descriptor for an ambitious, independent, and strong woman. But while this breed of bitch might be tough and confident, a man who's a bitch is instead seen as cowardly or weak. Bitch often reflects traditional gender roles. It's an emasculating insult; a man who's deemed to be a bitch is not doing a "good job" of being a man. On the other hand, son of a bitch is often an insult, but it can also conjure up images of badass cowboys, mavericks, and rebels, connoting courage, toughness, and grit.

Bitch has always had a split personality. It can pack a real punch. Alternatively, it can be benign, depending on its environment. In the distant past, bitch was invariably a vicious insult. Francis Grose, who wrote a dictionary of rude words in the eighteenth century, called bitch "The most offensive appellation that can be given to an English woman, even more provoking than that of whore."[6] Hundreds of years later, bitch was still viewed as profane, indecent, and obscene. Embroiled in controversy, bitch has been censored or entirely banned in books, newspapers, movies, on television, and in music. Today, much of the misogyny and violence associated with bitch is linked to rap and hip hop, although the word has its musical roots in jazz and the dirty blues. In recent decades, bitch has been unbleeped (for the most part) and it's gone on to become an everyday word. For some, bitch is so ubiquitous that it's simply lost its bite. Whatever we think of bitch, it's a prolific word that has spawned over one hundred different meanings and uses. These modern senses of the word, however, have not replaced older ones, because many continue to coexist in different contexts. And after all these years, bitch *still* means a female dog.

This book looks at the importance of bitch within broader issues of gender, sexism, and feminism. And it asks some nagging questions. Has bitch truly been rehabilitated to mean something wholly positive? Can bitch be reclaimed ... *should* it be? Does the word promote sexism and misogyny? We look at the ways that history has shaped bitch and how it's influenced by race, ethnicity, social class, age, gender, and sexuality. We explore real-life examples of usage from centuries-old manuscripts and literature through to modern-day use in music, television, and social media, in order to understand the historical and social factors that drive its use in its myriad contexts. We look at how bitch is used across the different varieties of English in Anglophone countries, and also how it has evolved in other cultures and languages. We delve into what bitch meant in the past, what it means today, and try to predict what it might mean in the future. We will discover why the word has had such an astonishing impact over the centuries. And we'll uncover what bitch reveals about our attitudes, beliefs, and values – and anything else this provocative word may say about us.

Join me for one bitching journey …

1

• • • • • •

A Female Dog

A bitch, as most people already know, is a female dog.

That *bitch* is a double entendre with an innocent literal meaning of "female dog" but also an offensive metaphorical one is often exploited for comedic value. In an episode of *The Simpsons*, ten-year-old Bart Simpson complains bitterly that his dog Santa's Little Helper has found a female companion: "He never wants to play fetch anymore, since his bitch moved in." Horrified, his mother Marge scolds him, "Don't ever say that word again!" Bart replies in his defense, "That's what she is. I looked it up." "Well," sniffs Marge, "I'm going to write the dictionary people and have that checked."[1]

If Marge Simpson looked up the word in the dictionary herself, she'd find that Bart is absolutely right: a bitch is defined there as "a female dog." This literal meaning is usually listed as the main sense of the word, but as we know from Marge's reaction, it's not the most common one. But it's also the very *first* use of the word. Although few people know just how far back this original meaning goes. As a trendy word we hear (and say) all the time, it might be tempting to guess that it isn't very old. But if we look up its etymology, that is the origins of the word, we discover that bitch meaning "a female dog" has a far longer pedigree that goes back over *one thousand years*. According to the *Oxford English Dictionary*, this earliest use dates to around 1000 CE,[2] although in those days the word didn't quite look the same. Bitch is an Old English word that was inherited from Germanic. Old English, or Anglo-Saxon, was the spoken and written language at the time (although most people couldn't read or write), and the word bitch would've been unrecognizable to modern readers, spelled as it was then as *bicce* and pronounced "bitch-eh."

To tell the story of bitch let's delve into the word's colorful and ever-changing history.

Where Did Bitch Come From?

To understand the origins of a word we need to consider its use in the past, which can be traced by looking at very old documents. The *Oxford English Dictionary*, which prides itself on being the definitive record of the English language, traces the earliest recorded use of bitch to the Pharmacopoeia *Medicina de Quadrupedibus*. The title translates to "Medicines from four-footed creatures," and this was a book of traditional remedies using bits and pieces of animals. The text was written in Latin and translated into Old English in the eleventh century. In this medieval manuscript there are two examples of bitch, meaning a female dog. The first reference was a cure for teething pains using "bitch's milk": *Biccean meolc gif ðu gelome cilda toðreoman mid smyrest & æthrinest, butan sare hy wexað.*[3] This translates to "If you frequently smear and touch a child's gums with bitch's milk, the teeth grow without pain." In folk medicine of the time, dogs were valued for the medicinal and magical properties that their body parts were thought to have. Apparently, "bitch's urine" had therapeutic benefits too, as a treatment for corns and warts: *Wearras & weartan onweg to donne, nim wulle & wæt mid biccean hlonde, wrið on þa weartan & on þa wearras.* This means "To do away with corns and warts, take wool and wet it with bitch's urine, bind it to the warts and corns."

The first thing that leaps out at us is that these examples look like they're written in a foreign language. Old English, or Anglo-Saxon, is a West Germanic language, which the Angles and Saxons brought with them from northern Germany and southern Denmark when they settled in Britain in the fifth century. As mentioned in the introduction, the epic poem *Beowulf* was penned in Old English, by an anonymous scribe. Old English was used around 450–1150, and it is the ancestor of the English language we know today, although the two bear little resemblance. As we've seen, Old English bitch was usually written as *bicce*, while we occasionally see examples of it spelled *bicge*. Hundreds of years later, when Old English had evolved into what we now call Middle English, the various spellings of bitch that were in use still look strange to modern eyes. Middle English was written and spoken between 1100 and 1500 or thereabouts, and for some historical context, it was the language Geoffrey Chaucer used to pen *Canterbury Tales*. An example of a different spelling of bitch from this era can be found in the *Coventry Leet Book*, which references a fifteenth-century ordinance that prohibited owners from allowing their "byches" to roam the streets, to prevent the dogs from defecating or fornicating in public. It says, *þat no man hold no grett houndes ne byches goyng in the hyghe way.*[4] Those who broke this rule were fined a hefty sum of forty pence for every violation.

The above quotes are among the earliest *recorded* occurrences of bitch, or bicce and byche as the case may be, which were discovered in surviving documents written in English, although the word's oral history probably goes back even further. Possible cognates (that is, relatives) of bitch from other languages may go back further still. The *Oxford English Dictionary* says that bitch is a cognate with Old Icelandic *bikkja*, Faroese *bikkja*, Old Swedish *bikia*, and Old Danish *bikke*, which all meant "a female dog" but are of unknown origin. Some sources say that the word derives from Lapp *pittja*, although to add to the confusion, others say the opposite is equally possible. Etymology requires a lot of detective work, but it's an inexact science, and word origins are the subject of much heated debate. Other contenders for the origins of bitch include Latin *bestia* "beast," German *Petze* "female dog," and French *biche*, from Old French *bisse* meaning "female deer"; and at least these words seem to resemble bitch. But there are many stranger theories out there too. Some people think that bitch has nothing at all to do with a female dog. They say that it comes from Middle High German *bicken*, meaning to pick or peck, which is probably imitative of the noises made by birds picking up food with their beaks. Early etymologies attempted to derive bitch from *bite* or *bicker*. It has been suggested that the word has Hebrew origins. It's alternatively claimed that bitch evolved from the Hindi word *bhang* that means cannabis. Others have even linked bitch to Sanskrit *bhaga*, meaning female genitals. As tempting as these more salacious theories are, none of them are very likely.

Over the centuries, bitch underwent changes in pronunciation and spelling. In various manuscripts and books like those we've looked at so far, bitch is found written in many different ways, from *bycce* in early Middle English through to *becch*, *bichche*, *bych*, and *bytche* in later versions of the language. Scottish had some additional variations, such as *beiche* and *beitch*. These variants exist because our spelling system hadn't yet been standardized. The arrival of the printing press, introduced to England by William Caxton in the fifteenth century, froze English spelling in time (for the most part). And so it wasn't until the 1600s that we finally had our current spelling of bitch, sometimes with an -e tacked onto the end of the word. We more readily recognize examples from this era, such as this one from a book of vulgar poetry: "Nor putting Pigs t' a Bitch to nurse; To turn 'em into Mungrel-Curs."[5] (At this time it was trendy to capitalize nouns, a convention that is retained in modern German.) The spelling of bitch has mostly stayed the same ever since, although when it comes to language, nothing is ever set in stone, as we can see with modern-day expressive variants like *biatch* and *biznatch*.

Bitch changed in the way it sounded and looked, while, more importantly to its story, the word also changed in meaning. As time went by, bitch evolved to mean much more than just a female dog. Its meaning extended to also refer to other female, four-legged, furry canines, including foxes and wolves. These animals have more user-friendly synonyms too, like *vixen*, *wolfess* or *she-wolf* respectively. Unlike bitch, these names now have positive connotations for female humans, referring to sexy or sensual women. In the past, dog also had the comparable female terms *she-dog* and *doggess*, with parallels to gender-specific nouns like actor and actress. (These literal senses are now archaic, although the words are still around as insults.) It is lesser known that bitch later referred to other carnivorous mammals too, including female bears, seals, otters, and even ferrets. It was not uncommon to have different words for the male and female of different species and many of these pairings are still in use today. Cattle are bulls and cows, horses are stallions and mares, and pigs are boars and sows. (It doesn't escape our attention that many names for the female animals double as insults for women.) When it comes to dogs, the name for the male of the species is unmarked; a male dog is simply called a dog, unless we're a breeder talking about sires and studs. (It doesn't escape our attention that these names for male dogs double as compliments for men.) Whereas the female of the species received an entirely different name: a bitch.

As many readers know, this original and literal sense of bitch as "the female of the canine kind" still exists today as a relic of the past, especially in the specialized contexts of zoology, veterinarian science, and breeding. As a technical term, you might overhear the phrase "bitch spay" when you take your dog to the vet, while a dog breeder might talk about a "breeding bitch." Some specialists might be aware the term is controversial and favor more euphemistic alternatives like lady, girl, the puppy's mother ... or just a female dog. The clinical sense of bitch has fallen out of fashion with the general public, while some aren't familiar with the literal term at all, like Marge Simpson. To their ears, the word may sound like an insult, implying that the dog in question is not a pleasant dog. And just like Marge, not everyone feels comfortable saying or hearing the word, even in this benign context.

Why is this so? Because when most people hear this word, they don't usually think about its inoffensive sense; they tend to think about its *offensive* one. Hundreds of years ago, bitch expanded from just meaning a female dog to becoming an insult for a person too, and especially a woman. (Interestingly, Old Icelandic *bikkja* was also used as a slur.[6]) This kind of semantic change happens a lot in language. New words appear, old words disappear, meanings evolve, and different dimensions of meanings emerge. Language can be unpredictable. But this changeability of the meaning of words is a gradual process. It happens very slowly, so gradually that we often don't notice it in real time. As an example, *girl* originally referred to a child of either sex during the Middle Ages. (Back then it was spelled as *gyrle*.) Over many centuries the word narrowed to mean less than it once did, to refer to a female girl specifically. Bitch went the other way, in which it broadened to mean much more than it once did. Most sources place the appearance of the insult at the fourteenth or fifteenth century; although there is some evidence to show that this shift occurred even earlier than that. (We'll discover that changes in language usually happen much earlier than we might think.) Among the many words for animals that double as insults, *bitch* and its more general meaning, *dog*, have the longest history of them all.

Man's Best Friend

We can't talk about bitch without also talking about dog. Long before *bitch* became an insult, *dog* was already an insult. The practice of referring to women as dogs is much older than the English language; it can be traced back as far as Ancient Greece and Rome. In Act 5 of *Curculio*, the Roman dramatist Plautus describes a heated argument between a man and a woman over a ring in which she ends up being called a dog: *ut eum eriperet, manum arripuit mordicus. vix foras me abripui atque effugi. apage istanc caniculam*; "To get it away from me, she seized my hand with her teeth. With difficulty I fled out of doors and escaped. Away with this dog of yours."[7] By biting the man, the woman was clearly behaving like a dog. The insult was also associated with lewdness. In Homer's *The Odyssey*, Helen of Troy regrets committing adultery, which sparked the Trojan War. Regarded as the most beautiful woman in the world, she berates herself as "dog-faced": ὅτ' ἐμεῖο κυνώπιδος εἴνεκ' Ἀχαιοὶ ἤλθεθ' ὑπὸ Τροίην, πόλεμον θρασὺν ὁρμαίνοντες; "... when the Achaeans went down to Troy on account of dog-faced me, raising up their audacious war."[8] This slur also played on Ancient Greek associations between women and dogs; both were expected to be loyal and obedient.

Men were also insulted as dogs in ancient societies; however, the implications were a little different. Dog usually implied that a woman was disobedient, immodest, or shameless, but when aimed at a man, dog referred to human vices such as greed, arrogance, and cowardice. In Homer's epic poem *The Iliad*, the demi-god Achilles implies that Agamemnon is fainthearted when he insults him as: οἰνοβαρές, κυνὸς ὄμματ' ἔχων, κραδίην δ' ἐλάφοιο; "Wine-sod! Dog-eyes! You have the heart of a deer!"[9] This sense of a dog as a wretched, debased, or cowardly man made its way into English too. Shakespeare had a talent for put-downs, and his numerous animal-related insults included references to toads, worms, weasels, and dogs. He mentions dogs hundreds of times in his many works, which were often portrayed as "thievish," "mangy," "unmanner'd," and "cowardly." In *Henry VI: Part One*, dog is wielded to mean lacking in courage when Charles, the King of France, complains about his soldiers, "What men haue I? Dogges, Cowards, Dastards."[10] (A *dastard* was a kind of coward who was also dishonorable or despicable. It's a term preserved in the name of Dick Dastardly, the super-villain in the Hanna-Barbera cartoon.) This use of dog as a coward has mostly dropped out of usage, although a few years ago when ISIS founder Abu Bakr al-Baghdadi died in a raid by US commandos, then President Donald Trump remarked, "He died like a dog. He died like a coward" and referred to the leader's men as "frightened puppies."[11] Nowadays, *pussy* has overtaken dog as the popular insult for a man who is considered to be weak or cowardly.

There are many positive stereotypes about dogs. We talk about them as being faithful, loyal, and obedient pets; they are man's best friend. But just like Shakespeare's criticisms of dogs, there are many negative stereotypes about them too. Bad dogs might be seen as aggressive, dirty, sly, or oversexed. When applied toward people, "dog" usually had negative connotations with a wide range of offensive meanings. By the twelfth century, a dog, then called a *hund* ("hound") in early English, also referred contemptuously to a man who was "a mean, worthless fellow, a currish, sneaking scoundrel."[12] A *cur* was a type of dog once used by cattle drovers in England; the breed is now extinct, and the term came to mean a ferocious dog or a mongrel. It also meant a man who was mean or cowardly. Over time, dog has become somewhat less offensive when applied to a man. By the 1600s, dog was often a playful, affectionate term for a mischievous, rakish fellow who had sex with lots of women. This evolved to our modern sense of a dog as a man with a reputation for chasing women, a playboy, or a player. In modern African American Vernacular English, a *dawg* is a friendly term akin to "brother" or "dude" that's used between boys and men. But for women, dog became no less offensive over time. While dog once referred to a disloyal woman with loose sexual morals, by the early 1900s it grew to mean an unattractive girl or woman.

Like bitch, dog underwent semantic change in English too. In Old English, *hund* was the everyday term for a canine. At that time, *docga* was a rare name for a powerful, fierce type of dog.[13] We only have one example of its use that comes from a Latin to English translation, and the word's origin and history remain one of the greatest mysteries of English etymology. (We might also remember that *bicge* was a rare spelling of bitch, while we can guess the modern descendants of other Old English words like *frocga* and *stacga*.) By Middle English the spelling became *dogge* or *dog* (or even *doge* and *doke*) and the word had broadened in meaning to be the all-purpose name for *any* type of dog. It was even picked up by other languages, including Danish *dogge* and German *Dogge*. Dog forced out *hund*, which narrowed in scope, and now only refers to a dog that's used for hunting. Many of these hunting breeds still have the word in their name, like bloodhounds; a large scent hound originally bred for hunting deer, wild boar, and even used for tracking people. We could say that all hounds are dogs, but not all dogs are hounds. (Case in point: Chihuahuas aren't hounds.) Hundreds of years ago there was also a specific term for a female hound used for hunting, a *brach*, which was borrowed from French. And yes, brach was used as an insult too. In *Wuthering Heights*, the cruel and wicked Heathcliff marries Isabella Linton as an act of revenge, and after killing her pet dog out of spite, he says, "Now, was it not the depth of absurdity—of genuine idiocy—for that pitiful, slavish, mean-minded brach to dream that I could love her?"[14]

Another animal insult that was contemporaneous with dog and bitch was *shrew*. A shrew was originally a name for a small, mole-like mammal that looked like a mouse, as suggested by the Old English term *screawa* "shrew-mouse"[15] (but they are not actually rodents). By the 1300s, shrew became an insult for a spiteful man or woman. The animal itself was held in superstitious dread, because it was thought that it had a venomous bite deadly to humans (which is not true, although they can kill frogs, mice, and other small creatures). Over the centuries, the slur narrowed to refer to women specifically. Shakespeare's *Taming of the Shrew* is a comedy about the foul-tempered, sharp-tongued Kate, who is the "shrew." She marries Petruchio, who behaves like a shrew himself to give her a dose of her own medicine. Using reverse psychology on Kate has the effect of reforming her or "taming the shrew." In Samuel Johnson's seminal *Dictionary of the English Language* he defined a shrew as a "peevish, malignant, clamorous, spiteful, vexatious, turbulent woman."[16] As a term for an argumentative, nagging woman, shrew is similar to the older use of *scold* as a noun, which was an insult for an angry woman. *Shrew* has survived as an insult for a bad-tempered woman, especially an older one, but it sounds a bit old-fashioned today. Shrew, dog, and bitch were once on a par with each other as insults for women, although the latter two have clearly won out in the popularity stakes.

A Promiscuous Woman

When bitch originally shifted in meaning from "female dog" to a slur, it didn't mean an unpleasant woman. Instead, a bitch was a promiscuous woman, just like the earlier meaning of "dog" when used toward a woman. A twelfth-century Catholic sermon written by the monk Aelfric railed against such lewd women: *ða fulan forliras, and ða fulan horan and byccan ðe acwellað heora cild ær þan ðe hit cuð beo mannum*; "The foul fornicators and the foul whores and bitches who kill their children before they can become adults."[17] This suggests that when bitch was first used against women in the English language it was comparable to *prostitute*. This use was still around hundreds of years later in 1610 when the poem "Westminster Whore" describes a woman as: "A damned lascivious bitch who fucks for halfe a crown."[18] In those days, bitch showed disapproval of a woman's sexual behavior. It was a metaphor that compared her to a female dog in its estrous cycle, that is, a "bitch in heat." (In terms of reproductive behavior, female dogs may show a preference for certain mates or have multiple mating partners, but technically, they are not promiscuous. Conversely, male dogs are sexually active year-round.[19]) Bitch was also an allusion to the fact that female dogs have so many puppies. (In another dog/cat analogy, the modern term *alley cat* refers to a prostitute or promiscuous woman.) In the past, bitch was also comparable to modern-day *slut*. In William Percy's play *The cuck-queanes and cuckolds errants*, the character Pearle berates his wife for losing a precious silver bowl when he abuses her as: "Hore, Hare, Harlot, Bitch, Fellatrice, Witch, Bawde, Ribaud, Tribade."[20] Among this list of archaic epithets, *fellatrice* was a woman who performed fellatio, *tribade* was a term for a lesbian, while here in this older sense, *bitch* meant slut.

So if bitch used to mean slut, what did slut mean? During the days of Middle English, slut coexisted with bitch, but it didn't mean a sexually promiscuous woman like it does today. Instead, *slutte* meant "a dirty, untidy, or slovenly woman."[21] Slut was related to *slattern*, an insult for a woman who was disheveled in her dress or who kept an untidy household. We find an early example of slut in the fourteenth century when Geoffrey Chaucer used the word in the Prologue to the "Canon Yeoman's Tale": "Why is the lord so sluttish, I thee pray."[22] That's right; by its context we can tell that Chaucer was using the word about a *man*, not a woman. But he wasn't referring to sex at all; he was talking about the lord's messy appearance, which was at odds with his noble social status. Later use of slut appears almost exclusively with women. Like bitch, slut has shape-shifted a lot, and by the fifteenth century it referred to a kitchen maid who did menial work, such as emptying the chamber pots. (She was often called a "drudge" too, from which we get the word *drudgery*, meaning work that is hard or boring.) The famous diarist Samuel Pepys meant this sense of slut when he wrote enthusiastically about his new maidservant: "Our little girl Susan is a most admirable slut, and pleases us mightily."[23] Over time, slut shifted again to mean a woman of low or loose character, although the sexual aspect wasn't entirely clear yet. By the 1700s, Dr. Johnson defined a slut as "a dirty woman" in its literal, not sexual, sense and he noted the word was only "of slight contempt"[24] (to him anyway). Surprisingly, it wasn't until the twentieth century that slut developed its modern meaning, condemning a woman who has many sexual partners. (We'll talk some more about this word soon.)

In the days when a bitch was a promiscuous woman, *bitchery* referred to prostitution. *A Caveat for Common Cursetors* estimates that a particular prostitute "would weekly be worth six or seven shillings with her begging and bitchery."[25] This use comes from a pamphlet that aimed to reveal the tricks that vagabonds (and prostitutes) used to deceive and steal money from gullible victims, otherwise known as "gulls." At the time, to go *bitching* meant to have sexual intercourse, especially with a prostitute, while a *bitch hunter* was a lecher, a man who went in pursuit of women for sex. The use of bitch meaning a sex worker was most prevalent in England, although it crossed the pond to the United States too. An 1830 issue of New York's *The Owl* reported the story of a man who "frequents a certain house in Orange Street, occupied by several black and white bitches. He must be void of shame and decency."[26] In some instances, bitch was used interchangeably with whore, harlot, or strumpet.

Over the centuries, bitch lost its explicitly sexual connotations, although this sense has never entirely gone away. In fact, it has experienced a resurgence, especially in modern African American Vernacular English. *Green's Dictionary of Slang* defines "bitch" as "a prostitute" and this use is still common in some parts of the US.[27] In an episode of *Chappelle's Show*, Wayne Brady plays a pimp who introduces his prostitutes to Dave Chappelle with "Hoes, Dave. Dave, Hoes." Dave attempts politeness with his incongruous reply, "Good evening, bitches."[28] This use of bitch as whore or hooker has spawned other phrases too. In American pimp culture, a *bottom bitch* is a sex worker who is at the top of the hierarchy of those working for a particular pimp, and who wields power and status over the other women. Bitch meaning whore is occasionally used for men too, especially in a humorous way. In the movie *Deuce Bigalow: Male Gigolo*, Deuce's pimp calls him a "man-whore" and a "he-bitch."[29]

An Unpleasant Woman

Over time, bitch developed the derogatory meaning of an "unpleasant woman" that we're most familiar with today. As we've seen, the original insult disapproved of a woman's sexuality, while later on it focused on her personality. It's difficult to know just when this meaning first appeared in use. It was evident in manuscripts and books by the 1500s, but it probably emerged in speech much earlier still. One early written example comes from the comedy *Gammer Gurton's Needle*. In this story, alehouse owner Dame Chat has been accused of stealing Dame Gurton's sewing needle. In turn, Dame Chat accuses Dame Gurton of stealing her rooster, then beckons her with, "Come out, thou hungry nedy bytche."[30] Bitch had become a catchall insult for a disliked woman, who was described variously as disagreeable, despicable, annoying, nagging, spiteful, or malicious; especially in the eyes of a man. For example, in the eighteenth-century satire *Law Is a Bottomless Pit*, the character John Bull (who was an English version of Uncle Sam) has a wife who enjoys the finer things in life, and she is slammed as "an extravagant Bitch."[31] It was around this time that the insult became increasingly taboo. References to the word were often censored, even in the tabloids that usually enjoyed a bit of smut. In the scandal sheet *The Female Tatler*, the *TMZ* of its day, the author recounts a conversation in which it was said to her, "Mrs Crackenthorpe. You are a dirty, confounded, impudent B—ch of a Harridan."[32] A *harridan* was yet another word for an unpleasant woman, especially an older one who was strict and bossy, although, unlike bitch, apparently it wasn't offensive enough to be censored.

By 1785, bitch was considered to be so improper that Captain Francis Grose, who compiled a book of obscene slang, declared the slur to be "the most offensive appellation that can be given to an English woman—even more provoking than that of whore."[33] Grose's *Classical Dictionary of the Vulgar Tongue* is the perfect dictionary for those who like to look up rude words. In fact, the book included some 9,000 words that had been omitted by Dr. Johnson in his famous *Dictionary of the English Language*, some of which the lexicographer denounced as "low bad words." Johnson *did* include bitch in his dictionary, possibly with the intention of recording its innocuous literal sense, which Grose described as "A she dog or doggess." Johnson defined a bitch as: "1. The female of the canine kind; as the wolf, the dog, the fox, the otter. 2. A name of reproach for a woman."[34] It may also have been the case that Johnson hadn't been exposed to many of the "vulgar" words faithfully recorded by Grose. Grose was a committed field researcher, along with his companion Tom Cocking, and the pair made regular trips into the slums, streets, docks, and drinking dens of London to pick up the latest slang terms. There they discovered St. Giles' Greek, a secret language spoken by beggars and thieves. And it was in this part of town that they encountered the street riposte "I may be a whore, but can't be a bitch," which was roughly equivalent to the modern, "I may be drunk, but you're ugly."[35] At this point in time it was better to be a prostitute, who was at least paid for her services, than it was to be a bitch.

Despite being considered a vulgar word in polite company, bitch survived, presumably through the efforts of enough vulgar people.

In the nineteenth century and beyond, a myriad of other meanings sprang to life, which we will explore throughout this book. Bitch expanded from just a noun to also being used as a verb and adjective. In the past, the word appeared in a few phrases too, but surprisingly, not all of them were offensive. Grose also noted the term to *stand bitch*, which simply meant "to make tea, or do the honours of the tea-table." This task wasn't always servile work but could be an honor that was bestowed upon an esteemed guest. This use is preserved in the Irish memoir *A Real Paddy*, "At breakfast the doctor insisted upon Sally standing bitch in his place, and making tea, to which she agreed and did the honours of the table handsomely."[36]

Standing bitch evolved into the quaint phrase "to bitch the pot," that is, to preside as hostess at a tea party. Hosting a tea party in the 1800s was a big deal for ladies; it was an important domestic ritual because they were excluded from coffeehouses. The Starbucks of their day, coffeehouses were places where elite gentlemen congregated to drink coffee, hold conversations, and conduct business, without women around. Tea was the preferred beverage of a lady. It was made fashionable among aristocratic women and it defined respectability. In terms of alcoholic beverages, champagne was considered to be an appropriate drink for women. Described as "pretty," "elegant," and "sparkling," champagne reflected views of femininity and feminine allure. And if we remember that a bitch was once a prostitute, *bitch's wine* was an indelicate name for champagne, a popular drink among sex workers and their clients in Victorian brothels, because of its association with wealth and prestige.

At this time, *to bitch* didn't always have the same meaning that it does nowadays, it might just mean to make a pot of tea, while a *bitch party* was a tea party. The pastime was associated with women and gossip, and tea became known as "chatter broth" and "scandal broth." This is the forerunner of the social knitting groups of today called "Stitch 'n' Bitch," where people, mainly women, meet to knit, stitch, and talk. (Those who choose to crochet instead are called "happy hookers.") The phrase "to bitch the pot" had some staying power, lasting as it did well into Victorian times. Part of its enduring popularity may lie with the fact that it was co-opted by university students, who were all male in those days. Women weren't allowed to attend tertiary institutions back then, much like the coffeehouses. Among a tea-drinking party of men one lucky man might be invited to be "old bitch," that is, the one to brew the tea. It was asked, "Who'll bitch the pot?" meaning who will pour out the tea? And if the gentleman did so gracefully, he was praised as an "excellent bitch." Although these phrases could be applied to both women and men, at their core there was gender bias because the bitch referred to a person catering to the needs of others, like a woman 'should' do, and performing what was perceived as "a female role." And we'll delve into gender issues a lot more soon.

An Unpleasant Man

The use of bitch toward men is not exclusively modern. While bitch has been invoked to insult women throughout history, it has also long been used as a derogatory term for men, just like *dog*. In fact, bitch has probably been used against men for as long as it's been used against women. One of the earliest recorded examples of a man being called a bitch comes from the Chester Mystery Plays, a series of productions based on Bible stories that were performed in the town of Chester, England, during the fifteenth century. (In more recent decades, this tradition has been revived and these plays are now staged every five years.)*The Slaughter of the Innocents* enacts the Massacre of the Holy Innocents, the nativity narrative of the Gospel of Matthew in which King Herod of Judea sends his soldiers to Bethlehem to execute all of the baby boys in an attempt to kill the newborn Jesus Christ. In one scene, a mother refuses to give up her infant son to a soldier. In his anger he insults her as a "quean." The forerunner of *queen*, this was yet another word for a prostitute, although in Old English it simply meant "woman" or "wife." In reply to the soldier, the mother retaliates bravely with, "Whom callest thou quean, scabd bitch?"[37] "Scabbed" was a reference to the pus-oozing sores, scabs, and scars from syphilis, known as "the pox," which was rampant during the Middle Ages.

Another early example of a male bitch that also comes from the fifteenth century is in the children's fairy tale *The Friar and The Boy*. In this story, the merry-hearted and mischievous Jack is accused of sorcery by his wicked stepmother: *Be God he ys a schrewd byche, In fayth, y trow, he be a Wyche.*[38] This meant "By God, he is a shrewd bitch. In faith, I know, he is a witch." (Presumably, she wanted to get rid of him. "Witch" was a dangerous accusation during the days of witch hunts and witch trials.) As we can see, calling a man or boy a bitch was a harsh insult in Middle English. This use probably dates back even further in spoken language. And as we know, it has survived to modern times. Just like today, to call a man a bitch in the past was to insult him by comparing him to a "bad" kind of woman, like the wicked stepmother branding her stepson a "witch." In the Middle Ages, *witch* was a common insult for a disagreeable older woman, along with the related slur *crone*. Alternatively, *white witch* and *crone* were names for wise women, cunning folk, and healers, who were typically older women. In more recent decades, witch and crone have been somewhat reclaimed in feminism and neo-paganism as symbols of mature female wisdom and power.

In early use toward men, bitch could also have connotations of promiscuity, just like it could for women. In 1542, the Catholic critic Henry Brinklow referred to a group of bishops as being: *as chast as a sawt bytch*, that is, "as pure as a randy bitch."[39] This book was written during the Reformation, when Catholic leaders were accused of various corruptions, particularly when it came to failing to uphold their vows of chastity. Brinklow likened these holy men to whores, and in applying feminine words to men, their very femaleness was part of the insult. Older sexual slang terms labeled promiscuous women in negative terms, as bitches, harlots, or whores, whereas promiscuous men were often portrayed in a more positive light as swaggering, romantic characters from history or novels, Casanovas, Lotharios, or Don Juans, depicting them as sexual conquerors and heroes. Calling a man a bitch, a derogatory word for a woman, therefore questioned his manhood and masculinity.

When used toward men, bitch was an insult that could mean many different things, but it always referred back to women in a negative way. Bitch could mean that the man was weak, timid, or delicate, just like a woman. In the 1840 novel *Border Beagles*, Mr. Bull offers his companions a swig of his strong peach brandy, "'Here, you b—hes,' he cried aloud —'here's stuff enough, and sorts enough, if your stomachs not too swingy proud for an honest liquor.'"[40] A male bitch might be seen as effeminate and girly, just like a woman. In the 1853 novel *Mr. Sponge's Sporting Tour*, Jack Spraggon and his sidekick Lord Scamperdale find a letter written on fancy "thick cream-laid" stationery paper: "'That must be from a woman,' observed Jack, squinting ardently at the writing. 'Not far wrong,' replied his lordship. 'From a bitch of a fellow, at all events.'"[41] Alternatively, a man who's a bitch might be criticized as domineering and bossy, just like a woman. In the 1797 bawdy *Burlesque Homer* appears the line, "That bullying, noisy, scolding bitch, Call'd Diomede."[42] The King of Argos and a hero in Greek mythology, Diomedes is here reduced to being an overbearing, nagging woman.

Bitch could compare a man to an unpleasant woman, while it could also insult a man by way of his beloved mother. The modern *son of a bitch* goes all the way back to Middle English where it was written as *biche-sone*, meaning "bitch's son." (Old Icelandic also had the comparable insult *bikkju-sonr*.) The earliest example is found in the tale of *Arthur & Merlin* written around the year 1330: *Abide þou þef malicious! Biche-sone þou drawest amis!* This meant "Stop you wicked thief! You son of a bitch, you draw wrongly!"[43] Son of a bitch, like *bastard*, while applied to a man ultimately insults a characteristic of a man's mother, not the man himself. By implication, it is the woman who is "the bitch." A related phrase was *of bicces lines*, meaning "of the lineage of bitches," that insulted a man's parentage, in particular, his mother and female relatives. To find the earliest example of son of a bitch in its current form we return to master insulter Shakespeare, who wielded the phrase in *King Lear*. In the play, the Earl of Kent attacks Oswald for his poor treatment of Lear and calls him "nothing but the composition of a knave, beggar, coward, pandar, and the son and heir of a mongrel bitch."[44] Shakespeare also liked using the phrases *whoreson* and *bitchwolf's son*. These were all scathing insults at the time. They were the kind of crass and vulgar language that playwrights and actors heard used in the taverns of London's underbelly; that Francis Grose would eventually collect over a century later.

But bad-mannered commoners weren't the only ones to use *son of a bitch*; even some noblemen used it, at least implicitly. In Lord Byron's *Don Juan*, the poet writes, "Like lap-dogs, the least civil sons of b-----s."[45] But at least Byron (or his publisher) had the decency to censor the offending word. Dr. Johnson, who we might remember didn't like "bad words," alluded to the phrase when he recounted an anecdote to his friend the diarist Hester Thrale: "I did not respect my mother, though I loved her; and one day, when in anger she called me a puppy, I asked her if she knew what they called a puppy's mother."[46] *Son of a bitch* finally made its way to the US in the late 1700s, where in the lusty and crude novel *The Adventures of Jonathan Corncob*, the hero says to Mr. Squeeze, "Why I beg your pardon, but you are a Judas, and a d----d son of a b----."[47] America would truly embrace the phrase as its own and there's a lot more to unpack with modern-day *son of a bitch*, so we'll return to it later on.

Further to the idea that a bitch was an effeminate man, the insult might also question his sexuality. While bitch gained currency in the twentieth century as an inclusive term inside the gay community, it was still a strong slur outside of the group (which will be discussed in future chapters). Some sources suggest that bitch meaning a "homosexual man" dates back to the eighteenth century. In 1726, the proceedings of the Old Bailey, London's central criminal court, show that Thomas Wright was charged for committing sexual offenses with Thomas Newton at a Molly House, a secret meeting place for men in London's gay subculture. On the night in question, a group of men were "dancing in obscene Postures," "Singing baudy Songs," "talking leudly," and "Acting a great many Indecencies."[48] The men "threatned that they'd Massacre any body that betray'd them." Despite this threat, fellow reveler Mark Partridge "blabbed something of the Secret" to others. This led to the arrest of the "Mollies" (a "Molly" was a slur for an effeminate gay man). They denounced the informant as a "treacherous, blowing-up Mollying Bitch." Sadly, on the basis of this testimony Wright and Newton were indicted for committing sodomy and buggery, and both men were sentenced to death. With this early use of bitch, there is a clear overlap between homophobia and misogyny. A gay man is the target of contempt, because he supposedly takes on the submissive role of a woman.

In a contrasting use that will sound familiar to modern readers, bitch could also have a positive use between men as a part of friendly banter. In an issue of the eighteenth-century *Chester Chronicle* we find the quote, "He comes up to me and says, 'Daffer, you b—h, what brings you here?'"[49] This kind of use wasn't intended to insult but to show familiarity. A nineteenth-century example from *The Rockhampton Bulletin* in Australia shows that even back then men could playfully tease each other with good-humored insults: "It was but a simple and primitive society when men caled each other Addlehead, Baldhead, Barebones, Bitch, Chisels, Dolt, Fogey, Gander, Maggot, Mangy, Muff, Muzzy."[50] This jocular use is similar to the modern-day one in which men jokingly call each other "cunt," "asshole," or "dick," among other insults, to signify friendship.

From emasculating insult to banter, these many different examples show that when it comes to calling a man a "bitch," not much has changed in hundreds of years.

A Bitch of a Thing

What's becoming clear is that *bitch* has meant many different things over a very long period of time. And while bitch usually referred to an animal or some*one*, it could also refer to some*thing*, and usually a thing or situation that was difficult or unpleasant. This use goes back at least as far as the Middle Ages. *The Castle of Perseverance* is a fifteenth-century mystery play about humankind's constant struggle between good and evil. In the story, the Seven Deadly Sins have foul mouths and constantly abuse the Seven Virtues as "bitches." At one point, the sin of Wrath calls Dame Patience: *Þou bycche blak as kole*, meaning, "You bitch black as coal."[51] The virtue of Patience is personified as a woman, a "Dame," and one who is difficult and unpleasant, likening her to a bitch. This kind of personification of bad things as bitches was the forerunner of modern idioms like *life's a bitch, and then you die*.

At this same time in history, people were terrified of a night-time visit from the "bitch daughter" or "bitch clout." This was a female demon who was believed to sit on her victim's chest while they were sleeping and suffocate them. The common expression was to be "ridden by the bitch daughter," who might be a succubus that had sex with a man while he was asleep. (Nowadays, we understand these nightmare assaults as episodes of sleep paralysis, a kind of nocturnal hallucination.) An early English to Latin dictionary defines this frightening creature as: "Þe Bychdowȝhter: Epialtis, Epialta, Noxa"; which translates to "The bitch daughter is an elf, sprite, or spirit."[52] This demon was often represented as an elderly woman, who was also known as the *old hag*. Medieval folk searched for rocks with holes in them and hung these "hag-stones" on strings from the ceilings of their cottages to ward off the nightmare hag. *Hag* was also a slur for a wizened old woman, a character found in folklore and children's tales such as "Hansel and Gretel." As yet another term for a disagreeable woman, hag is related to bitch and other insulting terms for older women like witch and crone. Following on from the idea of a bitch daughter as an evil entity, something that was *bitched* was cursed, wicked, or damned. In Chaucer's "Pardoner's Tale," the pardoner preaches against vices like drinking, swearing, and gambling, and he refers to a pair of unlucky dice as the "bicced bones."[53] (During the Medieval period, dice were usually made out of the bones of sheep or deer.)

We've seen that bitch could have a positive meaning, to show familiarity between people, much like today, and in the early modern period *bitch* referred fondly to an inanimate object, especially something like a boat. In *Tom Cringle's Log*, a crew of sailors bid farewell to their beloved ship: "'There she goes, the dear old beauty,' said one of her crew. "There goes the blessed old black b----h.'"[54] This use is similar to the modern practice of referring to ships and cars as "she" or "her." The English language probably borrowed this practice from Latin, in which words have gender and the word for ship, *navis*, is feminine.

Another theory says that this tradition relates to the idea of a mother or goddess guiding and protecting a ship's crew. On the other hand, *bitch* could be an expression of frustration at a boat or other object that was broken or an animal that was injured, in particular, a horse. In the 1832 *Book of Sports*, Bob advises his friend against borrowing a 'lame' horse when he says, "She's a stumbling bitch. You should not have her, Dick, unless I desir'd to see you laid dead in a ditch."[55]

Related to the idea of *bitch* as an expression of exasperation is its use to refer to anything that was unpleasant, difficult, or problematic. While fortune can be a "lady" she could also be a "bitch" when it came to gambling, according to *The Life of Richard Nash*: "That damned bitch fortune, no later than last night, tricked me out of 500 (guineas)."[56] And yes, this particular use dating back to the 1700s is related to the one we're familiar with today. This is the verb *to bitch* meaning to complain, which comes from the metaphor of a complaining, nagging woman. It's been suggested that *to bitch*, *bitching*, and *bitchy*, all allude to a feral mother dog protecting her young with her snarling, growling, barking, and biting, in order to keep people away. Another real-life example from the 1700s appears in a shocking tell-all memoir: "A Leaden-hall Butcher would be bitching his Wife, for not only opening her Placket, but her Pocket Apron to his Rogue of a Journeyman, and expensively treating the young strong back'd Rascal at the *Ship* Tavern whilst himself was entering his Puppy at the *Bear Garden*."[57] This colorful and long-winded sentence tells of a husband who complained because his wife was having an affair. Hypocritically, he was engaging in extramarital sex too. Bear gardens were blood sports arenas for the cruel practice of bear baiting, although the phrase was also slang for "vagina," while puppy meant "penis."

Such historical instances of bitch meaning to complain are rare, and it wouldn't be until the twentieth century that this use would truly flourish. But there were other verbs around that we don't use anymore. In Grose's *Dictionary of the Vulgar Tongue*, he notes a sense that goes back to a bitch being a coward. The act of bitching was "to yield, or give up an attempt through fear."[58] To bitch something could be to spoil, ruin, or botch it. In 1823, the muckraking newspaper *The Satirist* lampooned the new King George IV: "'Crocky, my boy, what do you think of the King, now?' – 'Vell, then,' quoth Crocky, 'I thinks as how he has bitched the business.'"[59] The unpopular monarch had a reputation for womanizing, gambling, and gluttony – he was once nicknamed the "Prince of Whales" – and George IV is generally regarded as one of the worst rulers in British history. This use of bitch is somewhat similar to the modern phrase "to fuck up."

Hearkening back to the meaning of bitch as slut, many older uses referring to objects had allusions to sex. Bitch was once an old mining term in which the "bitch" was a receiving tool used to recover rods from a bored hole. This is similar to today's naming convention for electrical cords and sockets, where the female connector receives and holds the male connector; a linking that is often called "mating." In the United States during the 1900s, a *bitch* was a makeshift lamp made with a twist of rag dipped in lard or fat that was stuffed into a tin can; the cloth wick crammed into the can hinted at sexual intercourse. There is a reference to this kind of lamp in the fishing and hunting magazine *Forest and Stream*: "Our light was furnished by a bacon grease lamp (called 'bitch' for short.)"[60] Predating the term, in Colonial America this was also known as a *slut lamp*. Other varieties of English have their own terms for these homemade lamps. In Caribbean English this kind of portable lamp is called a *cowgut* or a *kitchen bitch*. In the West Indies, the latter phrase can also refer to a person assigned to menial tasks in a restaurant's kitchen or a man who hangs around the kitchen, cooking and cleaning, instead of going out and doing "manly things."

Bitch morphed into some other miscellaneous meanings too that illustrate its broad usage. We might remember that Scottish had some unique variant forms of bitch. From Scottish English comes the term *bitch-fou* or "full as a bitch," meaning very drunk. Scotland's national bard Robert Burns, who was known for liking a drink himself, once wrote: "I've been at drunken writers' feasts. Nay, been bitch-fou 'mang godly priests."[61] In other assorted uses, the female character in tabletop games like chess might get branded a bitch too. The chessboard's most powerful and versatile piece, the queen, is often referred to as "The Bitch." In a deck of cards, the Queen of Spades is called "The Bitch" too. (In another similarity between bitch and slut, the queen has also been named "The Slut.") Alternatively, to have the "bitch end" of a hand of poker is to have the weaker version of the same hand as another player. In both the games of chess and cards, the queen is the only female character. She's a powerful woman who can use her influence to destroy a player, drawing parallels to a bitch. Meanwhile, in chess and cards, the king is never called a "bastard."

In the wide range of uses of the word, Bitch has been a name too. It's a place name for topographical features like Bitch Mountain, a summit in Chesterfield, New York. Bitch Creek is a stream in Wyoming that crosses into Idaho; the name is said to be derived from the French word *biche*, meaning "doe." (This is often used as a term of endearment in France, akin to "darling" or "love.") There's a village called Bitchfield in Lincolnshire, England. Some think it once referred to a field of female dogs or unpleasant women, but according to the Domesday Book, the name described an area of open land that once belonged to a man named Bills-felt, which later morphed into its present-day form.[62] Also in the UK, hundreds of years ago there was a Bitch Hill in Nottingham. This place *did* have a literal meaning; the name referred to a hill where hounds were bred. This was also the name of a town in Knaresborough that was changed to Beech Hill when bitch became offensive. In other countries, there's a village in Valais, Switzerland, called Bitsch. In a promotional stunt by Pornhub, the online pornography site once offered the 900 residents of Bitsch a free lifetime subscription to its service. The locals laughed it off. After being profiled in videos by influencers on Instagram and Tik Tok, the village keeps losing its road signs. There's also a town called Bitche in France that has suffered a lot of grief because of its risqué meaning in English. (But more on this later.)

Bitch was once a family name too. Church records, electoral registers, and censuses show that the name was introduced to Anglophone countries by immigrant families in the 1700s. For example, the 1911 Census of Canada shows that Frederick Bitch and his family, formerly of Russia, lived in the district of Medicine Hat, Alberta.[63] Use of the name died out by the early 1900s, because of the increasingly negative connotations of the word in English. Immigrants with the last name Bitch began to modify the spelling to something similar, like Birch, or they changed their name entirely to avoid the stigma associated with the word. Frederick Bitch's last name is spelled elsewhere as Bitsch, and then later changed altogether to Ditch. As a family name, Bitch is still found in other countries, including Argentina and Brazil, although it's rare. Names that look or sound similar to bitch are common in other languages, although they pose problems for immigrants in English-speaking countries. The popular Vietnamese first names *Phúc* ("blessing") and *Bích* ("emerald") are often mispronounced in English as "fuck" and "bitch" respectively. For this reason, some people with these names choose to adopt Western names as a cultural adaptation. In the *New Yorker* article "America Ruined My Name for Me," author Bích Minh Nguyen recounts how she was mocked incessantly because her first name looks similar to "bitch," although it's actually pronounced as "Bic."[64] Nowadays, Nguyen goes by the Anglicized name "Beth" instead.

How Do Good Words Turn Bad?

An indisputable fact about language is that it changes. Constantly. And as we can see, bitch has had a busy past. The word has changed a lot over time and has had many different meanings. Some are still around today, while many others have disappeared. But it retains its original meaning – a bitch is still a female dog. You see, when words develop a new sense, they don't instantly lose their old one(s). These rival meanings can coexist for centuries, until they eventually die out or win out. Over time, bitch has been used to label women as variously promiscuous, unpleasant, disagreeable, despicable, treacherous, nagging, spiteful, malicious, and much more. Bitch has been applied to men too, probably for as long as it's been applied to women, but it still suggests a negative attitude toward women. Calling a man a bitch, as an inherently female word, implied weakness, cowardice, and inferiority.

In modern times, the offensive sense of bitch as an insult for a woman is the dominant meaning. Even though there are many uses of the word, the insulting one has mostly muscled out these other meanings. Why did this happen? It's because of a linguistic phenomenon called "pejoration." (The name comes from *pejoratus*, the Latin word meaning "to become worse.") This is a process by which a word that once had positive or neutral connotations acquires negative ones. It's sometimes called semantic deterioration or degradation. The word "silly" is a great example of this. In Middle English, silly (then spelled "seely") meant happy or fortunate. As time went on, the definition shifted to mean someone who was innocent, holy, and pure. Then it came to mean a naïve person. By the 1500s the word became associated with its present-day connotations of something (or someone) that is foolish or ridiculous. Shakespeare used the word the same way that we use it today. In *A Midsummer Night's Dream*, Hippolyta watches a farcically terrible performance of *Pyramus and Thisbe* and complains, "This is the silliest stuff that I ever heard."[65]

Another unexpected example of pejoration is the word *discreet*. It once meant a person who was wise or judicious in avoiding mistakes or trying to be careful about what one says or does. Chaucer's "Physician's Tale" tells the story of Virginia, who is this kind of virtuous person: "Discreet she was in answeryng always."[66] Nowadays, discreet has become a euphemism for an illicit sexual meeting. In an article in the *Wall Street Journal* the manager of an online dating service for singles said he banned the word discreet from advertisements because, "it's often code for 'married and looking to fool around.'"[67] Occasionally, a word actually improves in its meaning or loses its offensiveness. In Middle English, *nice* meant foolish or simple, before it developed positive connotations in the 1800s to mean kind and friendly. When it comes to slang, negative words like *wicked, bad,* and *sick* have also developed positive senses. As we've seen, in some uses, both past and present, bitch has improved in meaning just like this, reversing its general trend of pejoration. The process by which bad words turn good is called amelioration, but this is far more rare than good words turning bad.

Pejoration has happened *a lot* when it comes to words associated with women.[68] *Mistress* was borrowed from French in the fourteenth century, when it meant a woman who was in charge of a household. Mistress was originally a respectable title, the female equivalent of *master*. But over time it came to mean the kept woman of a married man. In the thirteenth century, *wenche* simply meant a girl or young woman. *Wench* evolved to mean "servant girl" and was later used in the sense of a woman with loose morals. Similarly, *hussy* came from the innocent word *husewif* meaning "housewife" or mistress of a household. By the 1600s it developed a derogatory sense, referring to a girl or woman who behaved in an inappropriate way, while today it means a woman who has many casual sexual relationships (or is accused of doing so anyway). *Tart* was once just a shortening of *sweetheart*, but now means a prostitute or a sexually provocative woman. In this chapter we've seen the worsening of meaning happen to many other words related to women, like queen, shrew, slut, and, of course, bitch.

What forces prompt these changes in meaning? Word meanings change for many reasons, due to social, cultural, and psychological factors that shape our way of thinking and talking about the world around us. Meanings are directly connected to the attitudes, beliefs, and values of their time. Words can develop negative meanings because they become taboo, or they're somehow linked to a taboo. This can occur when an inoffensive word resembles a word that has become offensive. And when a word develops a new negative meaning, this offensive sense often supersedes any other ones. We've seen this happen time and time again in the English language. Hundreds of years ago, *coney* was the everyday word for a hare or rabbit. But coney sounded too similar to *cunny* that had become a slang term for cunt. Over time, coney was supplanted by rabbit, which had once specifically meant a baby bunny. Similarly, *donkey* has replaced *ass*, while *rooster* is preferred over *cock*. Sometimes the word becomes so tarnished by association that it drops out of use entirely.

In an example from the advertising industry, Ayds appetite-suppressant candy was popular in the 1980s, until the public awareness of AIDS as a life-threatening condition sullied the brand's name and led the company to withdraw the brand from the market. This can happen with technical terms too. In linguistics, *homophone* is used for words with different meanings that sound the same, like *pair* and *pear*, but it has become tainted because it sounds like *homosexual*, even though the words have nothing to do with each other beyond their prefix *homo-*. A few years ago, an English teacher blogged about the topic of homophones and was fired for supposedly promoting a "gay agenda" at the school.[69] By this same process, words like *denigrate*, *niggardly*, and *snigger* are on their way out because they look like the n-word, even though they are not etymologically related at all. When we hear an inoffensive word that sounds like an offensive one, or an inoffensive word that also has an offensive meaning, our minds tend to default to thinking about the naughty one, just like Marge Simpson when she heard Bart call the female dog a bitch.

Over the course of a millennium, bitch became stigmatized by its association with social taboos such as prostitution, promiscuity, "bad" women, and "unmanly" men. This led to its offensive meanings pushing out the inoffensive one. Bitch – which was once just the literal word for a female dog – eventually became what it is today, arguably one of the most insulting words in the English language. (And as we will see later on, English is not an exception.) There are thousands of unflattering words for women in English and bitch is one of, if not the most offensive of, these, along with *cunt, slut,* and *whore.* Linguist Deborah Tannen once said, "Bitch is the most contemptible thing you can say about a woman. Save perhaps the four-letter C word."[70] But on the other hand, bitch has developed positive uses in colloquial language and has even been reclaimed in some ways. We'll dig into all of this a lot more soon. Bitch is now an everyday word that we hear on TV and on the streets; a word we read in books, newspapers, and magazines, and see everywhere online.

But bitch might not have always been an everyday word. The many historical examples appearing in this chapter may have given us a false impression of the popularity of the word in the past. Despite a history spanning over one thousand years, bitch was not necessarily a common insult in Old English, Middle English, or even Early Modern English. We lack the evidence to say either way. Surprisingly, *bitch* may have existed at a lower level of use for a very long time before social changes catapulted the word into the spotlight.

The word's popularity has really exploded in modern times, so let's now turn our attention to the next chapter of the story of bitch.

2

* * * * * *

Feminist Bitch

Bitch lurked in the English language for centuries, but then in more recent times it emerged as an everyday word. Why? Bitch changed along with the changing social roles of women during the nineteenth and twentieth centuries. By the mid 1900s, the use of bitch exploded; its meteoric rise was – in part – a backlash against feminism. In response to this, the word was reclaimed by feminists, to some extent, that is. In modern times, bitch is still an insult for a woman who is considered to be unpleasant, disagreeable, or malicious. But in the word's evolution it has also come to mean a woman who is revered (or reviled) as tough, strong, and assertive. Nowadays, bitch wears many different faces. It's used against a woman who has opinions and doesn't shy away from expressing them. A bitch is a woman who stands up for herself in the workplace or earns a promotion in which she supervises men. She's a woman on the street who doesn't respond to men's catcalls, or frowns when told to "Smile, baby." She is often uninterested in pleasing men. She's a woman who rejects unwanted sexual advances from a man on a first date, or perhaps she refuses to go out with him in the first place. She's an ex-wife who's a "psycho bitch" for standing up for her children and demanding child support. Or she's a woman in power – a politician, a lawyer, or a boss. But on the other hand, bitch is frequently used in a positive way. "What's up, bitches?" is a greeting between friends. *Sexy bitch* and *good bitch* can be compliments, but so can *bad bitch*. Then there are the many uses of bitch that don't appear to have anything to do with people. It can all get pretty confusing.

Bitch is wielded against women, but also wielded *by* women. It can be an expression of sexism and misogyny, but also an empowering self-identity label. And bitch is a divisive word at the center of an ongoing debate. Has bitch been – can it be – *should* it be – reclaimed?

Lucy Stoners

In the mid nineteenth century, women couldn't vote or speak in public. Very few attended college, but even those women weren't allowed to earn a living other than as a teacher, seamstress, or domestic worker. A married woman couldn't divorce her abusive husband, gain custody of her children, or own property, down to the very clothes that she wore. By law and by custom, women were of an inferior status. The struggle for women's rights had been an important development of the Enlightenment in England, heralded by figures such as Mary Wollstonecraft and William Godwin (who were the parents of novelist Mary Shelley). The first organized movement for gender equality, however, was the Women's Rights Convention held in 1848. On a warm July day in Seneca Falls, New York, hundreds of women gathered to denounce inequalities in property rights, education, employment, and suffrage. Elizabeth Cady Stanton read a list of grievances based on the Declaration of Independence, and announced, "We hold these truths to be self-evident: that all men *and women* are created equal." This event launched the women's suffrage movement in the United States, which, many decades later, culminated in the passing of the Nineteenth Amendment in 1920, when women were given the right to vote (White women, that is. Black women didn't get the vote until 1965).

This era is known as the first wave of feminism. Throughout this time, women such as Elizabeth Cady Stanton, Harriet Tubman, Susan B. Anthony, and Margaret Fuller fought for suffrage in the US. They were joined by Barbara Bodichon and Bessie Rayner Parkes in the UK, and many other activists around the globe. Along the way they earned additional basic rights for women. Feminists in the US helped to attain the Thirteenth Amendment, which abolished enslavement in 1865, and they won the right to divorce, to own property, and claim their inheritance. They also earned the right to keep their last names, like Lucy Stone did when she married Henry Blackwell in 1855. Stone was an abolitionist and reformer, and one of the first women to rewrite the marriage vows to omit the word "obey."[1] She was also one of the first women to attend college, graduating in 1847 from Oberlin in Ohio, the first college to admit women, just as it had been the first to admit people of color. Stone's life was so inspiring that her name became synonymous with women like her. In her day, a strong-minded, independent woman was called a "Lucy Stoner." She may have been called a "bitch" too.

In the following century there was an apparent uptick in the use of bitch. Some people have suggested that this trend may be tied to the intense resistance toward the rise of the feminist movement and women's suffrage.[2] Early women's rights activists were christened "suffragettes," although the very name was an insult. Charles Hands, a journalist for the British newspaper the *Daily Mail*, coined the term in 1906, but his intention was to ridicule the women who were fighting for the right to vote. He created "suffragette" by adding -ette to the root word "suffragist," a more universal term that also applied to men. This suffix derives from French to mean something is feminine and small, like *maisonette* and *brunette*, but it can also suggest that it's an inferior or fake version of something, like a "leatherette" lounge. The word suffragette implied that the idea of women having the vote was simply ridiculous, frivolous, and a sham. (For this reason, modern historians favor the term *suffragists*.) "Suffragent" was also concocted to make fun of male allies who supported women's suffrage.

These courageous women risked all in their fight for the right to vote. They marched, petitioned, and campaigned, and for this they were assaulted, pelted with dead rats, and spat on with disgust. Many suffered imprisonment, and when they went on hunger strikes in protest, they were force-fed milk and raw eggs until they choked or vomited.[3] As a sexist slur, bitch echoed the message of the anti-suffrage movement, those men (and women) who pushed back against the suffragists. There is a wealth of early twentieth-century propaganda against women getting the vote. Campaigns promoted postcards and posters that portrayed suffragists as ugly, lazy, loose women, who were bad mothers and bad wives. In response, suffragists began their own postcard campaigns during holidays like Valentine's Day. Their cards were funny, serious, or sentimental, using patriotism and logical arguments to appeal to men for support. They explained that women respected and loved men who supported the cause of "Votes for Women." In those days, women were expected to "keep their place" in the home, as housewives and mothers. Those who opposed women's suffrage lamented, "Who will wash the dishes and raise the babies?" Women were also expected to keep their place in society; below men, as the weaker sex, the second sex. They were expected to be submissive, passive, and docile. In comparison, suffragists were seen as difficult, disruptive, and unruly women who didn't keep their place. They were criticized as "mannish," "unsexed," and "unnatural," because they didn't conform to the traditional feminine norms and stereotypes of women. But as the historian Laurel Thatcher Ulrich once wrote, "well-behaved women seldom make history."[4]

The suffragists were showered with fish heads, and also insults, although the newspapers were too decent and proper to quote them. Until the 1930s, "bitch" was mentioned in the papers solely with regard to dog competitions and classified advertisements in which puppies were for sale. In the 1939 movie *The Women*, Joan Crawford was only allowed to hint at the offensive word when she quipped, "And by the way, there's a name for you ladies, but it isn't used in high society – outside of a kennel." We don't know exactly how much bitch was used in speech at this point, in low society or elsewhere, but it was around this time that it started to appear with greater frequency in print. As restrictions on style in edited English loosened, the word began appearing in more works of literature. In these earlier uses, bitch is often conflated with feminist, showing the link between the slur and the feminism movement. In Idabel Williams' *Hell Cat*, the mayor's wife is dismissed as both:

"He's the mayor, isn't he? He's the most important man in town, isn't he? And married to that – that *bitch!*"

"Lula!"

"I don't care, I'll call her that to her face, and worse. I'll call her a – a *feminist!*"[5]

Even though we now call it the first wave of *feminism*, at the time the word was relatively unknown. *Feminist* was a comparatively new word too; it had only appeared in English in the 1890s, swiped from the French word *féminisme*. And right out of the gates these words were tinged with negativity. In an early use from 1895 the *Athenauem* sneeringly referred to an activist whose "coquetting with the doctrines of feminism are traced with real humor."[6] To combat these negative connotations, some writers used an alternative term, *womanism*, but unsurprisingly, this soon became used with the same hostility.[7] When the battle for the ballot was finally won, as early as 1893 in New Zealand but as late as 1928 in the United Kingdom, women were becoming increasingly liberated, confident, and worldly. And yet, the use of "bitch" increased exponentially in the coming decades. This was, in part, a counterattack to the changing social roles of women and the rise of feminism, revealing discontent with women's growing equality and the threat it posed to the patriarchy.

As society grappled with these shifting gender dynamics, writers coming of age during this period popularized the modern idea of the bitch. Ernest Hemingway, F. Scott Fitzgerald, Sherwood Anderson, and other Lost Generation authors of the 1920s–1950s created what has become known as the "bitch archetype," the domineering, indestructible anti-heroine, a tough woman who was waged in a battle of the sexes. Hemingway characterizes these women as man-eaters, "They are the hardest, the cruelest, the most predatory, and the most attractive, and their men have softened or gone to pieces nervously as they have hardened."[8] Hemingway became enamored with the word. Female characters in his novels and short stories were baptized "bitch goddesses," femmes fatales who used their beauty and sensuality to lure in men and then control them. He even called his own mother a bitch. Grace Hemingway and her son were at daggers drawn for most of their lives and he blamed her for his father's suicide. He wrote, "My mother is an all time all American bitch and she would make a pack mule shoot himself; let alone poor bloody father."[9]

Showing the gradual shift in meaning, Hemingway also adopted bitch to describe powerful qualities in women, such as edginess, strength, and grit. He had a turbulent relationship with fellow novelist and feminist pioneer Gertrude Stein and once said of her, "If anyone was ever a bitch that woman was a bitch." In Stein's famous poem "Sacred Emily," she penned the words, "Rose is a rose is a rose is a rose." After a bitter falling-out with Hemingway, he sent her a signed copy of his new book *Death in the Afternoon* with the parody inscription, "A bitch is a bitch is a bitch is a bitch."[10] Her response reveals women's changing social attitudes toward the word too. In defiance, Stein and her lifelong companion, cookbook author Alice B. Toklas, had special dinnerware handmade for them with the phrase written all the way around the edge of the plates.

Castrating Bitch

The first wave of feminism achieved some major accomplishments. But social equality had not yet been fully realized. Women began to organize again during the 1960s and 1970s, which heralded the second wave of feminism. While the first wavers were primarily concerned with suffrage and overturning legal obstacles to gender equality, the second wavers broadened the debate to include a wider range of issues, including the idea of women keeping their place in the home, at work, and in society. Feminists also began to challenge sexism in the English language. Like Elizabeth Cady Stanton had noted in her speech at Seneca Falls, the US Declaration of Independence (1776) effectively excludes women with the phrase "All *men* are created equal." Women often seem to be left out of history. In 1969, Neil Armstrong, the first person to walk on the moon, famously said, "One small step for *man*; one giant leap for *mankind*." Everyday language refers to men as the generic sex for "human" in words like *mankind* and *manmade*. Many job titles favor the masculine suffix in designations such as *chairman* and *mailman*. Feminists noted that these language conventions render women invisible and make men the norm.[11] Thanks to the efforts of feminism, many organizations now have guidelines for using inclusive language that recommend gender-neutral alternatives. (Having said that, there's still plenty of gender-biased language around today.)

The second wave of feminism was a turning point for women's identity. But right up until this time, the word "feminist" itself was pejorative. Ironically, very few women engaged in fighting for women's rights would've referred to themselves as "feminists." Just a few decades earlier, author Virginia Woolf was well known for her writings promoting the nascent feminist movement and she is regarded as a pioneering feminist figure, although she didn't label herself as one. The new movement that emerged in the 1960s was initially called Women's Liberation, while this era saw "feminism" being brought into general use. Even Simone de Beauvoir, the trailblazing feminist philosopher and author of *The Second Sex*, initially rejected the label, but she finally embraced it during the 1970s. De Beauvoir observed that language, including swearing, "is inherited from a masculine society and it contains many male prejudices." She added, "Women simply have to steal the instrument. Steal it and use it for their own good."[12] And in the 1980s, author Alice Walker reclaimed *womanist* and *womanism* as names for Black feminist and Black feminism respectively. Despite the rising stakes of these labels, feminist efforts resulted in more pushback. Self-proclaimed feminists were described in hostile terms as militant and radical, angry and rabid. They were mocked and nicknamed "women's libbers" and "bra burners." (The idea of bra burning was actually a media-generated myth, although the titillating story has served to further marginalize feminism as ridiculous and irrational.) A feminist, or any woman who stood up to a man, was supposedly guilty of penis envy; she was called a man-hater, a lesbian, and a castrating bitch.

The second wave of feminism was also a turning point for bitch. By this time, bitch had become a dog whistle for anti-feminists. In response, feminists began to reevaluate the meaning of the word, and in doing so they attempted to reclaim it. What is reclamation? Reclamation, sometimes called reappropriation, is a process by which an insult that was previously used to offend people is co-opted by the discriminated group as an empowering word. In the 1960s, feminists began to wrestle bitch away from the misogynists in this way. Reclamation is an effort to reshape language and attitudes, to reject stigmatizing labels that are imposed on a group by taking them back. The negative words are then used in a positive sense by the very people they had once been used against. As an example, the LGBTQ+ community has successfully reclaimed *gay* and *queer*, repurposing these former slurs as self-identifying labels.

Similarly, "suffragette" was coined to mock women fighting for the vote, but some reclaimed the word instead. In Britain, the Women's Social and Political Union named their magazine *The Suffragette* in 1912. They further took back the name by pronouncing it differently, with a hard *g*, like "suffra-get," reflecting their mission to "get" the right to vote. In an editorial the publication explained the difference as they saw it: "We have all heard of the girl who asked what was the difference between a Suffragist and a Suffragette, as she pronounced it, and the answer made to her was that the 'Suffragist jist wants the vote, while the Suffragette means to get it.'"[13] When a word is reclaimed, the negative sense is recast with a positive meaning within the group, becoming an expression of solidarity and pride in one's identity.

Efforts to reclaim bitch began with an essay written in 1968 by Jo Freeman, an American feminist, attorney, and editor of the *Voice of the Women's Liberation Movement*. Under the nom de plume of Joreen, she penned *The BITCH Manifesto*, which is now considered to be one of the leading texts of the second wave of feminism. This feminist tract ran alongside such celebrated articles as "The Personal Is Political" and "The Myth of the Vaginal Orgasm." In her treatise, Freeman gave an explosive description of bitches as: "Aggressive, assertive, domineering, overbearing, strong-minded, spiteful, hostile, direct, blunt, candid, obnoxious, thick-skinned, hard-headed, vicious, dogmatic, competent, competitive, pushy, loud-mouthed, independent, stubborn, demanding, manipulative, egoistic, driven, achieving, overwhelming, threatening, scary, ambitious, tough, brassy, masculine, boisterous, and turbulent. Among other things."[14] These descriptors have long been used against women, but Freeman reframed them as positive. She characterized a bitch as a powerful woman: "A Bitch occupies a lot of psychological space. You always know she is around. A Bitch takes shit from no one. You may not like her, but you cannot ignore her." With these revolutionary words, bitch received a feminist facelift and it became a flagship for feminism.

By redefining the word in a feminist context, *The BITCH Manifesto* turned the centuries-old definition of a bitch as a "bad woman" on its head. Freeman repurposed into a compliment what was originally intended as an insult. She writes, "BITCH does not use this word in the negative sense. A woman should be proud to declare she is a Bitch, because Bitch is Beautiful. It should be an act of affirmation by self and not negation by others." Freeman capitalized the word to differentiate it as a self-identifying label. She invited women to embrace their inner bitch, and to this day, her essay has inspired many others to "own" the word. Other women began to embrace the term, using it to uplift and elevate themselves and women in general. In this spirit, many famous women co-opted the label that was imposed on them. For years, Yoko Ono had been accused of being "the bitch who broke up The Beatles." In her 1974 song "Yes, I'm a Witch" she confronted this popular criticism head on: "Yes, I'm a witch, I'm a bitch, I don't care what you say. My voice is real, my voice speaks truth, I don't fit in your ways."[15] As these lyrics suggest, a bitch knows that she's different, but she doesn't care to conform to society's expectations of her.

Being a bitch was particularly fashionable during the "girl power" days of the 1990s, an era that is sometimes referred to as the third wave of feminism. Reclaiming sexist language was still of concern at this time, and powerful women were often proud to wear the label. Anna Wintour, the notorious former *Vogue* editor who left her assistants quaking in their designer heels, was the inspiration for Miranda Priestly, the tyrannical editor-in-chief in the movie *The Devil Wears Prada*. Nicknamed "Nuclear Wintour," she took on the descriptor unapologetically when she said, "I am very driven by what I do. I am certainly very competitive ... Yes, I'm a bitch."[16] Not *all* powerful women, however, accepted it willingly. Pop star Madonna initially rejected the title, "I am ambitious and I've worked hard to get where I am. But I'm no bitch." Although just a few years later, when the word had more cultural cachet, she reversed her stance and proved the word was in vogue. "I'm tough, ambitious, and I know what I want. If that makes me a bitch, okay."[17] Bitch became acceptable to the point that it was taken on as the name of an empowering anthem. In Meredith Brooks' "Bitch," she explicitly referred to herself as one: "I'm a bitch, I'm a lover, I'm a child, I'm a mother, I'm a sinner, I'm a saint, I do not feel ashamed." The song is a declaration of self-acceptance and authenticity that embraces bitch, not as a weakness, but as a strength.

In response to its growing prestige, countless women among the general public leaned into the word, calling their best friends "bitches" and even declaring themselves to be "bitches" too. In this same spirit, fans of actor Benedict Cumberbatch dubbed themselves Cumberbitches. "You say I'm a bitch like it's a bad thing" became a meme, appearing on buttons and bumper stickers, the phrase inspiring a song by the same name. Overturning centuries of mocking those who had the word bestowed on them as a name, bitch was finally acceptable enough to become one (well, for an artist anyway). In the mid 1990s fem-rocker

Karen Mould adopted the stage name Bitch, and she is also known by the nickname Capital B. It seemed as though everyone was jumping on the bitch bandwagon. The reclaimed word now had pop appeal although it still retained its feminist roots. The groundbreaking magazine *Bitch* emerged to explore feminist issues through the lens of popular culture, espousing the slogan, "If being an outspoken woman means being a bitch, we'll take that as a compliment." And no less a feminist than pioneer Gloria Steinem urged women to welcome the label. "The best thing I've ever thought of to say when someone calls you a 'bitch' is 'Thank you.' I mean, it totally disarms them. They don't know what to do."[18]

These women were part of a growing chorus of those who used bitch in a positive way. "Bitch" was suddenly everywhere, its affirmative message widely accepted and repeated.

This didn't mean, however, that the word had stopped being used in a negative way.

Difficult Bitch

The BITCH Manifesto not only drew attention to bitch, but it also drew attention to gender norms. In Western society, traditional gender roles haven't changed much since the time of the women's suffrage movement. These "rules" are only social constructs, but they dictate that men are to be dominant, strong, and tough, while women are to be polite, accommodating, docile, and nurturing. Freeman also exposed how these gender norms are illustrated by the way "bitch" is used. She writes that a bitch is a woman who is "accused of domineering when doing what would be considered natural by a man." Independence, ambition, and strength are defined as masculine qualities; however, if a woman displays these very same qualities, she is considered to be unfeminine. There is a double standard that characteristics valued in men are reinterpreted negatively when they're observed in women. What's seen as "dominant" behavior in men is construed as "difficult" in women. Men are assertive, but assertive women are "aggressive." Men are competitive, but competitive women are "combative." He's a boss, but she's "bossy." Tropes of dominant men versus difficult women play out in the media all the time. Over the years, reporters described former Yahoo CEO Marissa Mayer as "crazy," "too tough," and "difficult." In stark contrast, Amazon's Jeff Bezos is described favorably as "audacious," "determined," and "the dotcom king," a "rare leader who obsesses over finding small improvements."[19]

The difficult woman paradigm is pervasive in Hollywood. Many female actors have been labeled "tempestuous," "demanding," and "hard to work with." They've been blacklisted for simply complaining about poor working conditions, resisting the casting couch, or asking to be paid as much as their male co-stars. The "difficult" label has brought down the careers of many Hollywood women over the years. But it is a gendered word; their male counterparts are *never* described this way. Hollywood is still a boy's club, and being seen as dominant and strong is not a career killer for male actors. Katherine Heigl, Janet Hubert, Mira Sorvino, and Ashley Judd are among those "difficult divas" who stood up for themselves and their principles but were iced out of Hollywood for years. The mood has changed to a certain degree with the #metoo movement, which has dismantled some of the inherent sexism. (These events ushered in an era that is sometimes called the fourth wave of feminism.) But the stigma of the label was especially bad in the past. Film star Bette Davis was an icon of Hollywood's Golden Age who had a reputation for being strong-minded, which often resulted in her being called difficult. She once explained the disparity as "Strong men are praised, but strong women are regarded only as difficult." To put it another way, she added, "When a man gives his opinion, he's a man. When a woman gives her opinion, she's a *bitch*."[20]

This kind of gender bias is widespread in the music industry too. Male songwriters outnumber female songwriters, male producers outnumber female producers, and male artists are paid considerably more than female artists. Speaking out about these inequalities, rapper Missy Elliott said, "Music is a male-dominated field. Women are not always taken as seriously as we should be, so sometimes we have to put our foot down. To other people that may come across as being a bitch, but it's just knowing what we want and being confident."[21] She wrote the song "She's a Bitch" about having this kind of take-charge attitude. In her documentary *My Time Now*, rapper Nicki Minaj also shared her struggles as a female artist in a genre dominated by male rappers and how this got her characterized as a bitch. "When I am assertive, I'm a bitch. When a man is assertive, he's a boss. He's bossed up. No negative connotation behind 'bossed up.' But lots of negative connotation behind being a bitch."[22] Challenging this state of affairs, she covered PTAF's empowering (and explicit) song "Boss Ass Bitch." Minaj invokes "bitch" a lot in her music, like her hit *Bad Bitch* featuring Beyoncé, in which being bad is a good thing. In doing so, she reclaims a word that men had previously monopolized in the hip hop and rap industry. (And more on this topic soon.)

Ditch the Bitch

As an insult, bitch is commonly used to attack women in spaces that are male-dominated, particularly in politics and law. In addition, these women who break through the "Invisible Bar of the professions," as Jo Freeman calls it, are judged harshly in a way that their male colleagues aren't. They are judged, not only for their work performance, but also on their personality, clothing, and appearance. These women are often the targets of name-calling. In particular, bitch is a pervasive sexist slur in political culture. This is not the empowering "bitch" of Freeman's manifesto, a word adopted by women, but a word used against women to punish, demean, and silence them. Bitch is designed to put women back in their place. Ruth Bader Ginsburg, the former Justice of the United States Supreme Court, was nicknamed "Ruthless Ruthie" throughout her time in law school and frequently called a "bitch" behind her back. When she found out about this in later years she retorted, "Better bitch than mouse."[23]

Women who assert power and authority walk a tightrope between being seen as a bitch or just not being leadership material.[24] But it seems as though they cannot cultivate an image of competence and leadership without being dismissed as a bitch. In the past, there had been a certain amount of resignation and a tacit acceptance of this state of affairs. Political commentator Mike Kennedy once remarked, "The word 'bitch' hurts, but women concede that those kinds of insults and labels go with the territory."[25] But this is not the case for men. Women in politics are in a double bind. They're expected to be strong, tough, and to play the game in a man's world, but when they do so they're criticized for it. Bitch is aimed at women who behave in stereotypically male ways. For daring to act "like a man", women in the political spotlight are saddled with negative descriptors like angry, bossy, pushy, outspoken, and overbearing. In an attempt to invalidate their voices, these women are even criticized for the way they talk. In order to discredit and diminish them, politically active women are commonly characterized as loud, mouthy, nagging, shrill, strident, grating, and abrasive. These words portray them as emotional, irrational, and hysterical; but they're not words used to describe men in politics. Following a disagreement with her male colleagues, British politician Baroness Sayeeda Warsi once quipped, "the bitchiest women I've ever met in my life are the men in politics."[26]

Dubbed "The Iron Lady" for her uncompromising leadership style, Margaret Thatcher was the first female Prime Minister of the United Kingdom from 1979–1990. Thatcher was branded a "bitch" throughout her entire career. When she became the leader of the Conservative Party in 1975 the Vice-Chairman exclaimed, "My God! The bitch has won!"[27] In response to her history-making win, *Private Eye* magazine published a crude cartoon of Thatcher depicted as a dog, sitting on a podium beside a pile of its own excrement, with the caption "Top Bitch." During Thatcher's tenure, "Ditch the bitch" was a popular Labour Party slogan chanted among male members of parliament when she entered the Commons. At one point Thatcher said she didn't identify with feminism, which evolved along with her career, although she had to battle sexism constantly. Her voice was described as "shrill" and likened to a "perfumed fart." With a nod to the iconic black handbag she always carried, Thatcher was called "the Handbag," which her detractors gleefully shortened to "Bag." Former French President Jacques Chirac once belittled her as a "housewife." At the same time she was seen as unfeminine and manly, and compared to ruthless tyrants such as Caligula and "Atilla the Hen." Yassar Arafat once called her "the Iron Man." When Thatcher died in 2013, her critics waved banners, cheering "the wicked bitch is dead" and shouted, "ding dong, Thatcher's Dead," a play on "The Witch Is Dead" sung by the Munchkins in *The Wizard of Oz*.

These taunts were resurrected when Julia Gillard was elected as Australia's first female Prime Minister. Tony Abbott, the leader of the opposition party, frequently attacked her with sexist comments. He was photographed at public protests standing beside signs bearing the slogans "Ditch the witch" and "Bob Brown's bitch"[28] (Brown was Gillard's political ally). Abbott's act of being seen alongside these sexist sentiments implied his endorsement of them. In response, Gillard delivered to parliament a blistering monologue on sexism in which she referred to Abbott as a "misogynist." Her detractors denied that Abbott was a "woman hater" and accused her of not knowing the meaning of the word. The incident inspired Australia's *Macquarie Dictionary* to update its definition of misogyny from the former "pathological hatred of women" to "entrenched prejudice of women." In the early 2000s the slogan "Ditch the bitch" was part of a popular advertising campaign for Brookman, the London firm of divorce attorneys. Posters with the slogan appeared in the restrooms of fashionable city bars, along with the corresponding motto "All men are bastards" for unhappy wives. "Ditch the bitch" has also been invoked with reference to many other women in politics, especially Pat Schroeder, Dixy Lee Ray, and Hillary Clinton.

Numerous women in politics have had the "bitch" badge pinned on them, but perhaps no one more so than Hillary Rodham Clinton. Clinton has been called a bitch publicly ever since she was First Lady of the United States, when she was criticized for her alleged mishandling of issues including healthcare reform and the scandal surrounding her husband Bill Clinton's affair with intern Monica Lewinsky. Clinton was also branded a bitch for having ambition that people thought was above her station – her dream to become the first woman president of the United States. During the 2008 US presidential campaign, a woman asked Republican candidate John McCain about his opponent. "How do we beat the bitch?" she asked, to chuckles all around. McCain didn't admonish his supporter for using the slur, but instead replied, "That's an excellent question!"[29] During her 2016 political campaign against Donald Trump, anti-Hillary Clinton bumper stickers proclaimed, "Stop the bitch" and "Life's a bitch so don't vote for one." The slogan "Trump that Bitch" was cried at Republican rallies and splashed on badges and T-shirts. At one rally, a ten-year-old boy shouted, "Take the bitch down!"

Clinton's critics said she had a "likeability problem." TV and radio host Glenn Beck once called her a "stereotypical bitch," complaining about her "nagging" and that her voice sounded like "fingernails on the blackboard."[30] (Beck later denied that he'd called Clinton a bitch at all, arguing, "I said she *sounded* like one.") But the ad hominem attacks against her went beyond bitch. Critics demanded that Clinton know her place. At campaign rallies, she was taunted with jeers of "Iron my shirts!" while a Facebook group appeared that was called "Hillary Clinton: Stop Running for President and Make Me a Sandwich." In her *BITCH Manifesto*, Jo Freeman observed that women are unfairly judged for their looks, and in this way, press reports frequently focused on Clinton's appearance, from her figure to her hairstyle to her wide array of pantsuits. (Margaret Thatcher was also mocked for her steely image, with her power suits, string of pearls, and her iconic back-combed, teased hairstyle.) When an unflattering photo of Clinton appeared in the newspapers, Conservative pundit Rush Limbaugh asked, "Will Americans want to watch a woman get older before their eyes on a daily basis?"[31] Male candidates, however, don't face this same kind of sexist, ageist scrutiny. Further showing the threat of the power-seeking woman, Clinton became a caricature of the classic feminist emasculator. Conservative commentator Tucker Carlson once said, "When she comes on television I involuntarily cross my legs."[32] Playing on the ball-busting, castrating bitch theme, some stores sold a novelty Hillary nutcracker, which was able to crack a walnut between her pantsuited thighs.

Throughout her political campaigns, Clinton was explicitly called a "cunt" in public forums. A Republican strategist founded an anti-Clinton group he named Citizens United Not Timid, which went by the acronym CUNT. While opponent Donald Trump resisted calling Clinton a "bitch" in public, he did interrupt her speech during a presidential debate to call her "such a nasty woman." But this backfired when Clinton supporters co-opted the phrase. "Nasty woman" trended on social media and was emblazoned on T-shirts, badges, and coffee mugs. The attack resulted in playful internet memes celebrating strong women. This kind of reaction, however, has led some to observe that efforts to take back bitch and other sexist insults have sometimes been rooted in consumerism. They argue that the bad-girl bitch identity is friendly to corporations and abused as a marketing tool designed to sell songs, movies, and bumper stickers with easy empowerment slogans.

Over the course of her career as a presidential candidate, former Senator, Secretary of State, and First Lady, Hillary Clinton has been called all of the predictable insults: "shrew," "hag," "nag," and "witch" (which is often a euphemism for bitch), but by far the most common one hurled at her was "bitch." Noticeably, this slur isn't used against men in politics (except for Baroness Warsi's riposte). Bitch has always been a popular way to dismiss Clinton, and any woman in the political arena, without engaging in a legitimate discussion of their policies and politics. Clinton made an art form of turning the other cheek to such attacks. Some suggested, in the same vein as Jo Freeman, that Clinton just lean into the label. Tina Brown, former editor of *The New Yorker*, argued that Clinton needed to "own her inner bitch" to appeal to young women voters. But in the end, all of the incessant negative publicity torpedoed her campaigns for presidency.

Clinton, however, wasn't the first woman to run for president of the United States. That title goes to Victoria Woodhull, who ran in 1872, before women had even won the right to vote. For challenging the manly status quo in politics and society, she was nicknamed "Mrs. Satan," and called a "witch" and a "harpie."[33] Clinton has also been called a "harpy," a term that was inspired by the mythological winged monster that is often depicted as a bird of prey with the head of a woman. From Thatcher to Clinton, being branded a bitch sends a message to those women, and to all women, that they don't belong in these institutions and positions. When used in the political arena, bitch is about silencing women and keeping them out, warning them that they better not overstep their bounds. It's a word that seeks to control women and keep them in their place. Certainly, male politicians are not treated in this manner. It seems that modern efforts to take down women in politics are driven by the same fear of women taking power over a century ago.

Fucking Bitch

Bitch is an everyday word, although its acceptability and frequency of use is not to be mistaken with how highly offensive it can be. In fact, it can be so rude that some only dare to utter the word behind a woman's back, as in the case of Ruth Bader Ginsburg. They hope the slur will never reach the ears of the intended target, because they don't want to face the fallout. In a 1995 interview on the program *Eye to Eye*, Connie Chung interviewed Newt Gingrich's mother Kathleen "Kit" Gingrich and the following conversation ensued.

"Mrs. Gingrich, what has Newt told you about President Clinton?"

"Nothin'. And I can't tell you what he said about Hillary."

"You can't?"

"I can't."

"Why don't you just whisper it to me? Just between you and me."

Gingrich's microphone volume was turned up when she leaned in and whispered, "He thinks she's a bitch."[34]

Newt Gingrich was furious that the interviewer had tricked his mother into an embarrassing disclosure, breaking her confidence, and then sharing it with the world. And that's how the narrative played out: that Chung had manipulated Gingrich's elderly mother, not that he had called Hillary Clinton a "bitch," or what that might say about his attitudes toward women. Others deny they used the word at all, especially when it backfires on them, like it did with Glenn Beck and his "stereotypical bitch" comments about Clinton. And in the 1980s when George Bush ran for vice-presidency against Geraldine Ferraro, the first woman to run on a major party national ticket, his wife Barbara remarked that her husband's opponent was, "I can't say it, but it rhymes with 'rich.'"[35] Bush tried to cover her tracks by saying she had meant "witch." She later apologized to Ferraro, but backpedaled with the excuse, "I certainly didn't mean anything by it."

In a more recent incident of this kind, Congressman Ted Yoho accosted Congresswoman Alexandria Ocasio-Cortez on the steps of the US Capitol, calling her "disgusting" and saying, "You're out of your freaking mind" for her comments about unemployment and poverty. Ocasio-Cortez told Yoho he was being "rude" and she left the scene. When she was out of earshot Yoho mumbled "fucking bitch" under his breath.[36] A reporter for *The Hill* witnessed the exchange and broke the story. In a graceful response to the verbal abuse, Ocasio-Cortez reclaimed the slur when she tweeted "Bitches get stuff done." This was a nod to an iconic *Saturday Night Live* sketch in which Tina Fey and Amy Poehler discuss "bitch" and the word's frequent application to Hillary Clinton. "People say that Hillary is a bitch," says Fey. "Let me say this about that ... Yeah, she is. And so am I. You know what? Bitches get stuff done."[37]

Yoho denied he'd used the slur at all, claiming he merely muttered "bullshit" in reference to Ocasio-Cortez's progressive politics. Then he upped the ante when he refused to "apologize for my passion or for loving my God, my family, and my country." Ocasio-Cortez had intended to let the incident go, but in light of Yoho's lack of contrition and the invocation of his wife and daughters, she took to the floor of the House of Representatives and announced, "I am here because I have to show my parents that I am their daughter and they did not raise me to accept abuse from men." The Congresswoman proceeded to call out her colleague for his "sexist slur," which she described as disrespectful, dehumanizing, and emblematic of a culture of misogyny. Yoho's spokes-person later dismissed Ocasio-Cortez's speech as just an attempt to gain attention. But Ocasio-Cortez had broken the tacit rule that insults "go with the territory" and that women must tolerate being called a bitch.

Incidents such as these reveal an obvious but crucial point: "bitch" reveals negative attitudes toward women. It's wielded as an all-purpose insult against any woman who is deemed to be annoying, bothersome, insensitive, competition, or somehow "bad" in the eyes of the speaker. Bitch uses femininity as a weapon. A woman – and all that she is – is reduced to a single hurtful word. The insult is intensi-fied when teamed up with modifiers like fucking, fat, ugly, old, crazy, psycho, stupid, or dumb. These serve as double insults that further abuse a woman by attacking her appearance, age, or intellect. But the slur has an even darker side. Bitch promotes violence against women. In 2014, Kianga Mwamba was recording an arrest from her car when Baltimore police ordered her to move and suddenly pulled her from her vehicle as she attempted to comply. Her cell phone footage shows that the police attacked her with a Taser. Amid the sound of an officer handcuffing her, a male voice can be heard saying, "You a dumb bitch. Do you know that?"[38] In this context, bitch revealed con-tempt for this woman. And by extension, bitch can reveal contempt for all women.

Calling a woman "bitch" sends an aggressive and threatening message. It's used to bully, control, and intimidate. Bitch frequently precedes or accompanies violence against women, like sexual har-assment, domestic violence, and rape. Many studies have shown that men abuse their partners with "bitch" or "whore" as a means of objectifying the person before striking them or committing other acts of violence.[39] An equivalent to "she was asking for it," abusing a woman with "bitch" is used to justify violent behavior. During O.J. Simpson's trial for the brutal murder of his ex-wife Nicole Brown and her friend Ronald Goldman, there was much evidence of his physi-cal beatings and verbal abuse during and after their marriage. It was revealed that throughout their relationship he routinely referred to Brown as a "fucking bitch" and her mother Juditha as a "whore."[40]

Transcripts of calls Brown made to 911 when Simpson broke into her house, just eight months before her death, are peppered with Simpson screaming "Bitch!" at her. And a close friend of Brown's claimed that Simpson had once threatened, "I'll kill that bitch."[41] Cases such as this show that dehumanizing a woman as a bitch can ultimately have fatal consequences.

When used in combination with other words, bitch can reveal racism as well as sexism. Across the centuries, "black bitch" has been wielded against women of color. During the days of the women's suffrage movement in the nineteenth century, Lucy Parsons was a staunch fighter for the full equality of all women and an end to racial discrimination. The media sought to marginalize Parsons by labeling her a "Negro," "dark-skinned," and "colored." And while we can only speculate that white women protesters were called bitches, we have it on record that Parsons was physically attacked by police who called her a "black bitch" during an 1886 protest in Chicago.[42] Such abuse was common toward Black activists. In 1955, Rosa Parks helped initiate the US civil rights movement when she refused to give up her seat to a white man on a bus in Montgomery, Alabama. At this time of racial segregation, white bus drivers often mistreated their Black passengers. In particular, James Blake was notorious for abusing Black women. He forcibly threw Parks off the bus one day, while she recounted that he frequently targeted her and other women with the slurs "black bitch" and "coon."[43] Black bitch is still around today as an insult that shows contempt for women of color and depicts caricatures of them as aggressive, loud, rude, and pushy.

The connection between bitch and racism goes back to the time of enslavement in the American South and other slave-trading nations. Court records and various documents of slave-owners show the slur was a tool of violence used to hurt and control enslaved people.[44] Bitch was wielded against enslaved women, while son of a bitch was leveled at enslaved men. Plantation owners and overseers exploited the labor of these people and punished them with whippings, torture, and mutilation. When they were no longer permitted to use corporal punishment, they vented their spite with abusive and obscene language, which was always underpinned by the implicit threat and fear of violence. Through the use of racist slurs, planters denied enslaved people the status of "real" women and men by dehumanizing them as dogs or other animals. Bitch rendered enslaved people as possessions. They were listed alongside "stock" in plantation account books, while advertisements for "runaways" equated them with stray animals. Bitch also had sexual connotations. Enslaved women endured sexual abuse – harassment, rape, or being forced into concubinage – while sexualized insults like bitch, cunt, and whore implied promiscuity and reduced them to their sexual organs.

Bitch with a Capital "C"

A woman doesn't have to be a politician, business executive, film star, rocker, or feminist to be branded a bitch. She is called a bitch – just because. She may be branded a bitch for standing her ground and speaking her mind. She might be called a bitch when she's deemed to be "hormonal," which is usually blamed on her period or pregnancy. She could be called a bitch when she doesn't clean the house or dinner is late on the table. She is often dismissed as a bitch for not responding to a man's romantic overtures. As we've seen, bitch was once a word for a prostitute or promiscuous woman, and while it's still used interchangeably with whore and slut, it's also leveled against a woman who rejects a man's sexual advances. In the comedy sketch "Girl at a Bar" on *Saturday Night Live,* a woman waits alone in a crowded bar for her friend to arrive. In the meantime, she is repeatedly approached and propositioned by a string of "nice guys." Each man professes to be a feminist ally, until she politely declines his offer of a date or sexual encounter. Feeling entitled and angry at the rejection, even though he's "followed the rules," each rebuffed man retorts with the show-stopper "Bitch!"[45]

Bitch is part of a greater culture of abusive language used against women. As noted in the previous chapter, there are a staggering number of gendered insults for women in the English language. Among these, bitch, whore, slut, and cunt are the most prevalent, and also the most offensive. Let's take a closer look at these comparable sexist slurs. Whore is as old as bitch. The word dates back to late Old English *hōre*, which meant a woman who prostituted herself for money.[46] Unlike bitch, whore didn't go through as many and varied changes in meaning. But it did widen in scope to refer to an "unchaste or lewd" woman, without reference to exchanging money for sexual favors. Later on, it came to be a general term of abuse for women, and not much has changed to this day. Over time, there have been many synonyms for whore in the sense of prostitute, from harlot to hooker, while some of these make a comment on the woman's morality, such as fallen or loose woman. We talked about harridan in the previous chapter, which meant a bossy woman similar to a shrew or scold, but it originated as a slang term for an aging prostitute (the word probably coming from the sixteenth-century French *haridelle* for "old horse"). Butcher was once a male correspondent to bitch, in the sense of a male whore, but it didn't carry the same offensive connotations. Whore has been used to refer to male prostitutes for centuries too. It's still around, especially in modern phrases like man-whore, but it's more often humorous and doesn't carry the same moral judgment and sting of the word when it's applied to women. In the 1970s, whore was abbreviated to *ho* in colloquial African American English. Coming from this same dialect is *thot*, which is slang for whore and an acronym for "That Ho Over There."

In some ways, slut has become yet another synonym of whore. As we've seen, in its early days slut didn't mean a woman who had many sexual partners, because that was the earlier definition of bitch. Slut originally meant a dirty, slovenly, untidy woman, like a slattern, then later on it was a kitchen maid. (Around this same period, the amusing *fustilug* and *driggle draggle* were also insults for a woman accused of being untidy.) It wasn't until the time of free love in the swinging sixties that a slut became a woman who sleeps around. Slut joined the ranks of the many other words that imply a woman is promiscuous – moll, tramp, tart, floozy, skank, and Jezebel – words which are frequently paired with bitch. In 1950, the Hollywood scandal broke that Ava Gardner and Frank Sinatra were having an affair. The press branded Gardner a "home wrecker" and she attracted a stalker who repeatedly sent her hate mail that was addressed to "Bitch-Jezebel-Gardner."[47] Ol' Blue Eyes, however, was let off lightly for being a "ladies' man." Slut is also used in reference to men nowadays, but much in the same playful way that whore is. A promiscuous man is instead praised as a ladies' man, stud, or playboy. Unlike words for women, these names have positive connotations, suggesting he is handsome, charming, and virile. The difference in labels and attitudes across gender imply that when a man has sex, his worth increases, but when a woman has sex, her worth decreases. Women are slut-shamed for real or presumed sexual activity.[48] But slut has little to do with whether or not a girl or woman is sexually active. The slur has become a catchall to diminish and discredit women. She might be called a slut simply for having more guy friends than girl friends, wearing a short skirt, showing cleavage, or being attractive. Like bitch, any girl or woman might be called a slut for just about anything.

Cunt is another strong sexist slur that is used to discredit women, as we saw it used against Hillary Clinton. But well before it was an insult it was a literal word for the body part. When it emerged in the thirteenth century, cunt referred literally to "the female genitals, the vulva or vagina," but it wasn't considered to be obscene.[49] Around that time, cunt was an anatomical term that was used in medical writing. An early written reference appeared on a street sign in Oxfordshire called Gropecuntlane. (It's since been renamed Magpie Lane.) This was presumably the haunt of prostitutes plying their trade because it was common practice for medieval street names to reflect their function. The word even appeared in last names and documents record examples like John Fillecunt (1246), Robert Clevecunt (1302), and Bele Wydecunthe (1328). In Middle English the word was alternatively spelled as *conte*, *counte*, and even *queynte*. Chaucer used this last one in a bawdy way in "The Miller's Tale" when the young Oxford student Nicholas attempts to seduce his beautiful landlady Alisoun, "Pryvely he caught her by the queynte"[50] (which seems to be a medieval version of Donald Trump's infamous I'm such a big celebrity that I can "Grab 'em by the pussy" remark).

By Shakespeare's time cunt was considered to be obscene, so the playwright merely alludes to the word in *Hamlet* when the prince asks Ophelia, "Lady, shall I lie in your lap?" She replies, "No, my lord." To which Hamlet feigns shock and says, "Do you think I meant *country matters?*"[51] This may have referred to rural, unsophisticated matters, meanwhile punning on the word cunt. By the late 1600s cunt became a word for a promiscuous woman and a crude term for sexual intercourse. It was also a general term of abuse for a woman. Cunt eventually grew so offensive that Samuel Johnson decreed it to be one of those "low bad words" and he omitted it from his dictionary. Cunt was even too vulgar for Francis Grose's *Vulgar Tongue*, where he censored it as ****.[52] Cunt didn't appear in any major general dictionary of English from this time until the early 1960s, when it first appeared in *Webster's Third New International Dictionary*.

Even though cunt was a vulgar word for a long time, it wasn't a generalized insult until the nineteenth century. Today, cunt has the (dis) honor of being the most offensive insult in the English language, especially in US English. It's often represented with dashes and asterisks or avoided altogether. Sometimes it's referred to delicately as the c-word. In the movie *Stuck on You*, Cher calls herself "a total bitch with a capital 'C,'" with the suggestion of "cunt." While pussy, fanny, love taco, and vajayjay are among the many euphemisms for vagina, cunt is instead a dysphemism, a word that intends to be rude. And yet, there have been some attempts to reclaim cunt as a positive term by those who resent the misogynistic use of a word for a female body part. Feminists of the past have tried to take back cunt as a symbol of power and beauty, including Germaine Greer in her 1971 essay, "Lady Love Your Cunt" and Eve Ensler in her 1996 play *The Vagina Monologues*. There are ongoing efforts to reclaim the word, particularly by some feminists and members of the LGBTQ+ community, although these efforts tend to be short-lived. This could be due to censorship in mainstream media, but also because of ingrained cultural factors.[53]

The revulsion for the word and its referent – Grose defined cunt as "a nasty word for a nasty thing" – is thought to show contempt for women. Ironically, as an insult it's predominately used toward men, to imply that he is weak, like a woman, and also insulting him by association with femininity. But on the other hand, like bitch, cunt is sometimes used in a jocular way, especially in Australian English in greetings like, "How are you going, you old cunt?" Men can joke around with each other and use the word metaphorically, without any of them thinking about a vagina at all. Similarly, in Scotland cunt can be used as a nongendered and nonderogatory term. Cunt has boomed in usage over the years, especially in the relative freedom of the online world where it's easier to type things than say them out loud. But for the most part there remains a strong taboo around the word and it hasn't lost its stigma. It may never do so because of its long history of misogynistic use.

As we've seen, whore, slut, cunt, and bitch are tools that can be used to objectify women. But they're not the only gendered insults around. Others refer to a woman's appearance, such as *crone* or *bag*, while they further imply age and are often paired with old, like old hag or old biddy. Another common class of sexist slurs are animal metaphors in which women are likened to the stereotypical traits ascribed to a particular creature. An evil woman is called a dragon or a bat, a larger woman is a cow or pig, an ugly woman is a horse or dog, while a spiteful woman is catty or a bitch. To circle back to Donald Trump, who is known for his invective and name-calling, the former US President developed a reputation for using animal insults in which he abused women as "dogs," "horses," and "fat pigs" if he didn't like them. He once called a lawyer a "disgusting animal" when she asked to take a break during a deposition to pump breast milk for her baby.[54] He was also a fan of bitch. In a meeting at the Oval Office regarding US–German relations, Trump was caught on record referring to then German Chancellor Angela Merkel as "that bitch."[55] Some animal names are directed toward men too, notably snake, rat, and dog, although a disproportionate amount of them are used against women.

Even some women's names have turned into insults. A number of common first names are shorthand for an "annoying" woman who behaves badly. Karen, Becky, and Stacy are among a group of pejorative names that are associated with specific social stereotypes. Karen is a popular insult for a middle-aged white woman who is racist, obnoxious, and complaining; her demanding catch-cry is "I want to speak to the manager." Becky is a young white woman who is privileged, prejudiced, and superficial. Stacy is an attractive white woman who is vain, rude, and only interested in sex. These caricatures of women have become the subject of songs, memes, and viral videos. While they are often seen as harmless words that make fun of certain types of women, they have their roots in misogyny because they generalize women and perpetuate sexist stereotypes. Moreover, there are no true equivalent insults for calling out these same behaviors in men. It's argued that Chad is comparable to Stacy, although he's praised for his promiscuity as a good-looking stud while she's condemned as a slut. The names Ken and Kevin have been floated as corresponding (and alliterative) mates for Karen, although male Karen is generally used, which ultimately refers back to women in a negative way.

Bitch and other sexist slurs are used to police the behavior of women and to divide them into simplistic categories of "good" versus "bad." These slurs are everyday words that are pitted against women by men, but they are also used by women against women. This reveals and fosters an internalized sexism. Sexism is normalized from childhood; from a young age we're all groomed to be sexist. Negative stereotypes and cultural assumptions about women are learned subconsciously from family and friends, school, church, the workplace, laws, and society in general. Men and women are conditioned to accept these sexist beliefs and attitudes as normal, and then to enforce them. In this way, women impose sexism upon themselves, and against other women. A few years ago, Roseanne Barr was fired from her own TV show for racially abusing Valerie Jarrett on Twitter,[56] saying the former White House adviser looked like "the muslim brotherhood & planet of the apes had a baby." Barr, who is certainly no stranger to having the "bitch" moniker hurled at her, initially apologized to Jarrett, but then added fuel to the fire when she exclaimed in an interview, "I thought the bitch was WHITE! God damn it! I thought the bitch was white. Fuck!"[57]

The pejorative use of bitch by women against women perpetuates sexism. It encourages the popular stereotype that women don't like each other and simply can't get along. This belief holds that women are competitive, manipulative, and spiteful. Women are painted as petty, catty bitches who act in a bitchy way toward other women, especially those whom they somehow perceive as a threat. Women are often portrayed as rivals to win the attentions and affections of men. In 1989, Donald Trump's mistress Marla Maples confronted his wife Ivana Trump at a restaurant in Aspen, Colorado. Mrs. Trump chased Maples out of the room, shouting, "You bitch! Leave my husband alone!"[58] Other sensationalized accounts report that the altercation took place on a mountaintop where they threw snowballs and hissed at each other. Years later, in an interview with Howard Stern, Trump joked about pitting the two women against each other in a boxing ring. Women are portrayed as bitches, no matter what their age is. In the movie *Mean Girls* there is the trope of the backstabbing bitches in high school, who then graduate to being the "bitchy boss" in the workplace. In an article in *Forbes* about these stereotypes, one executive described a falling-out she had with her colleagues and the attention it received in the press. "If it had been men, it would have been all business. But because we're women, it's always portrayed as a catfight."[59] When used by women against women, sexist slurs like bitch can keep them from being allies and building solidarity and community.

Good Bitch, Bad Bitch

When all is said and done, has bitch truly been reclaimed? Unfortunately, there just isn't a simple answer to this question. It's complicated. Some of the examples mentioned in this chapter may suggest to us that bitch has been successfully reclaimed. When Jo Freeman penned *The BITCH Manifesto*, inspiring others to adopt bitch as an empowering self-identity, it was reclaimed, but only in those specific situations. Also, when Tina Fey and Alexandria Ocasio-Cortez enthused "Bitches get stuff done!" the word was reclaimed, but only in those situations. When feminist celebrities like Gloria Steinem thank people for calling them bitches, it's reclaimed, but only in cases like these. As we've seen, for some powerful women, from Yoko Ono to Nicki Minaj, bitch is a badge of honor they've worn proudly. Reclaiming bitch isn't only for celebrities, *any* woman can make the word her own, if she wants to do so. It's a personal choice. And if women want to take a bad word that has been used against them to make it better, who are we to say otherwise?

Today, bitch is used in lots of other positive ways too. Referring to a friend as "bitch" can show affection and familiarity; much in the way that cunt is used in a playful, joking manner between men who are close friends. Sexy bitch and skinny bitch are now widely acceptable and used not only about women, but also by women. Being called a good bitch can be taken as a compliment, but then so is being called a bad bitch. This phrase was inspired by Rihanna's song of the same name in which she describes herself as a bad bitch who is "Classy, seductive, a devil in Prada," and a woman who won't be messed with. Then there are the many oddball uses of bitch that don't seem to have anything to do with people at all. To describe something as bitchin' is to say that it's awesome or cool. While "life's a bitch" is a colorful way of saying that life is not easy, it isn't a nasty comment about a person. (And we'll revisit these uses and more very soon.)

These positive uses of bitch might further lead us to think that the word has been successfully reappropriated. On the other hand, the many counterexamples we've seen suggest that it hasn't. Unfortunately, the ways women try to reclaim bitch do not diminish its stigmatizing power in the hands of others, and especially men. When Ted Yoho called Ocasio-Cortez a "fucking bitch" it demonstrated that bitch hasn't been reclaimed. Similarly, when Kianga Mwamba was Tasered by Baltimore police and vilified as a "dumb bitch" it was further proof that bitch hasn't been reclaimed. And when O.J. Simpson repeatedly called Nicole Brown a "fucking bitch" in the midst of an abusive relationship, it shows that the word has definitely not been reclaimed. Bitch is a dangerous word. It can be an act of hate speech. Bitch reveals hatred toward a woman, or toward women in general. And like Ocasio-Cortez pointed out, bitch is not only disrespectful but also dehumanizing, and this puts women in a vulnerable position where they can be abused.

In rarer cases, the bitch is the one who is the abuser. Throughout history, powerful women who abuse their power have been regarded as bitches. As we've seen, Margaret Thatcher was frequently dubbed a bitch, often by working-class people from the north of England whose lives were ruined by her harsh policies. Bitch was also a common moniker given to the notorious Nazi women who participated in the Holocaust during World War II. Ilse Koch, who committed numerous atrocities at the Buchenwald concentration camp, became known as the "Witch," "Beast," or "Bitch of Buchenwald" for her senseless cruelty and brutality toward tens of thousands of innocent people. Similarly, Irma Grese, a warden of the women's section of Bergen-Belsen, earned the epithet "The Bitch of Belsen," while the blonde and blue-eyed Dorothea Binz, an officer at Ravensbrück, was known as the "Beautiful Bitch." Such arguably evil women, who fail to conform to feminine expectations and gendered stereotypes, risk being cast as bitches.

As we've seen, predecessors to bitch that have been successfully reclaimed include queer and gay. Some have even tried to reclaim other common insults like fat, nerdy, and slut. Infamously, the African American community has reclaimed *nigger*, often using different spellings and pronunciation like *nigga* to clearly distinguish the reclaimed word from the racist slur. We also see this differentiation with euphemisms of bitch, like *biotch* and *biznatch*. The catch is, however, that reclamation is always conditional. These words have only been reclaimed in part. That is, only those affected by the words can truly reclaim them. If bitch is to be reclaimed, only women can reclaim the word. But reclamation isn't the answer for everyone. Taking back a negative word can be empowering for some people, while others may continue to have strong negative associations to the word. Reclaimed words are only context-dependent, continuing to retain their negative connotations when used outside of the community that seeks to reclaim them. Both positive and negative meanings of the word continue to exist, side by side.

With such a checkered record, we have to concede that bitch hasn't been entirely rehabilitated. But we have to acknowledge its fluidity. Bitch is a flexible word that can be both good and bad. For centuries, bitch was an insult. In recent decades, some women have adopted bitch as an empowering label. Others reject the word. Bitch is battling a long history of invective use and many simply don't like the word and don't want to reclaim it. As we saw, *suffragette* was reclaimed by some women in the UK, but not in the US, where the term was used more by anti-suffragists than by the activists themselves. Bitch takes on a different power depending on who's using it. It is used by women for women, or used against them. We can't always control who uses the word and how, but we can control the way we conceive of it. For this reason, reclamation is seen as the antidote, and so the reclamation efforts of bitch are ongoing.

But can bitch ever be fully reclaimed? The truth is that it probably won't be. Speakers are likely to keep all of their options open to use the word for both good and bad.

In the previous chapter we talked about pejoration and how negative senses tend to muscle out the positive ones. In a related example, there was a pub called The Black Bitch in Linlithgow, Scotland. The establishment was named after a local legend about a loyal black greyhound that would bring food to her owner by swimming across a loch. A new owner wanted to change the pub's name, fearing it was sexist, racist, and offensive to his clientele. While he had the support of some people in the community, thousands of locals signed a petition to retain the name, arguing that it referred literally to a female dog and that it had no negative connotations. The city council, however, decided that the name wasn't an integral element of the historic interest of the building, which had previously gone by other names anyway, and agreed that the owner should choose a "more welcoming and inclusive name."[60] The pub was renamed The Willow Tree. These events show that the figurative racist and sexist associations of The Black Bitch overpowered any literal meaning of the individual words involved. And for this reason, the name obviously *did* have negative connotations. From Aunt Jemima to the Washington Redskins, hundreds of brand names, businesses, landmarks, and place names have been changed because their meanings have become offensive over time.

When attempts are made to reclaim a word it is often used in an ironic or satirical way, to add some levity and lessen its offensiveness. When Andi Zeisler and Lisa Jervis founded *Bitch* magazine they attempted to reclaim the word, inspired by the reclamation of queer by the LGBTQ+ community. They were also motivated by the word's myriad of meanings and the way it both intrigues and shocks people. Explaining the choice, Jervis said, "If speaking my mind makes me a bitch, I'm proud of that."[61] Bitch is a controversial word. Then they chose the subtitle: *Feminist Response to Pop Culture*. Feminist is also a controversial word. Zeisler remarked that "Having the word 'feminist' in the magazine subtitle has been far more controversial than having the word 'bitch' in the title ... the word bitch, for better or worse, has become part of our cultural lexicon. Yet feminist is still one of those words that people find very hard to understand."[62] The goals of the magazine, which started as a zine distributed out of the back of a station wagon in 1996, were to "point out the everyday sexism of popular culture, propose alternatives, and celebrate pro-woman, pro-feminism products." The magazine ran media criticism and cultural commentary on critical topics including nonbinary identity, body inclusivity, masculinity, and Black feminism. Sadly, *Bitch* closed its doors in 2022, although it was highly influential, inspiring feminist media such as *Feministe, Feministing, Jezebel,* Vice's *Broadly,* and the feminist comic book *Bitch Planet,* among many others in its lasting legacy.

Just like its early days, for many people feminism is very much the f-word. It is caught in a vicious cycle of bad and good. In some usage today, feminist carries negative connotations. Critics of modern feminism characterize feminists as angry and extreme, and over a century later, they're still demonized as militant and rabid. Conservatives mock them as *femtards*, *feminazis*, and *female supremacists*. Traditionalists argue that modern feminism has destroyed women. They say that the movement has abandoned the cause of gender equality to become antagonistic toward men. Feminists are misunderstood as man-haters and anti-male bigots who are on a mission to smash the patriarchy. Given the propaganda, some who would otherwise identify as feminists instead shun the label, like Simone de Beauvoir once did. Others find feminist to be a little outdated. Some even think the name should be replaced. Beyoncé once quipped, "I need to find a catchy new word for feminism, right? Like 'Bootylicious.'"[63] Having said all that, many women absolutely *do* embrace the label. But do they also embrace "bitch"? Can a feminist call herself a bitch? Some say she can't. Others do. Feminism has always been about independence of thought. In a throwback to *Hell Cat*, some women even use feminist and bitch interchangeably. In the novel *If I Stay*, the protagonist Mia says of her mother, "She didn't care that people called her a bitch. 'It's just another word for feminist,' she told me with pride."[64]

For better or for worse, bitch is interwoven with the history of feminism. It is a word that represents both feminism and anti-feminism at the same time. But for some, the difference is that "feminist" is a positive word that is tied to a movement for social change, whereas "bitch" is invariably a negative word with no movement behind it. Some argue that we shouldn't try to reclaim bitch anyway. They say we shouldn't use it at all. Bitch carries a lot of baggage. The word hasn't escaped its sexist past or its sexist present, and possibly can't. Bitch, and other sexist slurs, are thought to unintentionally hurt women as a group. Trying to reclaim the term by declaring oneself a "bitch" or calling other women "bitches" in a friendly way only provides a false power and unwittingly reinforces sexism, they maintain.[65] They assert that reclamation only increases the perception that the word is socially acceptable, and excuses men who use it against women. And that women who normalize bitch normalize sexism.

Everyone has an opinion about this word.

It seems obvious but needs to be said that most women don't like to be called a bitch. It's a personal attack. It's hurtful and it's meant to sting. Even Meredith Brooks, the singer and composer of "Bitch," once said, "All I can say is that no woman wants to be called a bitch." She added, "The actual meaning of the word for most people being a derogatory comment against a woman; that's *never* going to change. You can't un-ring the bell."[66] Bitch is offensive – in most uses – and it's intended to be that way. The bottom line is that the main meaning of bitch is that it's an insult for a woman who's doing or saying something, anything, that someone else doesn't like.

But when bitch is aimed at a man it means something entirely different ...

3

• • • • • •

Son of a Bitch

As we've seen, bitch has been wielded against men for almost as long as it's been wielded against women. Bitch is still used across the genders, but it's used somewhat differently. We've shown that when a woman reclaims bitch it can have positive connotations, however, when aimed at a man, it's rarely a compliment. While a bitch can be a strong woman, it usually means a weak man. Unlike women who are saddled with the word because they're powerful, men are targeted with bitch when they're considered to be power*less*. Bitch likens a woman to a man, whereas it likens a man to a woman. It's usually an emasculating insult that suggests he's lacking in courage, strength, and toughness. Bitch might also imply that he's effeminate or gay. There are many different versions of the slur for a man. He might just be a plain old bitch, but he may also be branded a little bitch, a prison bitch, or a son of a bitch. And while a man who's a bitch might be a coward, a son of a bitch can be courageous and strong.

Son of a Gun

Son of a bitch is a gendered insult; it's usually directed toward men. The dictionaries say it's occasionally aimed at women too, but that sounds a little strange to our ears. And so does "daughter of a bitch." It would just be easier to call her a bitch. It's typically seen as an insult for men, although son of a bitch is considered to be sexist because it refers back to women in a negative way. The son of a bitch is tainted through his association with "the bitch," but it's still a woman who's the bitch. The phrase is extra offensive because it implies the man's mother is the bitch in question. Perhaps he has inherited the same "bitchy" qualities that she has. If you look up the phrase in a dictionary, it gives the vague definition that the word is an insult for a disagreeable or objectionable person. Over the years, son of a bitch has become a generalized term of abuse, but it isn't as popular or offensive as it used to be. Leading with "son of a ... " tones down or softens the slur that follows and so the phrase has less of a sting than bitch all by itself. Depending on its context, however, the insult is not to be underestimated, because it can still pack a punch. Nowadays it has many different spellings, euphemisms, and meanings. It's predominately an insult, but it can also be an exclamation to show surprise or annoyance when something unexpected happens. In Texas, son-of-a-bitch is even the name of a hearty stew favored by cowboys that's made from beef heart, liver, kidneys, and vegetables.

Like its sister term, son of a bitch has a long history. As mentioned previously, Old Icelandic had the insult *bikkju-sonr*, which is a relative of the English phrase. The first recorded use in English is *biche-sone* ("bitch's son") that appears in the medieval romance *Arthur and Merlin*. Centuries later, it was flourishing in London's underbelly where it was picked up by none other than William Shakespeare, who used it, complete with the spelling we recognize today, in his tragedy *King Lear*. The Bard's friends, playwrights Francis Beaumont and John Fletcher, also took a liking to the vulgar phrase and used it in their works, including the 1625 play *Coxcombe*, "They had no mothers, they are the sons of bitches."[1] Half a century later, its use in Thomas Shadwell's play *The Humorist* reads like a modern text message and might be an example of how it was used in speech at the time. "Now I have it, ha, ha, ha! Though I am a dog, I am not the son of a bitch crazy, ha, ha, ha!"[2] Other related insults in Early Modern English were *son of a whore* and *whoreson*. These were extra offensive, because they implied the man was the son of a prostitute and probably a bastard too.

Over the centuries, use of the phrase waned, but it was poised for a glorious comeback. Just as son of a bitch was dying out in England, it was rescued by the United States. Early white settlers imported the phrase there, where it took hold and became America's favorite expletive from the eighteenth century until the middle of the twentieth century.[3] One of its earliest appearances in literature was in John Neal's 1823 book *Seventy-Six* about the American Revolutionary War. The protagonist, Jonathan Oadley, recounts a battle scene in which he's mounted on a horse: "I wheeled, made a dead set at the son-of-a-bitch in my rear, unhorsed him, and actually broke through the line."[4] At the time, the book was criticized heavily for its foul profanity and sexual content, although the author was unapologetic. As narrator, Oadley says, "My style may often offend you. I do not doubt that it will. I hope that it will. It will be remembered the better." The book is now praised as the closest representation of colloquial Yankee American English of its day, which gives us a glimpse into the use of son of a bitch in everyday speech. By the following century, the phrase had taken hold in popular literature. Just like bitch, son of a bitch was popularized by Lost Generation writers like John Steinbeck, Sherwood Anderson, and William Faulkner. We might remember that Ernest Hemingway used bitch liberally in his novels, and in his personal life, while he also loved using son of a bitch as well. In his letters he frequently reprimands himself as a "son of a bitch" for various reasons; out of guilt for his womanizing and for not keeping in contact with old buddies.[5]

Son of a bitch then achieved its longevity by becoming a catch-phrase in Western movies, where it became synonymous with the Wild West. In an iconic scene in *True Grit* the quintessential cowboy John Wayne, playing the role of one-eyed Marshal Reuben "Rooster" Cogburn, challenges the bad guys to a gunfight with "Fill your hand, you son of a bitch!" (Of course, he wins the showdown.) The insult of the phrase was greatly increased when preceded by words like *nothing but a, no good, dirty* or *damn*. In the movies, a tough guy might even refer to himself as a son of a bitch to prove just how tough he really was (evidently because he had grown up with a bitch as a mother). In *Cool Hand Luke*, the Captain, a sadistic and brutal prison overseer, threatens the inmates with "Now, I can be a good guy, or I can be one real mean son of a bitch." In the old Westerns, cowboys, outlaws, deputies, good guys, and bad guys alike brandish the phrase like a gun. Son of a bitch came to signify American hardness and toughness, resilience and grit.

It was an all-American phrase that was even acceptable for a president to say. In 1939, when the United States pursued friendly relations with Nicaraguan dictator Anastasio Somoza because the country was a non-communist stronghold, Franklin D. Roosevelt allegedly said of him, "He's a son-of-a-bitch, but he's *our* son-of-a-bitch."[6] Even if he didn't say it, the quote expressed the American attitude. The famous quote has since been attributed variously to former presidents Lyndon Johnson, Ronald Reagan, and Richard Nixon. A son of a bitch was a devious kind of guy who could be called upon to do the dirty work and get the job done. Nixon infamously invoked the phrase during the Watergate scandal when he sought a pawn to leak information to the newspapers. A taping system installed at Nixon's own request caught him saying, "I really need a son of a bitch like [Tom Charles] Huston who will work his butt off and do it dishonorably."[7]

Son of a bitch has also been wielded by famous American figures to describe the enemy. In a rousing speech made to his troops on the eve of the Normandy invasion, general George S. Patton said of Adolf Hitler, "And when we get to Berlin, I am personally going to shoot that paper-hanging son of a bitch. Just like I'd shoot a snake!"[8]

There are several theories to explain what this unusual insult meant. Some say "paper-hanging" was a reference to Hitler's failed pre-war career as an artist. Others say it refers to Hitler hanging military maps on the walls of his bunker. (The novel insult didn't have any enduring appeal, although Mel Brooks immortalized it in his fictional musical "Springtime for Hitler" featured in *The Producers*.) General Patton's speech was peppered with insults to rally the troops. He referred to German soldiers as "son of an asshole bitches." Then he ends his address by saying, "Why, by God, I actually pity those poor sons-of-bitches we're going up against. By God, I do." The fiery speech evidently worked, because the troops went on to victory, despite heavy casualties. Also known as Operation Overlord or D-Day, the Allied invasion of Western Europe in June 1944 marked the beginning of the end of World War II.

After Roosevelt died suddenly in April 1945, Harry S. Truman became US President and the one to lead his country through the final stages of the war. Military aide Harry Vaughan once praised his pal Truman as "one tough son of a bitch of a man."[9] As a wartime president, Truman is remembered as a strong, courageous leader and decision-maker, although not all of his decisions were popular. It was Truman's unenviable job to strategize how to end the war. He achieved this by dropping atomic bombs on Hiroshima and Nagasaki, forcing Japan to surrender to the United States. The bombs were created in a secret scientific effort called the Manhattan Project. After a successful test of the weapon, scientist Kenneth Bainbridge famously exclaimed to physicist Robert Oppenheimer, "Now we are all sons-of-bitches."[10] (The historic quote is conspicuous by its absence from the 2023 movie.) Bainbridge later explained his remark, "I was saying in effect that we had all worked hard to complete a weapon which would shorten the war, but posterity would not consider that phase of it and would judge the effort as the creation of an unspeakable weapon by unfeeling people. I was also saying that the weapon was terrible and those who contributed to its development must share in any condemnation of it."

Clearly, son of a bitch is a versatile phrase that can have positive or negative connotations, depending on its context. It has a wide range of uses. Poor son of a bitch can express pity or sympathy in a genuine way, or sarcastically, like General Patton's use. It can be used in banter as an affectionate term of address, rather like cunt, in phrases like I miss that old son of a bitch. It can also express admiration and approval: He's one lucky son of a bitch. Son of a bitch! exclaims surprise or shock, when we've stubbed a toe. Like Hemingway's use, it can be self-critical. It can also be intimidating, like the Captain's threat in *Cool Hand Luke*. Rock band Nazareth's "Hair of the Dog" has the menacing hook "Now you're messing with a son of a bitch." Or a son of a bitch could be someone who's unfeeling and lacking in empathy. During an interrogation by the police after his arrest in Pensacola, Florida, notorious serial killer Ted Bundy bragged, "I'm the most cold-hearted son of a bitch you'll ever meet."[11] As an insult, son of a bitch frequently implies a lack of intelligence and readily takes descriptors like dumb and stupid. 46th US President Joe Biden was once recorded on a hot mic responding to Fox News correspondent Peter Doocy asking, "Do you think inflation is a political liability ahead of the midterms?" Biden responded sarcastically, "It's a great asset – more inflation. What a stupid son of a bitch."[12] As if all of this wasn't enough, a son of a bitch can also be some*thing* rather than some*one*, a difficult task or a useless thing like a broken-down car.

Once a scathing insult, or the dominion of cowboys and war heroes, son of a bitch now sounds a little outdated and even precious, like saying *sugar* or *shivers* instead of shit. The caustic social critic H.L. Mencken once complained that it was embarrassing and weak compared to more creative insults in other languages. "Our maid-of-all-work is son-of-a-bitch, which seems as pale and ineffectual to a Slav or a Latin as 'fudge' does to us. There is simply no lift in it, no shock, no sis-boom-ah. The dumbest policeman in Palermo thinks of a dozen better ones between breakfast and the noon whistle."[13] Even though son of a bitch is already euphemistic, it has developed its own euphemisms like *sonuvabitch* and *sumbitch*, in which the words often run into each other to soften the slur. S.O.B. was once a popular euphemism in US English. It probably would've become an acronym if it wasn't for its similarity to "sob," as in to cry noisily.

Son of a bitch spawned numerous cutesy euphemisms like *son of a duck* and *son of a big shoe* ("son of a bitch, you"). *Son of a gun* is another "polite" watered-down version. It's said that the phrase is of naval origins, applying to boys who were born on ships during the days when women were allowed to accompany their sailor husbands to sea. Some claim that a son of a gun was a soldier's bastard.[14] Others say it was a British navy term for a boy of uncertain paternity born onto a ship, who was listed on the ship's log as a "son of a gun." Another theory tells that on a long sea voyage, a son of a gun was a child born on the vessel's gun deck. Yet another ties the phrase to the reason for shotgun weddings, the child of such unions was deemed a "son of a gun." We have to be suspicious when we come across so many different theories. Most of these colorful explanations appear more than a century after the emergence of the phrase so they're likely false etymologies, but they make for a good story. Nowadays, son of a gun is so whitewashed and acceptable that it's become the name of movies, restaurants, and even household cleaning products. In the modern era, son of a bitch and its many guises have mostly lost their sting.

Little Bitch

When it's used against men instead of women, bitch means something else. In terms of gender roles, men are usually considered to be the privileged and dominant group in Western society, while women are seen as the stigmatized or subordinate group, the second sex. But even within the privileged male group there is still a hierarchy of masculinity. Masculinity can be defined as our cultural view of "what men do to be men." Men who don't embody the idea of stereotypical masculinity, because of their gender expression, behavior, sexual orientation, or something else, are also stigmatized and oppressed by the narrow definition of what "being a real man" means. Being a real man can mean being tough. Bitch is commonly wielded by sportsmen who accuse a fellow player of unmanliness for not being tough enough. When the New England Patriots lost several football games, Martellus Bennett blamed team member Jimmy Garoppolo for failing to fight through a shoulder injury. "You can't win with a bitch for quarterback," Bennett said. "He didn't want to come out and do anything because his agent was trying to protect his body or some shit like that."[15] His replacement Jacoby Brissett "came out with a fucked-up thumb and played his heart out, but Jimmy was just being a bitch about it all." Garoppolo was labeled a bitch for not "sucking it up" and stoically enduring his pain like a "real man" supposedly should. Fellow player Julian Edelman agreed with this characterization, saying, "I got mad about it. I sacrifice my body all day long. I was taking shots for this, numbing up that. Broken ribs, shoulders, hanging on by limbs, just to play."

A man might be called a bitch for shirking his responsibilities as an adult and not "acting like a man." In James Joyce's *Portrait of the Artist as a Young Man*, Stephen Dedalus is a daydreaming, loafing, twenty-two-year-old college student. He's late for lectures one day, because his mother is still bathing him at that mature age, when his father Simon cries out to his sister, "Is your lazy bitch of a brother gone out yet?"[16] Ironically, Simon was the irresponsible one; he's incapable of keeping a job and prefers to spend his money on booze rather than taking care of his dozen children. Stephen described his father as an aimless type, "A medical student, an oarsman, a tenor, an amateur actor, a shouting politician … a drinker, a good fellow, a storyteller, somebody's secretary, something in a distillery, a tax gatherer, a bankrupt and at present a praiser of his own past." Being good at being a man meant performing the male role competently; being a proficient procreator, which Simon clearly did well, but also being a protector and provider.

Bitch might also be leveled at a man who has something stereotypically feminine about his appearance, like wearing earrings, growing long hair, being of short stature, or having "man boobs." The phrase *bitch tits* refers to a male bodybuilder with over-developed pectoral muscles through anabolic steroid use, and also a man who is overweight or has a hormone imbalance. For a man to have enlarged mammary glands, like a woman has breasts, makes him "like a woman" according to some. In the movie *Fight Club*, Robert Paulson, played by rock singer Meat Loaf, is a former bodybuilder who developed testicular cancer due to his excessive use of steroids. He underwent treatment for cancer, which resulted in gynecomastia. This condition is an increase in the amount of breast tissue in boys and men caused by an imbalance of estrogen and testosterone. Because of his enlarged breasts, Paulson was dubbed "Bitch Tits Bob."

When aimed at a man, or a woman, bitch means they are not performing their gender "properly." A male bitch is a man who is not considered to be masculine enough; he's a "man who's not doing a good job of being a man." As we've seen, a woman who's called a bitch is accused of being domineering, assertive, tough, or too sexual, like a man "should" be, whereas a man who's called a bitch is seen as submissive, sensitive, or too feminine, like a woman. If a man is *acting like a bitch* this often implies that he is behaving like a bitch of a woman; he's nagging, malicious, or spiteful. In Ice-T's song "Bitches 2," he raps about men he knows who've behaved in sneaky, underhanded ways such as to amount to being "bitches." He says, "So ladies, we ain't just talkin' bout you, cause some of you niggas is bitches too." Then he laments for each man, "How'd he go out? He went out like a bitch." This implies these men were beaten up or maybe even killed for their bitch-like transgressions, but that they didn't go out bravely like a man should. In the E-40 and Too $hort song "Bitch" we hear both versions of the word. E-40 warns men, "Don't act like a bitch" and criticizes those who have "feminine tendencies like a bitch," but he also calls a woman a bitch for having sex with multiple men. From African American English we also get the phrase *bitch ass* to refer to a weak, cowardly, unmanly man.

By the standards of rap and hip hop culture, calling a man a bitch is a substantial affront. This is because it emasculates him. Bitch is aimed squarely at his masculinity. In this machismo culture, boys are constantly being inundated with messages that being a girl is inferior. It's a compliment for a boy to be just like his dad. As they say, like father like son. But comparisons of boys to girls are often negative. A boy is told not to run like a girl or throw like a girl. He should not be a sissy or girly. A series of comedy sketches on *Saturday Night Live* featured Austrian bodybuilder brothers Hans & Franz and their show "Pumping Up," which was less about working out and more about humiliation as they abused their viewers, calling them "sissies," "crybabies," and "pathetic little girly men." The pair were characterized as cousins of Arnold Schwarzenegger, who in a case of life imitating art, adopted the phrase "girly men," which he used at several public functions, including an appearance at the 2004 Republican National Convention. Gay rights and feminist groups criticized Schwarzenegger for using the phrase and he later expressed regret, "At the time it felt like the right thing to do. It was in my gut. I improvised it. I called them girlie men because they weren't willing to take risks. They were afraid of everything. Politicians in general want to do little things so there's no risk involved. But it was shortsighted. In the long term, it's better to not say that, because you want to work with them."[17] Schwarzenegger's remorse was in the partisan nature of the word's use, not that he amplified a phrase representing a broader culture of misogyny and homophobia.

The effeminate, weak girly-man is contrasted with the *he-man*, *macho man*, and *manly man*, which bring together images of strength and superhero-like physique. Meanwhile they suggest the complementary stereotype that women are not as strong or courageous as men. Even for adult women, being a *girly girl*, that is excessively feminine, for liking pink clothes, wearing make-up, or dressing in skirts and dresses, is often seen as a bad thing. Girly girls are dismissed as unintelligent, vain, and superficial. Being a *man's man*, however, is a good thing. He's a man who's popular among men. A *mama's boy* is a weak, mollycoddled man who's unable to face the world's challenges like a "real man," while a close relationship between mother and son is deemed to be suspect. On the other hand, being a *daddy's girl* is romanticized, meaning that she's adorable and loved, she's a princess, while she knows how to flirt with men. Calling a man a "bitch" is the adult version of the schoolyard taunt "you fight like a girl," and this adds to the belief that anything feminine is a threat to masculinity.

If a man isn't deemed to be masculine enough in his actions, he may be branded a *little bitch* to shame him for his behavior. This implies that he's weak, pathetic, and too feminine. Therefore, he's not a "real man." *Bitchlet* and *bitchling* are also slang terms for a little bitch. Other insults are often tagged on to the phrase. He might be a *whiney little bitch* who is irritating because he complains or nags a lot, like a woman supposedly does. From a young age, boys and men are conditioned to not be little bitches. Whether it's getting injured on the football field or grieving the death of a family member, men in our culture are discouraged from expressing the effects of pain and suffering. There's a social rule against being a crybaby; boys and men are warned that they shouldn't cry. Like The Cure song says, "Boys Don't Cry." If a man cries like a little bitch, he's accused of being feeble, fragile, and showing too much emotion, like a woman would do. In *Corruption Officer*, a memoir by a former corrections officer, a new inmate at New York's notorious Rikers Island jail says of his night spent in a prison cell, "For the first time in my life my big 290-pound ass was lying on the bed provided for me, in a fetal position, whimpering to myself like a little bitch."[18] The little bitch is fearful, scared, and not "acting like a man." The implication is that he should toughen up and "man up." Even in the face of death. The 1953 poem *Death Row* tells the tale of Tony, "The man who didn't know the meaning of fright," a prisoner sentenced to death at New York's Sing Sing prison. He was described as "the dude who wasn't afraid to die," but as Tony awaited execution, "He broke down and cried like a scared little bitch and begged them not to throw the switch."[19]

Prison Bitch

In the US prison system "little bitch" has another meaning, referring to an exceptionally long prison sentence that is especially stiff due to repeat offenses. A "big bitch" is a conviction under any crime that carries a mandatory life sentence, or a sentence so long that it's an equivalent term. Within the colorful argot of prison culture, "bitch" has many meanings. It can refer to a female visitor, a prisoner's wife or girlfriend, and female prison staff such as correctional officers. A bitch might be a notably gullible inmate who is easily conned, or a "snitch," a tattletale who informs on other inmates when he provides secret information to prison authorities. In older slang, a *bitcher* was a habitual criminal. A bitch can even be the prison itself. In *Corruption Officer* a warden says, "Once they come through those doors we decide whether they're going to live in this bitch or whether they are going to fuck around with one of us and die up in this piece."

The phrase "being someone's bitch," a person who gets treated with little respect and is ordered around, began its life as a prison term for a male inmate who was low ranking, subordinate, or subservient. In the novel *Razorblade Tears*, Ike Randolph is sent to prison for manslaughter and as an inmate on the inside he says, "four brothers tried to jump me and make me their cell-block bitch."[20] In this context, making someone one's bitch means to assert dominance over an inmate, to subdue and control them. It suggests ownership of them, both within the social hierarchy of the prison, and sometimes sexually too. In prison lingo, bitch can also mean an effeminate man or a gay man, especially the "passive partner" in a sexual relationship. A *prison bitch* is a non-consensual sexual partner, a male prisoner who's used as an unwilling sex slave by another man (or men) in the absence of available women. Sometimes called a *punk*, the victim is used for sex and treated as property. He's often bought and sold as a commodity, like a pack of cigarettes. In a dehumanizing environment where inmates don't have many rights, this dynamic is also about power, oppression, and humiliation. This kind of abuse happens in women's prisons too, where *kittening* is the female version of having a prison bitch (the word has allusions to "pussy"). The *kitten* is "kept" by one inmate or shared throughout the prison block.

Same-sex relationships are common in men's prisons, where men seek a sexual outlet in an all-male environment. In what's called protective pairing, a weaker, vulnerable inmate is coerced into becoming a submissive sexual partner in exchange for physical protection from a "tough guy." The aggressor in the relationship is often called the *daddy* or the *husband* and his victim is the *prison wife, ho,* or *girlfriend.* In these relationships, the dominant man maintains his masculine identity, because his victim is symbolically placed in the position of a woman. Sex is only part of this arrangement, and the "wife" is often forced to perform non-sexual chores too, such as cleaning the cell, preparing food, and doing laundry. Sometimes he is forced to establish a female identity too, by taking a female name, shaving his legs, wearing make-up, dressing in women's clothes or underwear, and being emasculated to the point of not being allowed to stand while urinating.

Sexual victimization of adult inmates is an ongoing problem in US detention centers. A former inmate discusses the traumatic experience of prison rape: "I had no choice but to submit to being Inmate B's prison wife. Out of fear for my life, I submitted to sucking his dick, being fucked in my ass, and performing other duties as a woman, such as making his bed. In all reality, I was his slave."[21] The mindset is that the weaker inmate is a "bitch," because he can't defend himself or otherwise hold his own in the prison world of men. Another former prisoner describes these unequal relationships. "It's not that unusual. Men, well the young ones, they are scared out of their minds. They come in and, right off the bat, get jacked. They think this is never going to stop so if a guy tells him, 'Hey, I'll take care of everything' then sure, he'll do it. He'll act like the bitch and take it from another guy. I'm sure they would not do this outside, but prison is tough, so I get it." Sexual abuse in prison is perpetrated not only inmate-on-inmate but also staff-on-inmate, while incidents of misconduct are often underreported. No matter what crime a person has committed, rape is not part of the penalty.

Some of this slang has made its way beyond the prison walls where it's been co-opted by civilians too. In colloquial terms a bitch is anyone who adopts a subservient role, like an *office bitch* who performs menial tasks, such as fetching the coffee for coworkers. Bitch is often paired with a possessive word to signify ownership or control of someone. When Sammy Hagar replaced David Lee Roth in Van Halen it led to a feud, in which the original singer once bragged, "He works for me – he's my bitch. And when he says my name, we just sell that many more records. It reminds people of the glorious past even more. He doesn't even know it."[22] As mentioned, being someone's bitch is subordination or being told what to do, although outside of an oppressive prison environment this treatment may result in protest. In an episode of *Breaking Bad*, Jesse Pinkman warns Walter White, "Yo, stop treating me like I'm your assistant. I'm not your bitch to order around."[23] To be someone's bitch has invariably negative connotations; however, to make some*thing* one's bitch is often a good thing. People in remission declare triumphantly, "I made cancer my bitch." In such instances, the bitch is an adversity like sickness or a tough exam that is to be dominated and overcome.

Among the general public, these expressions don't usually have the violent and sexual connotations they have behind bars. Tropes of prison sexual assault, however, are common as jokes. The phrase of mock concern for someone going to prison, "Don't drop the soap!" implies that if they drop a bar of soap in a communal shower and bend over to retrieve it, they're in a vulnerable position to be raped by a fellow inmate. In a plot device on television, law enforcement officers warn young men who are in danger of incarceration, "Son, you know what they'll do to a pretty boy like you in prison?" In a racist meme, a Black character named Big Bubba metes out a kind of vigilante justice to his fellow inmates in the form of violent rape. Men treating men like women by dominating them sexually is often fodder for misguided humor too. Some websites have "prison bitch name generators." After entering your first and last name and clicking the "submit, bitch" button, these sites provide you with a new nickname, such as "butt whore," "mustache girl," and "ass master." In a society in which masculine dominance is normalized, these kinds of jokes are considered to be funny because they position a male "bitch" as feminized, that is, as a failed man.

Rodney Carrington's "Prison Bitch" plays to these well-worn tropes. The song tells the story of a tough guy who buys his cellmate for the cost of a candy bar and a packet of cigarettes. He's a "hardened criminal" who forces his "prison bitch" to perform various sexual acts, especially when the victim is picking up a bar of soap in the shower. It's joked that a pair of breasts was tattooed onto the submissive inmate's back to feminize him. The song ends with the "prison bitch" being resigned to his fate, but perhaps even enjoying it a little.[24]

There is a persistent myth that "prison is a gay man's dream." When Calvin Burdine was awaiting sentencing for allegedly stabbing his ex-boyfriend to death, the prosecuting attorney encouraged the jury in his closing remarks to award the death penalty rather than prison, because "sending a gay man to prison would be like setting a kid loose in a candy store."[25] The jury obliged, but the courts ordered a retrial because Burdine's lawyer was hostile, referring to his client as "fairy" and "faggot," while he slept through most of the proceedings. In the end, Burdine was sentenced to life in prison. Far from being a paradise or reward, the reality of life in prison for gay and transgender individuals is often a living hell of rape, beatings, and enslavement as a communal "bitch" or "prison ho." Gay prisoners are forced into passive and submissive roles, to abandon their male identity in order to survive a hypermasculine and homophobic environment. Jokes and slang about prison assault have homophobic undertones, and they also undermine the serious psychological trauma experienced by survivors of sexual assault.

Bitch Fight

As we saw earlier in this book, going back hundreds of years ago, bitch was a scathing insult for a "Molly," a man who today might identify as gay, bisexual, or queer. According to Francis Grose's *Vulgar Tongue*, at that time a "queer bitch" was an odd, unusual, or uncommon fellow.[26] By the twentieth century, however, bitch had entered common parlance among gay men, many of whom spoke Polari, a coded language used to communicate with others in the know. Polari was a jargon used within the gay community in Britain between 1900 and the 1970s, allowing gay men and women to hide and also reveal at a time when same-sex sexual activity was outlawed.[27] An eclectic mix of Italian, French, Yiddish, and London Cockney slang, Polari was spoken in gay pubs, fish markets, theaters, circuses, and on merchant ships. In the

Polari language, gay men were known as "omee-palones," meaning "men women." "Bitch" referred to an effeminate or passive gay man, while it could also mean a gay guy or drag queen who was rude, catty, or camp. "Camp" as in effeminate also comes from Polari (possibly derived from Italian *campare*, meaning "to exaggerate, make stand out"). Polari even had its own equivalent to son of a bitch: *cowson*. The word is immortalized in the lyrics of "Gertcha" by Chas & Dave. The song's hook is "gertcha cowson," which is akin to "get out of here, you little son of a bitch," which was something that Chas' father used to scream at him all the time when he was a kid.[28] The old-fashioned insult isn't around much today, but when the duo performed the song on *Top of the Pops* cowson was so offensive that the BBC producer demanded they omit the word. (They tried to do so, although they slipped up a few times.)

By the 1920s, bitch reached the gay community in the United States. Robert McAlmon, who published writers including Ernest Hemingway and Gertrude Stein, once wrote in a short story, "Isn't it strange though how all the queer men in the United States are friends of mine – the bitches all love me."[29] A bitch was an effeminate, passive man, but also a femme submissive lesbian who was highly feminine. "Bitch" was often contrasted with "butch," a masculine lesbian woman. Within the early LGBTQ+ community, bitch spawned lots of other new phrases too. In gay vernacular, *bitched up* meant fancily dressed, at the same time implying a certain amount of femininity in the attire. *Bitch's Christmas* was once a nickname for Halloween, an erotic and exotic celebration where queer men could dress in drag as they pleased. We might also remember that in former centuries, *bitchery* meant prostitution, while in the 1920s gay scene a bitchery was a gay bar. Many popular phrases come from this era, including *bitch fight*, which originally referred to an argument between gay men. A scene in the 1940s novel *O, Huge Angel* describes a vicious altercation between a group of intoxicated gay men, "The others sitting by them only turned around drunkenly and, accustomed to the bitch-fights in the City, they said nothing."[30] Bitch fight later shifted to the meaning we understand today of a fight between girls or women.

In an incident at the Academy Awards ceremony in 2022, host Chris Rock joked about actress Jada Pinkett Smith's shaved head, which she'd been shaving due to alopecia. Offended by the joke, her husband Will Smith leaped onto the stage and "gave Rock a good and vicious bitchslap," as it was described by the press.[31] Nowadays, a *bitch slap* refers to slapping someone angrily as an expression of dominance or contempt; it's to put someone in their place. (In African American English it can refer to killing a woman too. While a *bitch lick* is a hard blow and to *stamp a bitch* is when a man hits a woman hard enough to leave the imprint of his rings in her flesh.) In an ironic reversal of meaning, bitch slap used to mean a man who hit somebody in an effeminate way, with a slap rather than a punch, the implication being that he wasn't "man enough" to deliver a proper blow. Bitch slap and bitch fight are similar to *catfight*, an acrimonious fight between "catty" women. This is so named because, like cats, scratching is supposedly a common defensive tactic among bickering women, like hair pull-ing, ripping clothes, biting, hissing, and throwing their handbags at each other, as opposed to a manly brawl or fistfight between men. These gender differences in words for fighting imply that only men have serious, justifiable fights, whereas women fight over petty, trivial matters.

Like women, gay men are often stereotyped as mean, catty bitches. During a quarrel with Elton John, Boy George once called him a "humorless grand old dame." George later admitted he was at fault. "I did have a falling out with Elton a few years ago because I was being a bitch, but we made up and we're really good friends again."[32] From the idea of a catty gay man comes the adjective *bitchy*, to describe a spiteful, mean person, who is usually a gay man, or a woman. A remark can be bitchy too; in particular a comment that is cruel, sar-castic, or rude. The stereotype of the bitchy gay man and the bitchy queen has been around for a long time. Trading insults or the art of the putdown is important and celebrated within gay culture, in order for these men to defend themselves against bullies and harassment outside of the group. In the 1949 movie *Beyond the Forest*, Bette Davis' character marries a small-town doctor who introduces her to their modest marital home. She saunters down the stairs with a bored, snarky attitude and declares to him, "What a dump!"[33] (The scene was recreated by Elizabeth Taylor at the start of *Who's Afraid of Virginia Woolf.*) Davis is a gay icon (and so is Taylor) and the sassy remark in this scene is feted in gay culture as an archetypal example of bitchiness. But bitchy hasn't always meant an unkind person or comment; it originally referred to a sexually provocative woman. Even earlier still, bitchy described a male dog that appeared less muscular or aggressive and therefore looked and acted more like a female dog.

Bitch as a verb is also tied in closely with gay culture. Some say it's derived from bitchy; others think it comes from older uses of bitch as in to ruin or destroy something. Another theory is that it goes back as far as Chaucer's reference to "bicced bones," the unlucky dice. The verb was certainly adopted enthusiastically into the Polari language and popularized by gay culture. Bitching is about more than just complaining or arguing, it means to do so excessively and in an annoying way, akin to nagging or whining. This gave rise to the idiom to *bitch and moan*, which suggests the listener's annoyance. To *have a bitch* can also mean to complain in a gossiping way. The words gossip, chatter, babble, and bitch are all applied to communication between women. They imply that the discourses are at best trivial, and at worst, destructive. In the US military, a "bitch box" was a public address system, the loudspeaker's jarring alerts likened to a bitching, nagging woman. Similarly, in the Canadian Air Force, an automatic audible vocal warning system of danger is known as a Bitching Betty. The terms *bitch session* and *bitch sesh* are also associated with gossip and especially women; however, they originated with a US military phrase for a conversation in which (usually male) personnel aired their grievances with a senior officer. In a 1945 issue of *Yank*, Sergeant McDougall of the Air Force is praised for being "a kindly, fatherly type. He'd listen to any guy's bitching, never interrupting or making the guy feel like he was wasting his time."[34] When used as a verb, the act of bitching is almost always a bad thing, but as an adjective or exclamation, something that is *bitching!* has the opposite meaning; it's excellent or cool. While the gay community adopted bitching in this negative sense, the positive use of bitching as something awesome emerged in surfer slang in the 1950s and was popularized during the 1980s by teenage girls in California.

The use of the Polari language declined with the introduction of the Sexual Offences Act in 1967, which decriminalized gay sex, so there was no need for secret slang anymore. By the time of the gay liberation movement of the 1970s, many people found the jargon to be passé and sexist anyway. Nevertheless, a few Polari words have survived, most notably *camp, drag, butch,* and *bitch.* Gay culture has embraced the many different uses of bitch. Bitch can even be a self-identifying label. Depending on its context, bitch can be either an insult or a term of endearment, along with "honey," "sweetie," "girl," and the use of she/her pronouns. Polari was full of this kind of "she-ing," where queer men and women switched their pronouns so they could openly talk about sex and love in public without fear of arrest or persecution. For some modern gay men, using these feminine words with their friends is a way of embracing femininity and showing affection to others who share their identities. This in-group use, however, is somewhat controversial among feminists. Invoking bitch to create a shared culture is intended to be free of misogynistic intent, although in a society where women have long been demeaned by the word, there's a danger that men using it at all can perpetuate negative stereotypes of women. It's argued that gay men are men, and men can be prone to misogyny. Co-opting feminine language can be a reflection of their male privilege.

Bitch is often used within gay culture in a positive way, although it's also used outside of the group in a negative way. Much like women who reclaim bitch for themselves, only to have it used against them by men (and other women), bitch is used by gay men but also against them, especially by straight men. It's a common insult aimed at men rumored to be gay. American football star Odell Beckham Jr. has been targeted by slurs on the field; he was called a "bitch," "ballerina," and "female" amid speculation that he was gay.[35] The wide receiver was mocked as not being a "real man" because of his playing style, and also because he dyes his hair blonde and keeps his private life low-key.

Calling a player's manhood into question has long been considered the ultimate insult in sports. Slurs like bitch imply he's effeminate and not man enough to play football, hockey, or other manly (and violent) games. In the world of traditionally male sports, bitch denigrates boys and men who show a lack of aggression or masculinity. Reinforcing these gender roles, some sportswomen also abuse their fellow players with "bitch" during games, to subordinate their opponents and show their toughness.

When leveled against gay men by heterosexual men, bitch is almost invariably derogatory. Just as bitch is a tool of violence used against women, the word is wielded against gay men during hate crimes. It's a homophobic insult used toward gay people during incidents of gay bashing – an attack, abuse, or assault committed against a person who's perceived by the aggressor to be gay, lesbian, bisexual, or trans- gender.[36] Bitch often appears with other epithets that are intended to shame, like *homo, faggot, sissy,* and *poofter*. Words like *fucking, filthy*, and *dirty*, suggesting uncleanness and repulsion, frequently accom- pany these slurs too. Homophobia and misogyny are on the same continuum and many lesbian women have reported being abused as "bitch" along with other slurs during incidents of sexual violence. Pulitzer Prize-winning author Victoria Brownworth wrote about her traumatic experience of "corrective rape," a disturbing practice in which a gay man or lesbian is assaulted in an attempt to "cure" them of their sexual orientation.[37] During the attack, two men with knives proceeded to slap, punch, bite, choke, and rape Brownworth, mean- while abusing her verbally as a "whore," "pussy," "dyke," and "bitch."

Bastard, Blackguard, Bounder

We've already mentioned that there are thousands of sexist slurs for women. (We haven't listed them all, of course.) There are also many gendered slurs for men, but far fewer. As we've seen, *cur* was an older term for an aggressive mongrel dog that extended to people too, spe- cifically a despicable man. There were other insults for men that were contemporaneous with *dog* and *bitch*; these were usually vague character statements about his lack of honor or morality. A *bounder* was a dishonorable, unscrupulous man, while a *rogue* was a dishonest, unprincipled fellow. Some slurs referred to an ill-bred, ungentlemanly man, especially one who behaved badly in his relationships with women, like a *cad* or a *scoundrel*. A *rake* wasn't always a gardening tool, but was once short for *rakehell*, a rascal who was addicted to flirting, sex, and other sensual pleasures in life. Occasionally, a debauched woman might be called a rake too, but more often she was a whore or a bitch. But unlike whores and bitches, rascals, rogues, and scoundrels can still be described in flattering terms as "charming," "witty," and even "lovable."

Like bitch and slut, some gendered words for men have gone on an unexpected journey. Before the Joker, Loki, and Lex Luthor were infamous super-villains, *vilain* was originally a last name in Old French. By the 1300s, a *villein* referred to a peasant or tenant farmer who, as part of the medieval feudal system, was legally tied to a lord of the manor.[38] (This makes the word nearly equivalent in meaning to *villager*.) Villeins were poor and hardworking people, and their lives were difficult. Because of their low social status as commoners, villein became a scathing insult, especially for a man. Villeins were stationed below the ranks of knights and gentlemen, so their name implied that these people lacked chivalry and politeness and that they were uncouth in mind and manners. Villein was also closely influenced by *vile*, meaning wicked, morally flawed, and corrupt. In a plot twist, by the 1800s when the age of feudalism was over, villain came to mean a wicked character in fiction, a man (or occasionally a woman) whose evil motives and actions help drive the story. Other languages still bear a resemblance to the older meaning of the word. French *vilain* means "ugly" or "naughty," while Italian *villano* means "rude" or "impolite." The modern villain is still the bad guy, although he is often a celebrated, mustache-twirling character in books and movies, who is far away from the word's provincial roots.

Like villein, many older insults for men have classist origins, in which low socio-economic status is associated with low character and a lack of morality. *Blackguard* is one such word that became bad over time. In the 1500s, the term referred to a body of attendants or servants in a royal or nobleman's household.[39] The name might have been a reference to their black liveries or blackened shoes or boots, which were probably stained with soot. These were the lowest menials in a household, the scullions and kitchen-knaves charged with cleaning filthy pots and pans. Over the centuries, a blackguard came to mean a scoundrel, a man who was immoral and untrustworthy. By the 1700s, calling a man a blackguard was one of the worst things you could possibly say about him. Many of these insults sound like they're straight out of a Shakespeare play, and in fact, the playwright did love to have his characters hurl nasty insults like rascal, rogue, and knave.

In the time of Old English, *knave* simply meant boy.[40] This soon came to mean specifically a servant boy or "menial," a young person who performed unskilled labor. By the 1200s knave evolved from a person of low birth to one of low character, like the underhanded Knave of Hearts who stole the tarts in the nursery rhyme. Knave was once a withering insult. In Shakespeare's *All's Well That Ends Well*, the French nobleman Lafeu says to the unscrupulous soldier Parolles, "You are not worth another word, else I'd call you knave."[41] The /k/ sound in knave is silent today, although it was pronounced in Old and Middle Englishes. It was also pronounced in similar words like knife, knock, and knight, just like the scene in *Monty Python and the Holy Grail* when the Frenchman taunts King Arthur and his lance of knights and uses the old phonemic pronunciation of "knights." (Because this sound combination of /k/ followed by /n/ is difficult to pronounce, over hundreds of years we elided it until it disappeared completely.)

In another scene from the same movie, King Arthur vanquishes the Black Knight by slicing off the man's arms in battle. Unfazed, the Knight continues to bait him, so Arthur cries, "Look, you stupid bastard, you have no arms left!" During the Middle Ages, however, "bastard" didn't have the same meaning that it has today. In the 1300s, bastard usually referred to a child of illegitimate birth.[42] But being a bastard wasn't always stigmatized. In fact, Bastard could be a byname for a high-ranking nobleman. Anthony, Bastard of Burgundy, was the son of Philip the Good. (Anthony was one of eighteen illegitimate children born to one of Philip III's twenty-four documented mistresses.) William the Conqueror, the first Norman king of England, was the son of an unmarried duke, and in state documents he's often referred to by the epithet "William the Bastard." Royal bastards were so common that the last name Fitzroy, meaning "son of a king," was given to illegitimate royal offspring. King Henry VIII openly acknowledged Henry FitzRoy, his son born to mistress Bessie Blount, because until that point, his lack of a male heir had been a slur upon his manhood.[43] By the 1500s, bastard developed its figurative sense of something that wasn't pure or genuine, which also applied to a dog of mixed breed. By the 1600s, bastard had developed its modern sense as a term of abuse for an unpleasant man, now especially one who is callous or willfully cruel, or who acts ruthlessly out of self-interest. While a bastard is a "bad man," given the insult's implications of illegitimacy, it still refers back to a "bad woman," a woman who's stigmatized for giving birth to a child out of wedlock. Today, a weakened sense of bastard can also be a mildly dismissive term that expresses familiarity, affection, or commiseration, for example, a poor, old, or lucky bastard.

In the past, these insults were no small matter, but a serious type of slander. Men were obliged to defend their honor by answering these accusations, and often through the use of violence. This kind of society was known as a "culture of honor." In 1873, the dictionary writer Samuel Johnson said to his biographer James Boswell, "A man may shoot the man who invades his character, as he may shoot him who attempts to break into his house."[44] Perspectives about which words are considered to be offensive change, sometimes dramatically, across culture, context, and time. Calling someone a *fopdoodle* (a "fool") or a *cumberworld* (a "useless" person) would probably be laughed at today, although in the past, besmirching someone's good name with slurs like these offended their honor, and the offender might even be challenged to a duel. Boswell's son, Sir Alexander Boswell, would die in 1822 in such a duel with politician James Stewart after he publicly called him a "bully," a "coward," a "dastard," and a "sulky poltroon" (which was yet another name for a coward).[45] Stewart wasn't punished for his actions; instead, he was cleared of murder charges and the verdict of acquittal was received with loud cheers.

Of course, the modern bad man isn't a knave or a scoundrel. The significance of these and other antiquated slurs has faded over the centuries, to the point where they've lost their impact. They no longer carry the sting that they once did. This tells us that insults are always influenced by the contemporary society and culture to which they belong. Without lowly jobs like kitchen scullions and servant boys, blackguard and knave no longer have any relevance. And with changing morals and values, insults about disreputable character like cad and bounder are no longer offensive. Most people today wouldn't even know that these were once outrageous and shocking insults that might lead to a duel to the death. To be a bastard born to an unmarried woman has lost its stigma too, for the most part. And a villain is just a fictional character in a movie. Archaic terms of abuse like rake and rogue now sound almost quaint, like something out of a BBC period drama or a romance novel. As we can see, an insult outside of its time is powerless and impotent.

Modern insults won't result in a pistol duel at a distance of ten paces, but they can constitute what are called "fighting words." These are insulting words, "those that by their very utterance inflict injury or tend to incite an immediate breach of the peace." In the US, this kind of language isn't protected under the First Amendment of free speech. So what are fighting words? These aren't phrases like sulky poltroon anymore; instead, they're usually racial slurs and hate speech accompanied by profanities. Although they don't have to be. Fighting words are any abusive ones that are likely to provoke a fight, riot, public disturbance, or any other breach of public peace or order. In the 1942 landmark case *Chaplinsky v. New Hampshire* that established the fighting words doctrine, a Jehovah's Witness told a town marshal who tried to stop him preaching in public that he was a "God damned racketeer" and a "damned fascist."[46] These words seem tame by today's standards, but for this crime Chaplinsky was charged, convicted, and fined. The doctrine isn't invoked much anymore, but over the years "bitch" and "son of a bitch" have featured frequently as fighting words in the annals of court history.

The modern bad man is probably called an *asshole*. This contemporary insult and its British English version *arsehole* go back to Old English *earsþerl* and then Middle English *arce-hoole*.[47] This literally meant hole of the anus or rectum, much like nostril means hole of the nose. (Ass, not of the donkey kind but the US cousin of arse, is generally considered to be less offensive, and comes from 1800s nautical slang for "backside.") Arsehole had this literal meaning until the early 1900s, when it came to mean an unpleasant, remote, or unattractive place, like the asshole of the world. It wasn't until the 1930s that asshole became an insult for an irritating, contemptible, or selfish person. Like asshole, the insulting jerk, prick, and dick are generalized terms of abuse for people, and usually men, given their references to male genitalia. Surprisingly, none of these words were insults until the 1920s–1940s. These post-WWI years were fertile decades for language change during a time of immense political, economic, and social change – the women's right to vote, Prohibition, the Great Depression, and World War II among these events – which spawned lots of inventive insults for people, many of which are still around today, like twat and tit.

Prick started its life as Old English *prician*, "to pierce with a sharp point." Today it is a popular slur for a man who is insufferable, egotistical, and conceited. When New Zealand's outgoing Prime Minister Jacinda Ardern was asked a tricky question by political opponent David Seymour she was caught on a hot mic muttering under her breath: "He's such an arrogant prick."[48] She made the best of the situation by teaming up with the prick himself and auctioning off a signed copy of the transcript, raising $100,000 for prostate cancer charity. The event was called: "Ardern, Seymour join forces for pricks everywhere." Had Ardern lived in the 1500s, however, her insult might have been a compliment. At that time, prick was a diminutive, a term of endearment for a man; your prick was your darling. By the end of that century prick extended to also mean penis. Then much like bitch, prick underwent the process of pejoration over time, becoming a bad word and eventually an insult because of its association with something taboo.

But these words are only mild to moderate insults for men. As we've seen, cunt, whore, and slut are also directed toward men, although they don't pack as much of a punch as they do when they're used against women. In general, prick, bastard, son of a bitch, and other insults for men have less sting than insults for women. This is, in part, because society expects, and rewards, toughness in men. Sometimes a man's just gotta be an asshole to get what he wants outta life. Moreover, disparaging words associated with men and masculinity aren't used in the same way as disparaging words for women. We can say *life's a bitch*, but we don't say "life's a dick." We might say *I've had a bitch of a week*, but we don't tend to say "I've had a jerk of a week." We say *payback's a bitch*, but we don't say "payback's a prick." Men's words just aren't interchangeable with women's words, because they're simply not as potent.

Other insults for bad men still refer back to women, like *douche*, *motherfucker*, and again, *son of a bitch*. But the most offensive insults to hurl at a man are those that question his manliness. Words like *sissy*, *pussy*, and *wuss* are slurs for weak, timid, cowardly men. The charge that former US President George H. W. Bush resented the most was being called a "wimp." In 1987, *Newsweek* ran a cover story about the presidential candidate with the screaming headline: "George Bush: Fighting the Wimp Factor."[49] This wasn't the first time he'd heard the slur, even his predecessor Ronald Reagan called him a wimp, and later so would his successor Bill Clinton. The elder Bush was described variously as a "weakling," a "preppie," a "cloistered Ivy Leaguer," and even a "walking watercress sandwich," insults that all suggested he somehow lacked the toughness and inner fortitude necessary to lead the free world.

Other insults attack a man's masculinity by way of his sexual orientation. Whether the man in question is gay or not, homophobic slurs like *faggot, cocksucker,* and older terms like *poofter* and *pansy, fairy* and *fruit,* imply that he's unmasculine. Faggot has meant lots of different things over the centuries. The word dates back to the 1200s, when it originally referred to a bundle of sticks or twigs tied together for use as fuel.[50] Some people believe that the modern use of faggot refers to gay men who were burned at the stake as punishment for sodomy or buggery. This is a false etymology, although it was a common method of execution for heretics and those accused of witchcraft. In the world of prisons and schools, fag and bitch have sometimes covered the same territory. During the eighteenth century, *fag* was British public-school slang for a junior student who performed certain duties for a senior student, also implying that they had a same-sex relationship. (Fag is also slang for cigarette, which is a term that's still used in Britain and Australia.) Like many other insults we've looked at, the modern sense of faggot also dates back to 1920s American slang. It referred to a gay man, especially one considered to be effeminate, but more generally an unmanly man. It's little known, however, that like bitch and son of a bitch, faggot still refers back to a "bad woman."[51] From the sixteenth century until recently, faggot was also an insult for a woman considered to be old, lazy, troublesome, and useless.

Man Up

When a man is considered to be weak, cowardly, or submissive he's shamed with bullying expressions like "be a man," "take it like a man," and "man up." These pressure him to pull himself up, step up to his responsibilities, or to show less emotion, but they can leave him feeling inadequate and resentful. (Men are ordered to "man up," but we don't tell women to "woman up.") Man up is wielded a lot in politics when opponents challenge each other with ultimatums, implying their rivals are not man enough to be the leader. In one incident, British politician Jeremy Hunt urged then Prime Minister Boris Johnson to take part in a live televised debate with the call to action, "Don't be a coward, Boris, man up and show the nation you can cope with the intense scrutiny the most difficult job in the country will involve."[52] Hunt was criticized for using sexist language that is harmful and damaging to boys and girls. Ironically, just months later, Johnson would use the phrase himself, telling his opponent Jeremy Corbyn it was "time to man up" and accept his offer of a general election.[53]

Many abusive phrases exhort men to not behave like women: You're such a pussy. Don't be a girl. Don't be a little bitch. You don't have any balls. Grow a pair. Suck my dick. Blow me. He's got a small penis. Masculinity and power are often equated with penis size, and taunts about having a "small dick" suggest that an insecure man is boastful about his cars, money, gun collection, or other possessions as compensation for physical shortcomings. When former kickboxer and alleged human trafficker Andrew Tate taunted environmental activist Greta Thunberg with the tweet: "Please provide your email address so I can send a complete list of my car collection and their respective enormous emissions," she fired back with: "Yes, please do enlighten me. Email me at smalldickenergy@getalife.com ... "[54] Tate, who once admitted he was "absolutely a misogynist," and that women "belong in the home, can't drive, and are a man's property," was mortified by the suspicion that he had a small penis. Thunberg's quip was a nod to rapper Latto's song "Big Energy," the refrain of which features the phrase "big dick energy," referring to a man who shows confidence without cockiness or conceitedness.

All of these put-downs we've explored are insulting to men because they're emasculating. They "reduce" a man to a woman. Some compare him to a woman's body part that's still taboo and avoided because of a fear of its "dirty" taste and smell. Others lower a man to being a helpless child, with the implication that he's acting like a little boy, or even worse, a woman or girl. They diminish him as being "not a man at all." They suggest that certain behaviors, particularly those considered to be womanly, will feminize him in the eyes of his peers and society. They imply that admirable traits, like strength, bravery, and courage are found in men but not in women. At the same time they imply that human qualities like vulnerability, fear, and expressing emotions are found in women but not in (real) men. And in using these expressions as insults, the speaker is subtly insulting women as well, suggesting that a man who's being like a woman is undesirable.

But for all of these insults leveled against men, bitch has no equal. There is no exact masculine equivalent to bitch – not asshole, prick, dick, jerk, or even son of a bitch. Bitch can be a highly abusive insult for a woman, but it's also one of the worst insults for a man, because it compares him to a woman or a gay man. In our heteronormative society, bitch is the ultimate attack on masculinity. Calling a man a bitch is also loaded with misogyny. In the end, the use of bitch and other emasculating insults toward men reflects negative attitudes toward women. Anything that's feminine or traditionally associated with women is disliked and viewed as weak, trivial, and inferior. Even when it's used against a man, bitch is *still* synonymous with women (just like bastard, motherfucker, cunt, and older uses of faggot refer back to women too). Ultimately, there is no male counterpart to bitch because men are the privileged sex in Western society, while women are the stigmatized sex.

Because of its negative connection to women and femininity, bitch has been considered to be highly offensive over the centuries. At times, it's been so insulting that it has often been censored or even banned, but this hasn't stopped the word from proliferating in music, movies, and television.

If anything, it's helped.

4

• • • • •

The B Word

For some people, bitch is a four-letter word. Cast into the same category as expletives like fuck, cunt, and shit, bitch has at times been branded profane, obscene, and indecent. As a taboo word, it has often been censored or avoided altogether by the mainstream media, to protect tender eyes and ears. In its written form, bitch has been expurgated from books and newspapers. In the past, bitch was sometimes considered to be defamatory; it implied promiscuity and so it was a dangerous smear on a woman's character, and leveling the slur at an innocent party could land the offender in court. In its spoken form, bitch has been bleeped in songs and muted in movies. Some radio stations and television networks have even been fined for using it, the equivalent of having to pay money to a swear jar. Others have found creative ways to get around the censors. Bitch is switched with "witch" or euphemized as "the b-word," somewhat comparing it to "the n-word." It might be substituted with polite alternatives like bench or biscuit. But no matter how cleverly or cutely the word is camouflaged, people always know what is really meant.

Thanks to the many pioneers pushing the use of the word, bitch has undergone a dramatic unbleeping over time. As taboos changed, the word started to be used more openly. Nowadays, bitch is everywhere. It appears boldly in books, movies, and television, both subscription and network. It's sung in songs, especially in rap and hip hop music, where its use has a long and unexpected tradition. And it's omnipresent online. After centuries of censorship and lurking, bitch has emerged as an everyday word. In fact, it's so ubiquitous nowadays that some say they're numb to it. But that doesn't mean that bitch doesn't pack a punch anymore. Even today it's often censored. And it's still seen as derogatory, pejorative, and offensive, even if the dictionaries don't always label it as such. Let's take a look at the many bans on bitch and controversies surrounding the word, both past and present.

B—

One Sunday morning in Clerkenwell, London, during the spring of 1590, Joanna Gage paused her housework to eavesdrop on a noisy dispute between two neighbors. She went out into the yard, where she saw Edith Parsons leaning out of her cellar window to yell at Sicilia Thornton: "Thou art an whore, an arrant whore, a bitche. Yea, worse than a bitche. Thou goest sawghting up and downe the towne after knaves and art such a whott tayled whore that neither one nor two nor ten nor twenty knaves will scarce serve thee!"[1] This tirade was the Renaissance equivalent of calling a woman a slut. A few months later, three women who had witnessed the incident, including Joanna Gage, repeated these words to the Consistory Court in London, because Sicilia had sued Edith for "uttering the lewdest of slanders" and defaming her good name. The court found in Edith's favor, effectively deciding that Sicilia was indeed a bitch and a whore, although no penalty against her was recorded. This was a church court that dealt with hundreds of similar slander suits every year. It was known colloquially as the Bawdy Courts. As we've seen, society at this time was concerned with reputation and honor, so slurs like bitch and whore were smears against a woman's sexual and moral character. Men might sue for defamation too, rather than engage in a duel to the death. The insults that men reported, however, centered around words like "cuckold" and "whoremaster," which concerned not their own sexual behavior but that of the women over whom they were supposed to be in control. Men also reported non-specific invectives like "blackguard" and "knave," or accusations of fornication, rather than the sexual insults leveled at women. There is, after all, no way to truly call a man the female equivalent of a whore or a bitch.

These examples of the word appeared in court records of testimony, which were faithfully recorded verbatim. Although around this time bitch was probably said more often than it was written, so early books aren't a reflection of the true use and popularity of the word. As we know, Francis Grose, the collector of bawdy words, declared in the eighteenth century that bitch was "the most offensive appellation that can be given to an English woman, even more provoking than that of whore." In his own personal copy of the first edition of the book, Grose made thousands of handwritten annotations, and next to "bitch" he noted that it was a synonym of "carrion," a word for a corpse or the decaying flesh of dead animals. He wrote, "... instead of the appellation of *'bitch'* the blackguards sometimes say, *'your arse is a carrion gallows, because 'tis hung round with Dog's meat.'* "[2] This goes to show just how offensive bitch was, and that these kinds of crude words were favored by "low class" types. While Grose dared to spell out the word in full, many others didn't. Bitch was often censored in early books. In the 1759 farce *Low Life above Stairs*, Lord Lawless has a torrid fling with the Duchess of Lovesport, from whom he contracted syphilis, or the pox. When asked how his new relationship was faring he replied, "Damn the B-t-ch to Hell and the Devil, she has poxed me."[3] While it was acceptable to publish blasphemous words like damn, hell, and devil, bitch was considered to be *too* offensive to spell out in full, even in a comedy full of buffoonery and horseplay. This view of bitch as an obscene and indecent word that must be censored or even expurgated lasted for hundreds of years and well into modern times.

Bitch was censored in newspapers too, although the mainstream press tended to be the most squeamish of all media. An article in an 1851 issue of the *Hampshire Chronicle* describes an altercation but only hints at the word, "He heard the voice of a man calling out, 'Lay hold of the old b—,' directly after which he heard two women screaming."[4] Even during the days of the gutter press and yellow journalism, newspapers shielded readers from bitch with dashes, dots, and asterisks; they replaced it with rhymes like hitch and witch, or they substituted the word with "blank" and "expletive." When Adolph Ochs bought the *New York Times* in 1896 he declared that his family newspaper would not "soil the breakfast cloth" with indecency and salaciousness.[5] This saying soon morphed into the paper's famous slogan, "All the News That's Fit to Print." The insulting sense of bitch *wasn't* fit to print at the time. On the other hand, the literal sense of bitch was acceptable. A 1907 advertisement in the classifieds of *Dogdom* magazine tells the sad story of someone who had to rehome their beloved pet: "For sale – Boston bitch, good all over, fine pet, street and house broken. Reason for selling – can't keep her."[6] In 1944, the *New York Daily News* paved the way for the unbleeping of bitch when publisher Joseph Medill Patterson instructed his two managing editors by memo: "Please print the following words in full: Bastard, Son of a Bitch (no hyphens), God damn or Damn."

Nowadays, publishers have fewer inhibitions and bitch is usually printed without a second thought, but only thanks to the efforts of early authors who blazed the trail. When publisher Charles Scribner acquired the rights to Ernest Hemingway's *The Sun Also Rises*, its publication was nearly halted due to its use of the word. The character Lady Brett Ashley is strong and independent and often accused of being a bitch. She even calls herself a bitch. Offended by this vulgar language, Scribner announced that he'd no sooner allow profanity in one of his books than he would invite friends to use his parlor as a toilet room. Hemingway replied that he "never used a word without first considering whether or not it was replaceable."[7] Hemingway's editor, Max Perkins, warned him that the book might be suppressed if the word was kept in it, but he also supported his author by threatening to resign if Scribner declined to publish the book. In the end, "bitch" remained in the novel, but it was indeed banned in several cities, which just added to its notoriety. Even still, some critics believe it's Hemingway's most important work. His mother Grace, however, did not agree. The book's coarseness and vulgarity had embarrassed her at a ladies' book group meeting. She pronounced it "one of the filthiest books of the year." She added, "Surely you have other words in your vocabulary than 'damn' and 'bitch'—Every page fills me with a sick loathing. If I should pick up a book by any other writer with such words in it, I should read no more—but pitch it in the fire."[8] That he'd ticked off his mother only confirmed to Hemingway that he'd made the right choice to keep the word in the book.

Bitch *noun*

1. a woman

Even in modern times, bitch is occasionally censored in newspapers and magazines as b---h or "the b-word," if it's not removed entirely. Newspaper editors are often inclined to publish an offensive word verbatim in order to faithfully quote a song, movie, or book, but they don't always choose to do so. In 2005, the *New York Times* omitted the title *Chess Bitch: Women in the Ultimate Intellectual Sport* in a *review* of the book; as a result, the editors were criticized for their "astonishing squeamishness and misplaced political correctness."[9] Ironically, an op-ed about the book's notoriety appeared in that *same* issue, written by the author Jennifer Shahade, and commissioned *by* the newspaper. But neither piece mentioned the word at all. One of the paper's top editors admitted later that it was "an act of overly zealous concern for readers' sensitivities," but they didn't set the record straight. The process of censorship is often inconsistent and confusing. The diet book *Skinny Bitch* emerged around the same time and was reviewed in the *Times* with the word intact. The newspaper has an even longer history of printing the word in its pages, because it reviewed *Super Bitch* in 1975, a movie about a drug dealer who gets men to do her dirty work before having them killed. But then, at other times, editors choose to censor the word arbitrarily.

Some individuals and groups have gone on crusades to censor bitch from public conversations. In 2007, the New York City Council passed a symbolic ban on the word "nigger." In that same year, Brooklyn councillor Darlene Mealy tried to introduce a citywide ban of the "hateful and deeply sexist" bitch too, which was referred to as "the b-word" in the legislation. Citing its use in rap music, she said the word created "a paradigm of shame and indignity" for all women, describing it as "a vile attack on our womanhood."[10] Mealy acknowledged that the measure was unenforceable, but she argued that it would carry symbolic power against the pejorative uses of the word. Only eighteen of her fifty-one fellow-councillors voted with her, however, and so the measure failed. Had it passed, it would have likely failed in practice; such bans almost never work and only serve to heighten a word's power. That same year, civil rights activist Al Sharpton tried to ban "bitch," "ho," and "nigga" in the music industry as part of his "Decency Initiative." He was unsuccessful too. Then in 2014, Sheryl Sandberg, the former chief operating officer of Facebook, announced that she was starting a campaign to ban the b-word. But it turned out the word she had in mind was *bossy*, a PG version of bitch. The Ban Bossy campaign was criticized heavily, and it was pointed out that telling people what words they can or can't use is inherently bossy.

As recently as 2019, Massachusetts legislators proposed a bill that would criminalize certain uses of the word, stating, "a person who uses the word 'bitch' directed at another person to accost, annoy, degrade or demean the other person shall be considered to be a disorderly person."[11] The bill would've made these acts punishable by a fine of up to $200, or up to six months in jail. It turned out that the bill was filed by a constituent, not a senator. At any rate, many deemed the idea to be unconstitutional and the bill wasn't passed into law. Some activists are more concerned with raising awareness of how and why certain words can be offensive rather than trying to ban them. As part of the

"You Don't Say" campaign, students from Duke University in North Carolina started a public discussion about the offensiveness of hyper-masculine words and phrases like *pussy, that's so gay, man up,* and also bitch, because they imply that femininity is inherently negative.

Apps have been devised to "clean up" language that's judged to be offensive. Most software contains default profanity filters for naughty words, while autocorrect famously "corrects" "fuck" to "duck." One e-book reader app set out to enable readers to, in its own words, "read books, not profanity." Clean Reader applies a filter that censors bad language and replaces it with less risqué alternatives. Bitch becomes "witch," whore becomes "hussy," Jesus Christ is "geez," and blowjob is swapped with the euphemistic "pleasure."[12] Swear words like fucking and fucker become "freaking" and "idiot," hell becomes "heck," and shit is changed to "crap." It isn't only profanities that are scrubbed from books, but also body parts. Penis becomes "groin," vagina is swapped for "bottom," and breast changed to "chest." The program comes with three settings: clean, cleaner, and squeaky clean, which would "block the most profanity from a book including some hurtful racial terms." A number of authors, publishers, and distributors came out in protest of this censorship and lack of authorial consent, includ-ing novelist Chuck Wendig, who posted to Twitter, "Personally I think CleanReader is a bunch of hot jeepers mcgee and a bucket of monkey flopping cupcake batter oh gosh they got to Twitter." In response to the backlash, the company removed all book titles from its online catalog.

The Internet has always had something of the Wild West about it, including its lawless language. Bold behind a keyboard or hiding behind a handle, many people feel free to swear and insult others on social media in a way they wouldn't dare to do face-to-face. The Internet is a place of freedom of speech, but also a place of unbridled bullying, harassment, and abuse. One study found that bitch is the fourth most popular curse word on Twitter, after fuck, shit, and ass.[13] In general, bitch is a high-frequency word online. A Google search for "bitch" brings up almost one billion hits. The Internet is also the least policed of all media. But even without any censorship imposed on people, some choose to self-censor the word anyway; spelling bitch as b*tch, substituting it with a rhyming word like "rich," euphemizing it as "the b-word" or avoiding it altogether. Some try to censor other people's use of the word. In 2019, then US President Donald Trump complained on social media that he wasn't getting enough credit for a criminal reform bill that had passed through Congress and been signed into law. He referenced "boring musician @johnlegend and his filthy mouthed wife [who] are talking now about how great it is – but I didn't see them around when we needed help getting it passed."[14] This obviously referred to television personality Chrissy Teigen, who responded by calling Trump a "pussy ass bitch." This implied that Trump was talking big, but his bark was bigger than his bite. The White House immediately contacted the platform to demand the tweet be removed. However, they don't screen content or remove potentially offensive language, so the remark was not taken down.

Some people have even attempted to remove "bitch" entirely from the dictionary, while others have, more realistically, petitioned to have the definitions updated. In 2019, more than 34,000 people signed a petition calling on Oxford University Press to change their dictionary definition of "woman," which included "bitch" as a synonym. In several other dictionaries, "bitch" is also defined as "a woman." In certain slang, bitch is invoked to refer to women, but of course, this use has additional, and usually negative, connotations – "bitch" is definitely *not* a direct synonym of "woman." The petition noted other offensive words that were listed as synonyms of woman, including "bird, biddy, bint, mare, and wench."[15] The document also cited example sentences of the word listed in the dictionary that portray women as sex objects or subordinate, including such gems as: "Ms. September will embody the professional, intelligent yet sexy career woman" and "I told you to be home when I get home, little woman." Oxford University Press responded that excluding derogatory terms in the dictionary would be "akin to censorship."[16] They argued that dictionary makers have a responsibility to accurately describe how language is used and that includes sexist terms. Despite the dictionary's defensiveness, the petition prompted an extensive review of its entry for "woman." The OED finally conceded that it's important for sexist words to be contextualized, "So if a word is derogatory or highly offensive we should say it."[17]

And yet, despite centuries of censorship and suppression of the word, bitch was not marked as offensive in dictionaries until recently. Hundreds of years ago, Samuel Johnson qualified "bitch" as only "a word of slight contempt" (to him anyway). A few decades later, Francis Grose described it as "the most offensive" name for a woman, but in modern-day English marking the word as offensive is only a recent phenomenon. In an episode of the *History of Swear Words*, host Nicholas Cage reads from the dictionary, "Bitch: a female dog." Shaking his head he adds, "No mention of how 99.99 percent of the people use the word. I mean, what year is this from, 1885? No! It's from 2015. That's right. The *Merriam-Webster Dictionary* didn't label the word 'bitch' offensive until the same year it added the word 'twerk!'"[18] When Merriam-Webster lexicographer Kory Stamper was charged with the task of updating the definition of "bitch" in the 1990s, she noticed the entry didn't have any warning labels to explain that some meanings of the word are offensive.[19] She delved into the dictionary's archives and discovered it wasn't until the 1960s that bitch was flagged as an abusive term, when the editor was a woman. But her recommendations were completely ignored by another editor – a man – who didn't have the same real-world experience with the word that the woman editor did. And that's how bitch stayed for the rest of the twentieth century. Stamper's efforts eventually resulted in the entry being updated to reflect the insulting uses of the word, while the aforementioned petition was instrumental in the *Oxford English Dictionary* finally following suit years later. Similar campaigns have been launched in other countries and languages. One such effort in Europe led Italian dictionary *Treccani* to scrap the use of *puttana* ("whore"), *cagna* ("bitch"), and other words for sex workers to define *donna* ("woman").[20]

Nowadays, most dictionaries acknowledge that many senses of "bitch" are insulting and sexist, while the word is finally labeled as "offensive," "vulgar," "coarse," or "derogatory."

Super Bitch

The inaugural use of bitch in cinema coincides with its first use in modern literature, although initially its rise wasn't as stratospheric. The 1930 film *Hell's Angels* starring Jean Harlow has the distinction of being the first movie in which someone utters the words "son of a bitch," along with other profanities like hell, ass, bloody, goddamn, for Christ's sake, and shut up. Language like this had never before been heard in movies, but that's because this period marked the gradual transition from silent films to talkies. The movie's producer, eccentric entrepreneur Howard Hughes, was able to avoid censorship because there *weren't* any censors at the time. During the Roaring 20s, the movie industry was notoriously lawless, so in response, the Motion Picture Producers and Distributors of America was founded. The goal of the organization was to "clean up" the image of the movie industry, especially in the wake of a scandal surrounding actor Roscoe "Fatty" Arbuckle and the rape and murder of actress Virginia Rappe. The Motion Picture Production Code was introduced in the early 1930s. Informally known as the Hays Code, named after Chairman (and Presbyterian deacon) Will H. Hays, this was a set of moral guidelines that major film studios were forced to follow if they wanted their films to play in American theaters. The code stated that, "No picture shall be produced which will lower the moral standards of those who see it."[21] The rules included prohibitions on profanity, nudity, the superfluous use of liquor, the use of illegal drugs, the mocking of religion, lustful kissing, scenes of passion, and even interracial romance. Hughes, who was known for stretching the boundaries on sex and violence, would go on to challenge the supremacy of studio moguls and the industry's restrictive moral codes. But most producers and directors toed the line to avoid their movies being banned. The Hays Code ushered in the era of a more "wholesome" and "innocent" Hollywood.

The Hays Code was in place until the late 1960s, when American culture was shocked out of its innocence with the assassination of John Kennedy, the assassination of Martin Luther King Jr., and the general civil unrest at the time. The authority of the Code waned over the years too, and many films began to openly flout the rules. The 1959 courtroom drama *Anatomy of a Murder* was one such movie. This was the story of a lawyer who took on a difficult case, defending a young army lieutenant accused of murdering a local tavern owner who he believed had raped his wife. The movie was groundbreaking for its frank discussion of sex, which included the use of shocking words like panties, penetration, rape, sperm, and bitch. It starred James Stewart, whose father called him at four in the morning to let him know that he was upset by customers coming into his hardware store to disapprove of his movie-star son appearing in a "dirty picture" that was full of profane language. Stewart said, "He took an ad out in the local paper saying: 'My son, Jim, has just made a nasty picture and I advise no-one to go see it.' Well, of course, the film did much more business than it would have done otherwise."[22] Some time later, Stewart's father called him again at four in the morning. He admitted he'd sneaked into a drive-in screening of the film to see it for himself, but he didn't think it was dirty after all.

Anatomy of a Murder was the gateway for bitch to become a mainstream word in Hollywood movies. Although just like in the Westerns, son of a bitch was often preferred over bitch, because it was a softened version. In 1966, Elizabeth Taylor won a Best Actress Oscar for her role as Martha in *Who's Afraid of Virginia Woolf*, a movie that stands at the crossroads of old and new Hollywood. The boisterous Martha is intoxicated throughout most of the movie, and as a mean drunk she utters the insults "bastard" and "son of a bitch." But within a few years, bitch was so acceptable in cinema that it even appeared in the title of the 1973 film *Super Bitch* that we've already mentioned. Fast-forward to today, and dozens of movies include "bitch" in their titles, while many thousands more feature the word in their scripts. That is, unless the movie is G-rated. In 1968, the Hays Code evolved into the Motion Picture Association (MPA) film rating system. The scheme is voluntary, although most cinemas refuse to exhibit non-rated films. The MPA system is used to help parents decide what films are appropriate for their children, although some kids' films do allow a little salty language. G-rated (General Audience) films don't permit strong language. Mild language is permitted at the PG (Parental Guidance Suggested) level, but bitch only when it means a female dog. PG-13 (Parents Strongly Cautioned) allows a little more, including violence, partial nudity, and language like bitch, dick, ass, cock, and even the occasional f-bomb. In the PG-13 film *The Monster Squad*, the villain Count Dracula is in search of a powerful amulet so he can take over the world. In one iconic scene, he lifts up little five-year-old Phoebe by her throat, bears his fangs, and snarls, "Give me the amulet, you bitch!"

Words You Can Sometimes Say on Television

In 1972, George Carlin took to the stage in Santa Monica, California, to debut his now legendary monologue, "Seven Words You Can Never Say on Television" for his album *Class Clown*. These "Seven Dirty Words" were: shit, piss, fuck, cunt, cocksucker, motherfucker, and tits. "Those are the heavy seven," said Carlin. "Those are the ones that'll infect your soul, curve your spine and keep the country from winning the war."[23] This was Carlin's attempt at exposing the absurdity of outlawing words, but the comedian knew he was treading in dangerous territory that could put his career in jeopardy. He'd been hanging out with Lenny Bruce a decade earlier when his mentor was arrested on obscenity charges for saying, "fuck" and "tits" during a show in Chicago. Bruce was blacklisted from performing in US clubs because of his profanity-laced shows. He'd previously performed a ribald routine of the "nine dirty words," a list that included ass and balls too, which had inspired Carlin's stand-up routine. Sure enough, Carlin met the same fate as Bruce a few months later when he was arrested for disturbing the peace while performing his "Dirty Words" show in Milwaukee. The charges were thrown out, luckily for Carlin, but the bigger battle was just beginning. When the show was replayed on radio during the afternoon, the Federal Communications Commission (FCC) determined that it was "indecent." The FCC prohibits profane content on broadcast radio and television between the hours of 6am and 10pm. The

Carlin case went all the way up to the Supreme Court, which ruled in favor of the FCC's right to restrict adult language on television and in radio broadcasts, just in case children were listening. Carlin's routine, however, raised questions about censorship that remain unresolved today. The "Dirty Words" are, for the most part, still dirty.

When Carlin created his list, bitch didn't make the cut. Depending on its context, he reasoned, the literal meaning of bitch as a female dog was safely allowed on television and radio, along with cock, as in rooster, and ass, as in donkey. Bitch, ass, and cock might be acceptable on air if referring to animal husbandry. Lenny Bruce's "balls" were okay too, because sports announcers said this innocent word all the time. Prick could even be appropriate, but only in the right context. As he noted, "you can prick your finger, but you can't finger your prick."[24] Carlin called these "part-time" dirty words, because they were acceptable when literal, but still considered to be taboo when used in a figurative way. But the comedian wasn't reporting actual network policy as some might believe; the FCC had vague standards for indecency and obscenity. Profane speech was defined loosely as material that "depicts or describes sexual or excretory organs or activities" in terms that are so "grossly offensive" that it becomes a "nuisance."[25]

Television was strict in those days. In the 1960s, talk show host Jack Paar stormed off the stage when censors wouldn't allow him to tell a joke in which a toilet was called a "WC," short for water closet. Lucille Ball was pregnant during an entire season of *I Love Lucy*, although the word "pregnant" wasn't allowed on air because it was considered too suggestive. The writers settled for "expecting" instead. And as late as 2006, the doctors on *Grey's Anatomy* were not allowed to say "vagina" during a childbirth scene, so they opted for "vajayjay" instead. (This catapulted the word into mainstream speech, along with Oprah Winfrey's enthusiastic embrace of the euphemism.) As for the "Seven Dirty Words," Carlin seems to have chosen them more for comedy rhythm than fact. The full list of forbidden words didn't include just seven of them; it also included asshole, goddamn, bastard, bitch, and many others.

The first uncensored use of "bitch" on American prime-time television is often claimed to be its appearance in a 1979 episode of *M*A*S*H*. In "Guerilla My Dreams," Lieutenant Park, a South Korean intelligence officer, wanted to interrogate a North Korean patient. The young woman was accused of being a spy. The commander was known for his brutal interrogation tactics, and it was assumed that he would torture the woman into a confession, before killing her. As it was put, "To take your mind off the pain, he kills you."[26] Knowing this grim reality, surgeon Benjamin "Hawkeye" Pierce tries, but fails, to save her life by getting her transferred as a US prisoner of war. As the officer hauls away the hapless woman, Hawkeye angrily calls him a "son of a bitch." The show's producers had to receive a special dispensation from the FCC to be allowed to use the profanity, which was justified as necessary to emphasize the gravity of the scene. The shocking decision received a high level of media coverage ahead of time, and so when the show aired, millions of people tuned in to hear Alan Alda utter the scandalous words.

But this well-publicized use of the phrase eclipsed an earlier one. Contrary to popular belief, the first use of "bitch" on network television appears to be an episode of the sitcom *Maude* that aired five years earlier in 1974. In "Walter's Heart Attack," Maude's husband Walter suffers a mild heart attack while trying to save his accountant from taking her own life because her husband was leaving her. At the hospital, Walter tries to hide from his wife the fact that he'd visited the young woman's apartment. When he recovers, and the threat of infidelity has subsided, Maude cries, "Oh Walter, I'm the happiest woman in the world!" She hugs him, but then mutters through clenched teeth, "You son of a bitch!"[27] When the Head of Program Practices at CBS first read the script he insisted, "You're kidding about that last line. You can't use that language!" The show's scriptwriter Norman Lear replied, "If you can come up with a line for Maude that's every bit as good as saying 'son of a bitch,' every bit as right, I'll do it."[28] In the end, the episode was filmed with the offending line intact. Amazingly, the show went to air without any fanfare, unlike the media circus that preceded the episode of *M*A*S*H*. The use of the phrase caused some shock among viewers, but it largely went unnoticed, even by the FCC.

Broadcast channels broke FCC rules often, either accidentally or by deliberately pushing the boundaries. In some cases, rule breakers faced fines for using profanity. In others, the FCC decided arbitrarily that the rules didn't apply or they simply didn't bother to enforce their own penalties. In 2003, when U2's Bono accepted the Golden Globe award for best original song, he exclaimed, "This is really, really fucking brilliant!" The FCC reviewed the incident and determined that Bono had used fuck as "an expletive to emphasize an exclamation" rather than using it to describe "sexual organs or activities."[29] So they decided that he didn't violate their regulations. Bono's use of this "fleeting expletive" set a precedent for other celebrities, like Cher and Nicole Richie, to cheekily use the word in the same way during live television performances. These incidents occurred around the same time as Janet Jackson's "wardrobe malfunction" during her live performance at the Super Bowl, in which her right breast was bared, but adorned with a nipple shield. (This became such a controversy that it's sometimes referred to tongue-in-cheek as Nipplegate.) Bowing to ever-increasing moral pressure, the FCC immediately cracked down on obscenity. It also changed its mind and ruled against Bono, but declined to fine him.

When Bono cussed, NBC was broadcasting the awards live around the world. The network's engineers had failed to hit the censor button during his speech, so the expletive went uncensored. Broadcast delays have their roots in 1950s radio, when the method was used, not for censorship, but to increase sound clarity and depth.[30] But the delay became a standard both in live radio and television to keep the public "safe" from indecent exposure. Often called the seven-second delay or profanity delay, this allowed a few seconds for editors, directors, or engineers to catch anything they deemed to be indecent content before it hit the airwaves. This delay gave them time to replace the offending language with a 1000 Hz tone, known as a "bleep," because this onomatopoeic word echoes the actual sound. Unsure about the confusing nuances of FCC regulations, broadcast networks tried to skirt the rules by writing profanity into scenes and then obscuring it with taxi horns or other background noise. The bleep has become so embedded in popular culture that some shows employ it for comic effect. In a famous cinematic example, at the climax of the spaghetti western *The Good, the Bad, and the Ugly*, Tuco the bandit shouts at Blondie the outlaw, "You know what you are? Just a dirty son of a —." Bitch overlaps with the trademark coyote howl that transitions into the movie's iconic theme song.

Yo, Bitch!

Well into the early 2000s, bitch was still causing waves on network television, but mostly among audiences. The word appeared frequently on *Friends* over the years, which earned the show many angry viewer complaints to the FCC. In one episode aired in the show's final months, Ross takes a photo of his baby daughter in the park when a bigger child on the swings slams him to the ground. "Son of a bitch!" he moans, much to the wide-eyed amazement of nearby youngsters. "Oh relax," he snaps at them. "I didn't say the f-word." Criticisms of this particular episode also included other characters' use of the words crap, hell, pissed, and bastard. One viewer even objected to Ross merely alluding to "fuck" by saying "the f-word."[31] The reviewers of the complaints, however, decided that the words weren't sufficiently graphic or explicit in context to be grossly offensive and therefore were not considered to be indecent.

When bitch was still taboo on network television, it was already acceptable on pay TV. Subscription-based media providers haven't faced regulatory scrutiny in the past because they were not licensed by the FCC, and therefore received strict First Amendment protection. Many shows took advantage of this freedom to do and say as they pleased, like the AMC network's *Breaking Bad*. The methamphetamine-cooking Jesse Pinkman is celebrated for his relentless use of "bitch." His signature phrases were "Yeah, Bitch!" and "Yo, bitch!" which became fandom favorites and made the word synonymous with the show itself. Observant fans have calculated that the anti-hero utters the word fifty-four times during the show's run. Today, bitch is so commonplace that networks have even greenlighted the word in the title of television shows, like the supernatural teen sitcom *Boo, Bitch*. In a news story related to subscription television, one customer reported to the media that she'd complained about her cable service, only to receive her next bill addressed to "Super Bitch."[32] Other customers have reported similar account name changes to insults such as "dummy," "asshole," and "whore."

In recent decades, television taboos have been tumbling left and right, and bitch was among the words that were finally unbleeped. Nowadays bitch is ubiquitous on network television. Some shows go out of their way to say the word as frequently as they can. *How I Met Your Mother* became feted for its use of "bitch." The sitcom ran for nine seasons and 208 episodes, during which "bitch" was uttered a total of 121 times.[33] But even recently, the use of bitch has been bowdlerized. The word was censored in the title of the comedy drama *GCB*, based on the novel "Good Christian Bitches," and also the sitcom *Don't Trust the B---- in Apartment 23*. (In the French version of the show, *Garce* ("Bitch") isn't censored, while the German adaptation is just called *Apartment 23*.) Sometimes the word is removed altogether. *Black Bitch* was the working title of a political drama about systemic injustice toward Indigenous Australians. The producers said they were trying to reclaim the racial slur, but its use caused a media storm among members of the Indigenous community. Amid the backlash the show was renamed *Total Control*. In comedy, bitch can carry a certain grrl power, but in drama, the word still retains its sting.

The different rules and regulations for movies versus television have often clashed. With the stereotype in mind of the family gathered around the TV set, television has often been more concerned with propriety than cinema. In the edited-for-television cut of *Jaws*, Martin Brody growls at the shark, "Smile, you son of a —" before he fires a gun. "Bitch" is muffled by the gunshot and explosion. When *Smokey and the Bandit* was shown in cinemas in the 1970s, Buford T. Justice's catchphrase was "sumbitch," usually uttered in reference to Bo "Bandit" Darville. But when it first aired on television a few years later, sumbitch was overdubbed with "scum bum." The nonsensical phrase achieved a cult level of popularity with kids and teenagers, so the scale-model car company Hot Wheels released a replica of the 1970s Firebird Trans Am with "scum bum" emblazoned on its tail.[34] Sometimes the replacement choices for taboo words were ridiculous. In the edited-for-television version of *Back to the Future*, "damn," "hell," and "bastard" were acceptable, but "bitch" and "ass" were redubbed when Biff the bully grabs Marty McFly and says, "You caused 300 bucks worth of damage to my car, you son of a butthead, and I'm gonna take it out of your hide." But the censors weren't fooling anyone; any kid who'd ever heard the words before knew what was really being said, and besides, viewers could often lip-read the badly dubbed rude words.

Fans often railed against these edits because they changed the meaning of the dialogue and the intensity of the scene. In the iconic climax to *Aliens*, Sigourney Weaver's character Ellen Ripley tries to protect the little girl Newt from the alien queen when she screams, "Get away from her, you bitch!" In the original cut-for-television version, bitch is replaced with "butcher." TV censorship had altered one of the most memorable lines in film history. "Get away from her, you bitch!" underlined not only that specific moment, but every moment like that in real life where a mother will do *anything* to save her child. "Butcher" just wouldn't cut it …. This kind of censorship annoyed not only the fans but also the artists themselves. Artists often had to compromise their art in exchange for exposure on television. In 2005, the theme song "It's Hard Out Here for a Pimp" from *Hustle & Flow* won an Academy Award for Best Original Song. There was a live performance of the song at the Oscars, but given its salacious theme, the lyrics posed a problem for the censors. During the live rendition, "witches" replaced "bitches" and other words like "hoes," "shit," and "fuck" were cleaned up as well.

Although bitch is considered tame by today's standards, sometimes it's still abridged, bleeped out, muted, and substituted with popular euphemisms like *beech* and *biotch*, or even more creative ones. Censoring bitch is sometimes done, not because it must be, but because it's funny. In *The Big Bang Theory*, for example, Sheldon was well known for his favorite curse "Son of a biscuit!" In one episode, Leonard refers to "bitches" and Sheldon rebukes him with "I call the B word!" The euphemism in this scene ends up getting more studio audience laughs than the naughty word. In many shows, the script-writers let the viewers' dirty minds do the work for them. The sitcom *Son of the Beach* was a spoof of *Baywatch*, with much of its humor based on double entendres and innuendo like this. Similarly, *The Good Place* was a comedy about a virtuous afterlife where *bitch* was replaced by "birch" and "bench," *ass* became "ash," *fuck* was "fork," and *shit* became "shirt." On the other hand, cursing was allowed, and even encouraged, in the hellish "Bad Place." This gimmick is also used in marketing. In an advertisement for the Hyundai Santa Fe, instead of bleeping out the offending word, "bitch" is swapped with the innocent "blueberry." With so much public exposure to "bitch" and other "dirty words" nowadays, sometimes a euphemism can have more shock value and impact than a swear word among jaded audiences, because it catches people off guard.

Bitch was banned from television for decades, but by 2009, the *New York Times* reported that the use of bitch on prime-time TV had tripled between the years 1998 and 2008.[35] Some think that the increase in swearing on television reflects a general increase in swearing in society, and also reflects a moral decline. But as we've seen, swearing has *always* been around, although it has often been censored to avoid offending some people. Others speculate that television is just catching up with the actual use of swearing in society. If nothing else, the increase in profanity on television definitely shows that there is an increase in public displays of profanity, and an increase in the acceptability of swearing. Nowadays, instead of avoiding "dirty words," television writers pepper their scripts with them in the hope of attracting a wider audience. Profanity may still be offensive; it might drive away some viewers, but it also *attracts* viewers. Swearing, like sex, sells.

The Bitch Is Back

Well before there was Meredith Brooks and her 1990s anthem "Bitch" (the title of which was often censored as "Nothing in Between"), the word had already appeared in many songs in the past. In terms of music, bitch has its roots in jazz and the dirty blues, a sub-genre of blues that dealt with taboo topics like sex and drugs, couched in blunt and sexually explicit lyrics. And while "Bitch" seemed groundbreaking for its time, it's rather tame compared to the scandalous songs of the past. Jazz pianist Jelly Roll Morton composed some raunchy dirty blues tunes that he used to play in the Storyville saloons and brothels of New Orleans at the turn of the twentieth century. (His nickname "jelly roll" was slang for female genitalia, a reference to a jam-filled, rolled up sponge cake.) Morton's epic blues tale "The Murder Ballad" is about a lover killing her rival, and "bitch" amps up the intensity of the story. The woman threatens that if the mistress won't leave her man alone, "Bitch, I'll cut your fucking throat and drink your blood like wine."[36] The mistress fires back, "I'd like to see a bitch like you stop me. This ain't no slavery time and I'm sure that I'm free." In a fit of jealousy, the heroine declares, "Bitch, your day has come. You fucked my man, but you will never fuck another one." She pulls out a pistol and orders the woman to, "Open your legs, you dirty bitch, I'm gonna shoot you between your thighs." And she does. Charged with murder, she is sent to prison for fifty years. Completely unaffected by her plight, her man just moves on with his life, taking yet another lover. She ends up regretting her violent actions, warning other women to appreciate their independence and not follow her path of destruction.

In 1938, the folklorist Alan Lomax recorded Morton performing this half-hour extended blues song for the Library of Congress and gave it a title, because it didn't have one. Morton was initially reluctant to sing the explicit lyrics, but aided by Lomax's gentle encouragement and a bottle of whiskey, he played the tragic, hard-bitten song uncensored. He also played a bawdy version of Mississippi John Hurt's "Make Me a Pallet on the Floor." In this rendition, a pimp is having an afternoon tryst with a working man's wife. Morton sings, "Come here, you sweet bitch. Gimme that pussy. Let me get in your drawers. I'm going to make you think you fucking with Santa Claus." These history-making recordings reveal and preserve a now-vanished world of barrelhouse bards. Because of their profane language, the songs weren't released, and neither were the lyrics printed, until 2005.

The word "bitch" was less exploited in country and folk music because it was deemed to be offensive, but it was still used by some stars to shore up their outlaw cred. Woody Guthrie is famous for the populist "This Land Is Your Land," but in the 1940s he penned the hard-edged "Dopefiend Robber" about a World War II veteran who becomes addicted to morphine after recovering from a combat-related injury. The man's addiction escalates into robbery and murder. Guthrie sings: "One seventeen-year-old bitch tells me, 'Now you've knocked me up. You'll have to fork me a thousand to pay my knocker doc.' Here take this gun and come with me tonight. I'll teach ya how to rob and you can payoff your doc." In the song, "bitch" shows that the hero is a tough and rough rebel who doesn't care for rules or decorum. But the bad boy image didn't suit Guthrie, so he returned to his traditional ballads and children's songs, and Dopefiend Robber remained unreleased. Bob Dylan rewrote the lyrics in the 1960s, sans swearing.

Johnny Cash, who was a true bad boy known for his antics on and off-stage, sings the word in "A Boy Named Sue," based on the Shel Silverstein poem. The song chronicles a young man's quest for revenge on his father who abandoned him at the tender age of three, leaving him with a guitar and the name "Sue," as an act of tough love. One day, Sue confronts his father in a saloon. The two draw guns and then the old man finally recognizes his estranged son.

> Now you just fought one hell of a fight
> And I know you hate me, and you got the right,
> To kill me now, and I wouldn't blame you if you do
> But you ought to thank me, before I die
> For the gravel in your guts and the spit in your eye
> Because I'm the son-of-a-bitch that named you Sue.

Cash replaced Silverstein's "heartless hound" with the more hard-hitting "son of a bitch." The profanity was bleeped out on the single and album, although it went uncensored in Cash's original performance for the inmates at San Quentin prison in 1958. In a live show at the White House years later, he uttered a bleep-censored sound in lieu of the phrase. Cash also inserted "bitch" into the rockabilly "Cocaine Blues," his reworking of the traditional folk song "Little Sadie." This is the tale of Willy Lee, who, under the influence of whiskey and cocaine, murders his unfaithful girlfriend. Cash sings of her, "I can't forget the day I shot that bad bitch down." He famously played this song at his 1968 Folsom Prison concert, in which he sang the provocative lyric to an enthusiastic audience. The occasion was recreated in the biographical movie *Walk the Line*, although it fades into the next scene before the offending line is sung.

Men in music have often commandeered bitch as a way to dominate and diminish women. In the days of classic jazz, women singing the dirty blues wielded the word too, but in a different way. "Mother of the Blues" Gertrude "Ma" Rainey, together with her protégée Bessie Smith, used bitch as a way to empower themselves in a world where men were in control.[37] Their songs were about women who celebrated their right to conduct themselves as expansively, and behave as badly, as men. Like Jelly Roll Morton, their hardcore songs were full of sexual braggadocio and often sung in brothels and bar rooms or recorded for clandestine distribution as a "party record." But no one is known for lewd lyrics more than 1930s singer Lucille Bogan, especially in her absolutely obscene song "Till the Cows Come Home." Calling herself "the bitch from Baltimore," Bogan sings, "If you suck my pussy, baby, I'll suck your dick. I'll do it to you honey, until I make you shit." Like male blues musicians, women also used the word to claim virility for themselves. Trailblazing funk singer Betty Davis, the onetime wife of Miles Davis, was also known for her sexually explicit lyrics. In "Nasty Gal," she invokes the word to claim power over a lover who tried to use it to shut her down. She roars, "You said I was a bitch now. Didn't ya? Didn't ya? You said I was a witch now. I'm gonna tell 'em why."

The first artist to use "bitch" in an album title was Betty's husband Miles Davis. In 1969, the jazz trumpeter released his seminal jazz fusion album with the then-shocking title *Bitches Brew*. The album was groundbreaking, from the music to the cover art depicting free love and flower power, to its stark title. What the name actually means, however, is a mystery, although there are many theories floating around about it. Without an apostrophe at the end of the plural noun "Bitches," some speculate that "Brew" is intended as a verb, not a noun, meaning "a thing that bitches do, is brew."[38] Given the cover theme, the name might refer to brewing a strange potion that could help them achieve voodoo possession, or brewing a concoction used to create zombies. Carlos Santana suggested that the album was a tribute to the "cosmic ladies," Davis' wife Betty and her friends, who surrounded him at the time and introduced him to the music, clothes, and attitudes of the 1960s counterculture.[39] Others say that the "bitches" were the artists themselves, because the label was once a compliment for a highly skilled jazz musician. Whatever the title meant, it was provocative, just like the music. In modern slang, a "bitch's brew" is similar to a "girly drink"; a disparaging term for a cocktail or flavored alcoholic beverage that women drink but supposedly "real men" don't.

With the word's seal of approval from none other than the "Prince of Darkness" Miles Davis, bitch quickly became central to the vocabulary of popular music. In 1971, the Rolling Stones released "Bitch" as the B-side to "Brown Sugar." Mick Jagger penned the lyrics, and it's suggested that the song was about his disastrous breakup with girlfriend Marianne Faithfull. Some say the song wasn't about a specific person, but that it's about love in general; "It must be love, it's a bitch." Others say it's about Jagger's substance abuse, with lyrics like, "You got to mix it child. You got to fix," supposedly being a reference to a "heroin fix." In the lines "I'm feeling hungry. Can't see the reason. Just ate a horse meat pie," horse is said to be slang for "heroin." Some radio stations declined airplay of the song because of its profane title. Similarly, David Bowie's "Queen Bitch" was banned that same year because it was thought to be in bad taste, as much for its title ("bitch" doesn't appear in the lyrics) as its theme, with a story line about the singer's boyfriend who looks for drag queens and hookups on the street. Bitch pops up in a number of Bowie's songs, including the famous line in "Ziggy Stardust" in which his band The Spiders from Mars plan to exact revenge on their egotistical front man, "So we bitched about his fans and should we crush his sweet hands?"

Elton John's 1974 song "The Bitch Is Back" was the first hit song with the word unapologetically in its title. Many radio stations refused to play it when it was released, but when the song charted they relented and added it to their playlists. A few DJs tried to edit out the word, which proved to be an overwhelming task because it appears in the song forty-two times. Some wags nicknamed the censored version, "The Bleep Is Back." There's much speculation about the lyrics, with fans asking: who is the bitch? The song was apparently inspired by Maxine Feibelman, then wife of John's collaborator Bernie Taupin, who tutted, "Uh-oh, the bitch is back" every time John was in a bad mood.[40] (Some sources claim the song is about Feibelman herself, whom Taupin divorced a few years later.) Emboldened by David Bowie's recent use of the word in a song title, Taupin wrote the lyrics with the refrain, "I'm a bitch. I'm a bitch. Oh, the bitch is back." Instead of being offended by the characterization, John embraced the label and put music to the lyrics, saying, "It's kind of my theme song." At a 1974 concert he prefaced his performance with, "This is a song not referring to anyone in the audience, but mainly to me." Some segments of the LGBTQ+ community have taken the song as a signal of John's sexuality; at the time he hadn't yet come out. The title has since become part of pop culture lexicon. With a nod to Sigourney Weaver's famous cry "Get away from her, you bitch!", "The bitch is back" became the tag line for the sequel *Alien 3*.

Bitch now appears in thousands of song titles and it's embedded in many more verses and choruses. There are just too many songs to name. Even still, the acceptability of bitch, or its unacceptability, has been fluid over the years. While Elton John's song was being played on the radio, other songs containing the word were banned. In 1992, rock band Spinal Tap's "Bitch School" was censored by MTV for its controversial title and lyrics, which include the verse:

> *You been bad. Don't do what I say.*
> *You don't listen. And you never obey.*
> *Try to teach you. But you just won't be good.*
> *You won't behave the way a big girl should.*
> *It's time to give that whip a crack.*
> *I'm gonna have to send you back to Bitch School.*

On the surface, the lyrics sound extremely sexist, but this was actually a tongue-in-cheek song about obedience classes for disobedient dogs.

And speaking of satire, with songs like "Wet Bikini" and "Shark Attack," Slovenian punk band the Bitch Boys was a parody of the 1960s surf band the Beach Boys.

Other songs containing the word were banned for their implications of violence and misogyny. In 1997, Prodigy's "Smack My Bitch Up" caused controversy for its suggestive title. The refrain consists of the line, "Change my pitch up. Smack my bitch up," which is sampled from the hip hop song "Give the Drummer Some," performed by Rapper Kool Keith. "Smack" is actually a heroin reference, while "bitch" refers to the vein in the arm used to inject it. (Of course, the band reveled in the lyrics' double entendres.) The song performed well in the charts, even though it was banned from most television and radio stations; some played the instrumental version only and referred to the tune as "Smack." The song was also controversial for its explicit music video, which depicted scenes of drug and alcohol-fueled sexual assault. Band member Liam Howlett joked, "No radio station was gonna play the song, so we thought we'd make a video that no one would play either."[41] In a twist at the end of the video, the protagonist is revealed to be a woman.

Other musical uses of bitch were banned only by certain genres that didn't approve of the word. In 1979, the country music group the Charlie Daniels Band released their song "The Devil Went Down to Georgia." This was a ballad about the devil's failure to gain the soul of young Johnny via a fiddle-playing contest. The album version of the song goes, "Devil just come on back if you ever want to try again. I done told you once, you son of a bitch, I'm the best that's ever been." The censors had no problem doing deals with the Devil, but cursing was clearly out of the question. The controversial lyrics were censored to, "Cause I told you once, you son of a gun," to accommodate radio airplay for country music. It seemed to be a matter of country music stations being more conservative than rock ones. Like complaints about movies cut for TV, fans were annoyed by the prudish radio edit, arguing that it blunted the song's intensity. In 1998, the song was re-released with the offending word intact, while the record company "accidentally" sent this uncensored version to country music stations too. When the error was discovered, much to the embarrassment of DJs around the US, the records were quickly replaced with a "clean" version.

Censorship of the music industry, or the threat of censorship, was about to get much worse before it would get any better. In 1983, an American committee was formed called the Parents Music Resource Center (PMRC), who advocated for warning labels to be placed on music deemed to have violent, drug-related, or sexual themes. Mary Elizabeth "Tipper" Gore, former wife of politician Al Gore, founded the committee because she heard her eleven-year-old daughter listening to the "embarrassingly vulgar lyrics" of Prince's song "Darling Nikki" that refer explicitly to female masturbation. Gore dubbed this kind of music, "a poisonous source infecting the youth of the world with messages they cannot handle."[42] Through their intensive campaigning, the PMRC were successful, and it became obligatory for record labels to place black-and-white "Parental Advisory Explicit Content" stickers on records featuring violent or sexually explicit language, especially from the heavy metal, punk, and hip hop genres. Some retailers refused to sell those stickered albums, affecting the visibility and income of many artists.

The campaign ultimately backfired, however, because the label was no longer a protective device but a guarantee of forbidden fruit. In an infamous photo of Gore, she's posed holding the album *Be My Slave* by the heavy metal band Bitch, which she singled out as an example of "vulgar" content, although the artist thanked Gore in the album's liner notes for this exposure, which greatly increased her album sales. These events also inspired many angry songs about Gore, including "Pro Me" by BWP (Bytches With Problems) and Ice-T's "KKK Bitch." In "Freedom of Speech" Ice-T raps, "You're bitching about rock 'n' roll; that's censorship, dumb bitch." In the rapper's memoir he wrote, "Tipper Gore is the only woman I ever directly called a 'bitch' on any of my records, and I meant that in the most negative sense of the word."[43] In the end, this crusade didn't affect the use of bitch in music, which was steadily increasing, especially in rap and hip hop.

Perfect Bitch

When Jelly Roll Morton performed for Alan Lomax, he explained why his songs were so "smutty," as he called them. During his days of playing piano in the red-light district of New Orleans, the instrument was considered to be effeminate. For turn-of-the-century Black and Creole women, learning to play the piano meant respectability and class status. Famous contemporary pianists included Mamie Desdunes (who had instructed Morton) and also Dolly Adams, "Sweet Emma" Barrett, and many other talented female musicians. This was a time, however, when the male-dominated jazz scene didn't fully accept women as performers or professional musicians. And while instruments like the trumpet and trombone were seen as masculine, the piano was viewed as feminine. As Morton put it, "When a man played piano, the stamp was on him for life, the femininity stamp, and I didn't want that on. So of course, when I did start to playin', the song were kinda smutty a bit."[44] Playing smutty music made him more masculine in the eyes (and ears) of his audience. Morton proceeded to play "Winin' Boy Blues" for Lomax, one of his own compositions, which was another smutty song about a sexual conquest. The lyrics include, "I had that bitch and had her on the stump. I fucked her 'til her pussy stunk." The aggressive cries of "bitch" seem to embody both desire and scorn for women at the same time. The song was written in the late 1800s, although it's reminiscent of contemporary rap and hip hop. It's clear that Morton's smutty lyrics rival the most explicit language of today's rappers. In other words, the roots of modern gangster rap and hip hop music go back to the dirty blues of the nineteenth century.

Throughout the 1980s and 1990s, rap and hip hop laid claim to "bitch" and promoted much of the violence and misogyny associated with it today. Grandmaster Caz claims he was the first to use the word in the 1970s, in an unrecorded song about a girl who "wouldn't give me any play."[45] Although the first to say it on the record was English-American rapper Slick Rick in the 1985 beatboxing classic "La Di Da Di" with Doug E. Fresh. Rick sings about a jealous and violent older woman who tries to flirt with him, "The bitch been around before my mother's born." A year later, Ice-T rapped about beating up a "bitch" who dared to talk back to him in "Six in Da Morning." With the original gangsta rapper Ice-T giving the word his blessing, the use of bitch rapidly escalated from this point. Bitch went hand in hand with unflattering stereotypes of women. In NWA's "Bitch Iz a Bitch" Ice Cube raps, "Now the title bitch don't apply to all women, but all women have a little bitch in 'em." The song characterizes women as manipulative, materialistic, and money hungry. Public Enemy's "Sophisticated Bitch" does this too, as a scathing takedown of a gold-digger in which Chuck D raps, "Get ready to only throw money at the bitch." Bitch also dehumanizes women as sex objects, implying they're sluts and whores. In "Bitches Ain't Shit," Dr. Dre sings, "Bitches ain't shit but hoes and tricks. Lick on deez nutz and suck the dick. Gets the fuck out after you're done." A bitch was someone without value, a woman to be used and discarded.

Rap and hip hop have been heavily condemned for their misogynistic and violent imagery and lyrics, and also their sexist music videos full of scantily clad women. Some studies conclude that rap music is problematic, claiming that exposure to it increases negative stereotypes of women, and especially Black women.[46] Its language is also believed to glorify and promote real-world acts of violence against women. During a joint concert in 1998, the Beastie Boys called Prodigy beforehand and asked them not to play "Smack My Bitch Up" in their set, because of the song's sexist and violent implications. On stage, Prodigy's Maxim lambasted the Beastie Boys for this request, telling the audience, "They didn't want us to play this fucking tune. But the way things go, I do what the fuck I want!" before launching into the song.[47] Adam Horovitz of the Beastie Boys later commented on the incident, saying, "You know, a woman in America gets murdered every 20 minutes every day in domestic violence. So 'Smack My Bitch Up' isn't that funny."[48]

Rap artists defend their music as an art form, saying that rap and hip hop have been unfairly demonized. It's often argued that rapping is just rhythm, but not "real music." Rap and hip hop have been criticized and compared unfavorably to Eurocentric standards of what music should be. The debate around rap music's validity is often rooted in racism, which has affected every African American music style, from jazz to blues to rap. Rap artists explain that rap music is the voice of the street, telling it like it is. Their lyrics are raw, honest, and authentic. Rap and hip hop music are often described as the soundtrack to modern social issues in Black communities across the United States, like drug use, gang activity, prostitution, poverty, and gun culture. Their music is a reflection of the harsh realities of people of color, and so they call it "reality rap." Speaking about these issues, Ice Cube refuses to compromise or apologize for the subject matter of his band's lyrics, explaining, "Our raps are documentary. We don't take sides."[49]

Bitch features heavily in rap music, and also the trash talk tradition that gave birth to the genre. Originally known as "The Dozens," this is a street game rooted in the art of the insult. In another example of everything old is new again, we go back to Jelly Roll Morton and the dirty blues. In the 1930s, Morton played another smutty tune for Lomax called "The Dirty Dozens." Some of the verses come straight from the insult game: "Oh you dirty motherfucker. You old cocksucker. You dirty son of a bitch. You bastard. You're everything; and your mammy don't wear no drawers."[50] The "smutty" language of the dozens game is intended to be humorous, boastful, insulting, and provocative, and it's always performed in front of an appreciative audience. This tradition clearly influenced rap and hip hop music, and also modern "Yo Mama" jokes. Another verse of "The Dirty Dozens" begins with a couplet that was a common street rhyme in the 1970s. "Said, look our bitch, you made me mad. I'll tell you 'bout the puppies that your sister had. Oh, it was a fad. She fucked a hog. She fucked a dog. I know the dirty bitch would fuck a frog. 'Cause your mammy don't wear no drawers." Insults about mothers or sisters having sex with dogs have always been common in dozens playing, by way of extending the metaphor inherent in "bitch." Whether uttered in a blues murder ballad, a street game, or a rap song, bitch can be a weapon of sorts, a way of demonstrating dominance and power over other people, and especially women.

Since the time of Lucille Bogan, the self-professed "bitch of Baltimore," Black female artists have reclaimed bitch as both a gun and also a bulletproof vest. Like Bogan's X-rated dirty blues, the rapper Trina's use of the word goes back to the earlier meaning of bitch as a highly sexual woman. In "Nasty Bitch" she describes her sexual prowess in graphic detail, she's a dirty girl who'll do anything, while in "Da Baddest Bitch" she sings, "If I had the chance to be a virgin again, I'd be fucking by the time I'm ten." The explicit sex raps of Nicki Minaj's "Boss Ass Bitch" are also reminiscent of Bogan's sexual bragging in her raunchy tunes of the 1920s and 30s. In other modern songs, "bitch" is about female rappers asserting their dominance in the "man's world" of music. Rihanna's "Bitch Better Have My Money," often censored as "bbhmm," is a revenge fantasy story that's inspired by the artist's real-life experience with an accountant who mismanaged her finances and cheated her out of money. In using the word, Rihanna shows us that she's tough, formidable, and not someone to mess with. Hip hop artist Lizzo declares that a bitch is a woman who believes in herself and never gives up when she raps unapologetically, "I did a DNA test and found out I'm 100% that bitch." Lizzo liked the phrase so much that she trademarked it.

But not all artists have embraced the role of bitch. Some female rappers have railed against the label, including MC Trouble and Lauryn Hill. Queen Latifah's U.N.I.T.Y. speaks out against the disrespect of women in society, addressing issues of sexual harassment, sexism, and slurs against women in rap and hip hop culture. In the song she asks, "Who you calling a bitch?" Then she tells her listeners, "You got to let him know, you ain't a bitch or a ho."

In the ongoing debate about who gets to dictate the word's use, a few male artists have stood up for women. In Lupe Fiasco's song "Bitch Bad," he made a heroic attempt to address the issue, "I say bitch bad, woman good, lady better." But most rappers use it as a pejorative. In "Call Her a Bitch," Too $hort raps, "One thing's for sure, you *will* get called a bitch ... Bitch." And bitch is still used to objectify women. In Tyler the Creator's "Bitch Suck Dick," he suggests women should use their mouths for giving blowjobs, not talking. Appealing to the "psycho bitch" ex-girlfriend trope, "bitch" is also wielded to get revenge on exes. In his song "I Don't Fuck with You," Big Sean refers to his former fiancée Naya Rivera as a "stupid-ass bitch," "crazy bitch," and "dumbass bitch." In fact, he invokes the word dozens of times in the song to refer to her. In Jay-Z's "That's My Bitch," he teams up with Kanye West to diss their ex-girlfriends. In reference to the song's title, Jay-Z also name checks his wife Beyoncé, warning any men who leer at her to "Get ya own dog, ya heard? That's my bitch."

In the rap lexicon, "bitch" is infamously used as a synonym for "woman" (as we've seen reported by some dictionaries). In Jay-Z's "99 Problems," for example, he uses the word as a stand-in for "woman." Fans speculated that he would renounce the word, based on a widely circulated poem that surfaced when his daughter Blue Ivy Carter was born. The poem read: "Before I got in the game, made a change and got rich. I didn't think hard about using the word bitch. I rapped, I flipped it, I sold it, I lived it. Now with my daughter in this world I curse those that give it." It turned out, however, that the poem was penned by a blogger as a prank.[51] The birth of his baby daughter did *not* stop him from using the word. It was only a few years before that Al Sharpton had tried to ban "bitch," "ho," and "nigga" from music, but Jay-Z refused publicly, protesting that Sharpton didn't represent him. In "Say Hello" he raps in response, "I'll remove the curses if you tell me our schools' gon' be perfect, when Jena Six don't exist, tell him that's when I'll stop sayin' bitch, bitch."[52]

Jay-Z's collaborator Kanye West is also fond of the word and has created controversy with his frequent use of it. He dedicated the song "Perfect Bitch" to his then-girlfriend Kim Kardashian. (Makeup artist Charlotte Tilbury later launched a cult peachy-colored lipstick called "Bitch Perfect".) Kardashian reportedly told friends that West's gesture made her feel special. "I'm honored. I love it. I know he doesn't mean it in a negative way when he says the word 'bitch.' The song talks about how he was with so many other girls but could never find the right one until he met me."[53] A few years later, however, when Kardashian was his wife, she's no longer branded a bitch in his song "Bound 2," but instead she's a "good girl" who's worth "a thousand bitches." West later had second thoughts about whether bitch was acceptable in rap and hip hop. He took to Twitter to ask fans their views on its use in music, musing that "Stevie Wonder never had to use the word bitch." He concluded, "Perhaps the words BITCH and NIGGA are now neither positive or negative. They are just potent and it depends on how they are used and by whom?"[54] West's final verdict was that it's okay to call women bitches. He continues to use the word in his lyrics, including the notorious song "Famous," in which he says of artist Taylor Swift, "I feel like me and Taylor might still have sex. Why? I made the bitch famous." This referred to his interruption of Swift's acceptance of the award for Best Female Video at the 2009 MTV Music Video Awards, in order to proclaim that despite her victory, Beyoncé still had "one of the best videos of all time." Criticized heavily for his use of the slur in the song, West claimed he "did not diss" Swift, but had first obtained her approval of the lyric. Swift, however, denied this version of events and denounced the line as misogynistic. West argued in his defense, "Bitch is an endearing term in hip hop, like the word Nigga." This is, of course, all in the interpretation.

Given the word's long tradition in rap and hip hop music, it's unlikely that male artists will stop calling women (and some men) "bitches" anytime soon, as long as they also continue to call themselves "niggas" and "dogs."

B*#%$

People have always complained about so-called "bad" language. It's not just a modern trend. Social critics in the 1940s railed against the colorful language of the GIs returning from World War II. In the 1920s, some condemned the "mucker posers," the well-bred young people who emulated "the manners and language of the longshoremen."[55] And so on down to the Victorians, whose sermons and statutes were full of references to public profanity. Earlier still, Samuel Johnson eschewed the "low bad words" in his famous dictionary, while even Francis Grose censored "cunt" in his *Dictionary of the Vulgar Tongue*.

As the philosopher Charles de Montesquieu once observed, people have been complaining about the decline of manners and morals since the time of Aristotle.[56]

Some may complain about "indecent" words, fine people when they use them, or even try to censor or ban them, but no matter what any organization or committee says or does, these efforts are not likely to have much of an effect on the way we talk. Profanity, obscenity, and taboo words in general seem to fill a basic need of human communication. This category of words has probably always been around, and probably always will be. But the moralists are correct about one thing: this kind of language *has* become more widespread and audible than ever before.

Whether it's perceived as profanity, a part-time dirty word, or simply benign, it's undeniable that bitch is a controversial word. It's also an everyday word. Bitch is so common nowadays that we take for granted how hard it was for early writers, actors, and artists to write, speak, or sing the word at all. Little did they know how much the word would eventually take off. Because it's so commonplace today, bitch doesn't quite have the shock value that it once did back in the days of Francis Grose. Some remark that the word is so prevalent nowadays, on television and the Internet and in books, video games, movies, and music, that bitch has lost its bite. But is this true?

Let's now look at the way bitch is used today and how it might be used in the future.

5

• • • • • •

Basic Bitch

Even though the word has been around for over one thousand years, bitch has proven that an old dog *can* be taught new tricks. Over the centuries, bitch has become a linguistic chameleon with many different meanings and uses. It's a shape-shifter too, morphing into modern spinoffs like *biatch*, *biznatch*, and *betch*. Bitch is a versatile word. It can behave like a noun, an adjective, a verb, or an interjection, and it also makes a cameo appearance in lots of idioms. In these ways, bitch is similar to *fuck*, another taboo yet flexible word with many different guises.

Bitch can be a bitch of a word. Calling someone a bitch once seemed to be a pretty straightforward insult, but today – after so many variations, reinventions, and attempts to reclaim the word – it's not always entirely clear what bitch really means. Well, my good bitch, there are basic bitches and bad bitches; sexy bitches and psycho bitches; boss bitches and even perfect bitches. A bitch can be a female dog or a bad woman, although in the past a bitch could also be a cool jazz musician or a freewheeling hobo. You can ride bitch, go bitchcakes, wear a resting bitch face, or just drop the word onto the end of a sentence like, "It's Britney, bitch!" Things can be bitches too, a difficult task, an old broken-down car, or a natural disaster. Even love is a bitch. Ultimately, life's a bitch, and then you die. But is the word going away anytime soon? Bitch, please.

The word came down to us from Old English, but we modern speakers have really made the word our bitch. Nowadays, bitch is everywhere. It's a global word. Bitch is found not only in Anglophone countries and cultures like the United States, Canada, Australia, New Zealand, and the UK, but also as far away as China and India. The word appears in numerous other languages too, from Arabic to Zulu. But where is it going to from here? Let's take a look at bitch in the present day, and beyond.

Biznatch

As we know, there were many different spellings of bitch before the introduction of the printing press in the 1400s, because it hadn't yet been standardized. Over recent decades, even with a standardized spelling, bitch has spawned many slang variations, with just the insertion of a few different sounds. These are euphemisms that are sometimes called minced oaths or polite substitutes which still convey the word's core meaning, like heck for hell, shoot for shit, and fudge for fuck. Some of them are used when bitch seems too severe, like *binch* or *bish*. *Biatch* and *biotch* are also intended to be expressive and theatrical. Others can be used as pet names among close friends, like "Wassup, biznatch?" But under the right (or wrong) circumstances they can still be deeply offensive. In an episode of *Better Call Saul*, two con-artists try to extort money from drug kingpin Tuco. They burst into Tuco's house with his frail, elderly grandmother in tow. "This crazy old biznatch ran over my brother," claims one of the men. These were fighting words for Tuco, who asks incredulously, "You called her 'biznatch'?" The guy shrugs, "Whatever." To prove that no one disrespects his *abuelita* by calling her "biznatch," Tuco brutally attacks them with his grandmother's walking cane. As they lie on the floor, writhing in pain, Tuco spits "Biznatch" right back at them.

So where did biznatch come from? Since the 1970s, inserting sounds such as -z-, -iz- and -izzle into words became a game in African American slang, originally forming a secret language similar to Pig Latin. This practice was popularized by rappers like Jay-Z, Snoop Dogg, and Missy Elliott, who were all inspired by Frankie Smith's 1980s R&B hit "Double Dutch Bus," which had lyrics like "Hizzey, gizzirls! Y'izzall hizzave t' mizzove izzout the wizzay sizzo the gizzuys can plizzay bizzasketbizzal." This can be roughly translated as, "Hi girls, you have to move outta the way so the guys can play basketball." Biznatch arose from this tradition, along with *fuznuck* (fuck), *hizo* (ho or whore), and *shiznit* (shit). This kind of inventive language is a way to stand out against the background of American culture, an instrument of both fitting in and standing out.[1] Biznatch is a euphemism, but it's also an intensifier that gives force and emphasis. The process of inserting sounds into words is known as infixing, and it's just like dropping bloody, freaking, fucking, or other expletives into the middle of words, such as abso-fucking-lutely.

Some variations of bitch have specific meanings, like *betch*, which labels a type of rich, shallow, consumeristic white woman who loves things like having brunch and taking selfies. As the *New York Times* defined betch, "What do you call a young woman who is materialistic, sustains herself on iced coffee and Diet Coke, and believes the three cardinal rules to getting ahead in life are 'don't be easy,' 'don't be poor' and 'don't be ugly'?"[2] Betch is foremost an insult, but it is also used self-referentially as an affectionate term among fellow betches. A betch is related to the *rich bitch*, a mean, snide woman who flaunts her outrageous wealth. She may also be classified as a *rude* or *selfish bitch*.

The rich bitch is a popular trope of television drama, like the scheming, backstabbing, designer clothes-wearing Alexis Carrington played by Joan Collins in the 1980s soap opera *Dynasty*. *Bish* is another playful alternative, along with *bunch* and *binch*, which may have begun their lives innocently enough as typos of *bench*. (But binch is not to be confused with Binch, the popular chocolate cookie made by the South Korean company Lotte.) All of these euphemisms are softened, less offensive versions of bitch, like *freaking* instead of fucking or *sugar* as an alternative for shit. They're also handy workarounds for getting past profanity filters. (While everyone knows what they *really* mean.)

These variations seem to stem from one original variant: *biatch*. This was first recorded in the mid 1980s and comes from a drawn-out, exaggerated pronunciation of bitch that originated in gangster rap and hip hop culture. Biatch was first uttered in rap music by Too $hort in "Call Her a Bitch" and "Cusswords," where it's used as a kind of mic drop at the end of a diss. In all of its many forms, bitch became one of the rapper's trademarks and he defended his use of the word in his song, "Ain't Nothin' but a Word to Me." Biatch was then popularized by other rappers like Snoop Dogg and Dr. Dre. The word took off among the general public and morphed into new spellings, like *biotch*, *byatch*, and *beeyotch*. These are generally taken to be euphemisms that are less offensive than bitch, but they can still be disparaging and even threatening. When rioters attacked the US Capitol in 2021, protester Richard "Bigo" Barnett broke into Nancy Pelosi's office, sat in her chair and put his feet up on her desk, before stealing a private document and leaving her a note saying, "Nancy Bigo was here biatd."[3] In the aftermath of the events, Barnett's lawyers argued that "Biatd" was meant to read "biatch" and that this was intended as a "term of endearment." A condition of biatch being interpreted as endearing is that it's used among friends to show familiarity, which in this case, it was definitely not. Biatch is a popular word. Slang is ephemeral, and most colloquial speech doesn't make it to the dictionary, but occasionally some words do. Biatch had the honor of being added to the *Oxford English Dictionary* a few years ago, the same year as *craptastic*, *butt fuck*, *drunk text*, and *sausage party*.

Resting Bitch Face

Resting bitch face is another relative of bitch that made it into a number of dictionaries. Resting bitch face, otherwise known as RBF, is a facial expression that unintentionally makes someone look angry or irritated, especially when the person is resting, relaxed, or not expressing any particular emotion. Sometimes called the "not face," it's described as a furrowed brow, pressed lips and a raised chin giving the person an unfriendly, bored, or annoyed appearance. Resting bitch face has been widely referred to in the media, especially in the pages of lifestyle and fashion magazines. Many famous women have been accused of wearing this expression simply for not smiling in photographs, including golden age actresses Bette Davis and Vivien Leigh, and more recently, Kristen Stewart and Victoria Beckham. The phrase is usually uttered in criticism of women. In her comedy show "Douglas," Hannah Gadsby jokes, "Only women have *resting bitch face*. Men simply have very important thoughts you'd best not interrupt them having."[4] Men have, however, been accused of having RBF too, sometimes masculinized as resting asshole face. Kanye West is an enthusiast of the expression. He explains, "Not smiling makes me smile. When you see paintings in an old castle, people are not smiling 'cause it just wouldn't look as cool."[5]

Historical figures have been accused posthumously of wearing a resting bitch face, as revealed by their grim expressions and scowls in portraits, namely the Mona Lisa, Louis XIV of France, and George Washington. The phenomenon is real, according to some scientists. One study found that the expression was as common in men's faces as women's but posited that there's an expectation that women should smile and not scowl, added to social pressure that they maintain an aura of approachability and likeability.[6] Told that she needs to smile more, a request that would make any woman frown, Kanye West's ex Kim Kardashian replied, "I *do* smile, even laugh on occasion. Not too often though because it causes wrinkles."[7] Plastic surgeons say that resting bitch face is caused by gravity and genetics; as a result, some people get cosmetic surgery to rid themselves of the droopy, saggy look. There's also a "resting bitch voice" in which a person, usually a woman, is said to be unable to contain the bitchiness and irritation in the tone of her voice.

Just as resting bitch face is usually connected to women, *something* that's a bitch is often associated with women too, or it's considered to be a subordinate version of something. To *ride* or *sit bitch* is to be a passenger on the pillion of a motorcycle, known as the woman's or *bitch seat*. It can also be a passenger sandwiched in the middle seat of a car or truck with passengers at either side. The terms originally come from "biker bitches" who would ride behind their male companions on a motorcycle in biker gang caravans. A bitch might be something that's second rate, like a *bitch bath*. This is a makeshift "bath" in which the usual bathwater or shower is replaced by the application of deodorant, perfume, and other scented cosmetics, masking the dirt and odor rather than removing it when lacking proper bathing facilities. Sometimes it means to wash only one's private parts after having sex, when it may be called a whore's bath, as the bare minimum of cleaning that someone can get away with, presumably before seeing their next client. Bitch is often trivializing too. *Bitchwork* is a name for menial or tedious work, with the implication that it's the kind of work that women should have to do. Bitch is also used to refer to something inferior or of poor quality. In stoner culture, *bitchweed* is adulterated, contaminated, or otherwise 'bad' marijuana, while a *bitch* is someone who knowingly dispenses it. Among heroin users, the major vein used for injection is known as the "bitch," just like the drug references in the Prodigy's track "Smack My Bitch Up."

A bitch can be some*thing* inferior, but also some*one* inferior, like the *basic bitch* type. On an easyJet flight from Turkey to England, model Kate Moss was met by police at the airport and escorted off the plane for disorderly conduct. She'd thrown her weight around during the flight, demanding attention because of her celebrity status, and swigging vodka from a bottle stashed in her handbag. Allegedly, she called a flight attendant a "basic bitch," because the woman refused to peel her a grape.[8] Other sources claim that while she was being ushered off the plane, her parting words to the pilot were, "You're a basic bitch."

Whichever version of events is accurate, there's no doubt that Moss popularized the term with this infamous incident. It's tricky, however, to pinpoint the exact origins of basic bitch. The original meaning may have been an insult for someone who was "basic" in the sense of simple, uncomplicated, and perhaps a little boring. In her *Unabridged Journals*, poet Sylvia Plath invokes basic to refer to her dislike of dull society small talk. Recalling an attempt to make conversation in a fraternity room, she says, "You've had all you can take of good-looking vacuums and shallow socialites. So you try to be basic."[9]

There were a few other forerunners of the term too. In the 1989 film *Say Anything*, Diane (Ione Skye) fears she's offended her suitor Lloyd (John Cusack) when she dismisses him with, "I've never gone out with someone so basic." *Generic* has been used in a similar way. In *Clueless*, Alicia Silverstone's character Cher Horowitz mocks a group of rival peers in the mall with the harsh diss, "Could they please be more generic?" By 2010, the phrase sounds familiar to modern ears when rapper Kreayshawn's song "Gucci Gucci" slams commercially "girly" things with the lyrics, "Gucci Gucci, Louis Louis, Fendi Fendi, Prada; the basic bitches wear that shit; so I don't even bother." When Moss wielded basic bitch a few years later, the term took off, being lobbed at any woman whose behavior, interests, and style was deemed to be mainstream, predictable, or unoriginal. Basic bitch shares some similarities with the shallow, superficial betch and also the *average bitch*, an ordinary, mediocre, girl-next-door type. Amid rumors of Jay-Z's infidelity, Beyoncé warns her husband to appreciate her in the ballad "Sandcastles," "You're not married to no average bitch, boy." The rapper had a reputation for being a womanizer and a "bitch magnet."

A *bitch magnet* is a man who's irresistibly alluring to women. But this isn't only about his good looks. It can also be an object that's said to make him more attractive to women, like having lots of money or driving an expensive sports car. Bitch Magnet was also the name of a 1980s punk rock band. In his memoir "Your Band Sucks," guitarist Jon Fine reflects that although his band was a cult favorite with a loyal fan base, they never really made it big. He suspects their controversial name had something to do with it. "We were 18 years old when we chose the name," he said. "I think we thought it was funny. As a 47-year-old man, it's probably not a name I would choose, but I'm not going to walk away from it."[10] Bitch magnet arose from the similar terms *babe magnet* and *chick magnet*, although unlike the positive connotations of babe and chick as desirable young women, bitch implies contempt for the women who are magnetically attracted to the man. Going back to rapper Jay-Z, on his album *Vol.3 Life and Times of S. Carter*, he's portrayed as an abusive, manipulative, and dismissive bitch magnet, implying that these women don't matter to him, they're disposable. For this reason, some eschew the label when it's pasted on them. Notwithstanding a lifetime of Hugh Hefner's problematic exploitation of women, when challenged on Twitter to explain why he was such a bitch magnet, the late *Playboy* publisher tweeted back, "I have a lot of girlfriends because I don't call them 'bitches.' A little respect goes a long way."

Bitch, Please

In rap and hip hop culture, *ho magnet* is yet another variation of the phrase and it's something to brag about. In "Doin' What I Do" Mac Dre boasts about his ability to attract women with ease when he raps, "I'm a ho magnet," as proof of his success in the music industry. In Snoop Dogg's "Bitch Please," he also crows about being a ho magnet with the lyrics, "Bitch please! Get down on your goddamn knees, for this money, chronic, clothes and weed." The amended radio versions of the song were released under the names "B Please" and "Trick Please," while Eminem later released the sequel song "Bitch Please II." In African American English, *bitch, please* is synonymous with *nigga, please* as both are expressions of annoyance or impatience. The latter is used mostly toward men, although it isn't deemed to be appropriate when used outside of the African American community.

In the movie *Mean Girls*, two teens dubbed "cool Asians" are shown arguing in Vietnamese with one of the subtitles reading, "Nigga, please" or "Bitch, please" depending on the version. The scriptwriter, comedian Tina Fey, was criticized when it was later discovered that the actual translation was akin to the innocuous, "Please, I wouldn't dare." Fey admitted that the incorrect translation was added in for shock value. Bitch, please became a popular way of expressing that something is ridiculous, akin to "Oh, come on!" Bitch, please has birthed many internet memes, but probably the most famous one depicts Chinese basketball player Yao Ming laughing heartily and looking like he's saying "Bitch, please," captioned with the phrase. Bitch, please went viral online, although it was in existence long before the Internet. It has been suggested that bitch, please has its roots among inner-city prostitution rings in the 1970s.[11] And while it's often tongue-in-cheek nowadays, in the past it carried connotations of violence and hostility.

Bitch can be suggestive of anger, aggression, and also instability, with allusions to a snarling, barking, biting female dog. In a popular trope already mentioned, an ex-wife, ex-girlfriend, or ex-mistress is painted as irrational, unbalanced, and unstable. As the saying goes: *bitches be crazy*. The woman is often described as a *batshit* or *crazy bitch*, like the bunny-boiling "psycho bitch" Alex played by Glenn Close in *Fatal Attraction*. Similarly, a *ratchet bitch* is an ill-tempered woman who escalates a situation or argument by ratcheting things up. It has the implication that she's provoking a fight or altercation and is reminiscent of the domestic violence trope "she pushed me too far." Ratchet also conjures up imagery of Nurse Ratched, the cruel and controlling psychiatric nurse in *One Flew Over the Cuckoo's Nest*. Yet another term for an angry woman is *raging bitch*. Raging stems from Latin "rabies," implying a madness and fury that likens her to a rabid dog. Other insults suggest a woman is acting "hysterical" or "too emotional," such as *real* or *total bitch*. A *cranky* or *moody bitch* is accused of being hormonal or it's assumed she's "on her period." According to Domino's Pizza secret jargon, a *bitch pie* is topped with pepperoni, mushroom, and sausage, the initials standing for "PMS."

Bitch on wheels is a related term for an angry woman known for her incessant, circular ranting and bitching, when she "goes on and on" like a continuously spinning wheel. Notorious Black Widow murderer Sharon Nelson, who killed several of her husbands to cash in on their insurance policies, was dubbed the "Bitch on Wheels" by those who were closest to her. There's even a mythical place where such enraged bitches supposedly hail from. In the 1994 romantic thriller *I Love Trouble*, during a heated argument Nick Nolte challenges his rival Julia Roberts with, "Where did you say you were from? Bitchville?" There's also a film by the same name, in which three sisters are desperate to escape their family home in rural Croatia. The story is partly told from the point of view of the neighbor, who portrays the family as a bunch of whores and angry bitches. These bitchy insults are thrown at women, although sometimes women themselves take on the mantle to say, "don't fuck with me." A popular meme on bumper stickers threatens that the driver can "go from zero to bitch in 2.5 seconds."

Many phrases invoke the image of an angry person, usually a woman, who starts screaming, crying, and throwing objects when things don't go her way. To *bitch someone off* is to piss them off, while telling someone to "bitch off" is akin to saying fuck off. Like a counterpoint to the cutesy *cupcake*, *bitchcakes* is an insult for someone, and usually a woman. It evolved into the phrase *to go bitchcakes on someone*, meaning to become wildly or uncontrollably angry. An early use appeared on the 1990s TV show *NewsRadio*. In one episode, Beth decides to make up a word and see if she can get others to use it by dropping it into conversation. Testing her theory, she says, "If my boyfriend acted like that, I would go absolutely bitchcakes." Her friend Lisa asks, "Bitchcakes?" To which Beth replies, "I just made that up. You think it's gonna catch on?"[12] By the end of the day, everyone is using it. The word was picked up by the general public to refer to a person, and usually a woman, who flips out or freaks out. It's related to other expressions that mean to pick a fight, complain, or cause a disturbance, like to *pitch a bitch*. A *bitch fit* is a temper tantrum, which is also an emasculating phrase for a man who's upset. These are all similar to the sayings to *go apeshit, ballistic,* or *postal,* which often refer more to testosterone-fueled angry and violent men than women.

Sexy Bitch

Bitch has a long relationship with sex and sexuality. As we know, early versions of the word referred to a woman who was promiscuous or sensual. A bitch was a slutty woman, as a metaphorical extension of the behavior of a canine "bitch in heat." Bitch could also mean a prostitute or whore, and bitchery was prostitution or harlotry, while it was a onetime name for a brothel as well. *Bitch money* referred to earnings from prostitution or pimping, and to go bitching was to seek out a prostitute for sex. Some towns became known for their houses of ill repute. Long before Boston, Massachusetts, was famous for the Red Sox and its trendy brewpubs, the city earned the reputation of "Bitches' Heaven" among railroad tramps and hobos for having an abundance of cheap sex workers.[13] Bitch was also slang for a hobo. In the present day, there's still a strong connection between bitch and sex and sexuality. In street slang, a bitch is a sexual partner. In kink culture, a dominatrix is also called a *dominant bitch*, a woman who assumes the dominant role in BDSM scenes, or the female equivalent of a dominant.

Bitch also has a place in the colorful vocabulary of erotic or dirty talk. While this kind of language is not for everyone, some find it to be a turn-on in the bedroom. (Talking dirty is often associated with pornography too.) *Sexy bitch* can be a compliment that conveys a woman's sexual prowess. A *dirty bitch* is a woman who loves sex and enjoys having it. Like the rapper Trina, a *nasty bitch* is a woman who's up for trying anything sexually, even the really "nasty" stuff. Female sexuality has long been considered to be negative and shameful, so it's of little surprise that pejorative terms like dirty and nasty appear with bitch, even if it's to describe something positive like sexual liberation. Of course, these phrases are often used in a derogatory way too, imply-ing that a woman is unclean or a slut. A woman who rejects a man's sexual advances may be deemed to be a *frigid bitch*, suggesting she has a physical shortcoming or sexual anomaly, rather than that she's just exercising her free will to not have sex. Bitch often accuses women of using their sexuality as a weapon, granting sex as a reward for men, or withholding sex as a means of punishment.

Bitch also appears in crude colloquial names for sexual body parts and functions. *Bitch hammer* is slang for the penis, while *bitch bag* refers to the testicles. Bitch bags may also refer to a woman's mammary glands, or equally a man's, rather like the man boobs or bitch tits that we mentioned earlier. *Bitch butter* and *bitch juice* might mean a woman's vaginal secretions. Alternatively, *bitch juice* refers to coffee, cocktails, or wine; that is, the drink of choice of the so-called bitch.

Science Works, Bitches!

In the myriad uses of bitch, sometimes it's simply tagged onto the end of a sentence for emphasis. It's a mic drop. Known as a discourse marker, other words are, like, also used in this same way, dude. This emphatic use of bitch is a popular TV trope, like Jesse Pinkman's catchphrase "Yo, bitch!" in *Breaking Bad*. In one infamous episode, a drug enforcement agent tries to bust Pinkman who's hiding in his meth lab, so he yells out, "This is my own private domicile, and I will not be harassed … bitch!" This quote became a popular meme on cross-stitch patterns and welcome mats. Emphatic bitch is also exploited in many movies. In *Nightmare on Elm Street 5*, Freddy Krueger is famous for whispering menacingly, "Die, bitch!" before killing his victims. In one scene he cries "Bon appétit, bitch!" before forcing a starving model to eat her own internal organs. Emphatic bitch can also express excitement. It's popular on tourist souvenirs in coastal towns. In Florida, T-shirts are emblazoned with "I'm in Miami, Bitch!" which doubles as a witty pun on "beach."

Like these examples, bitch is dropped onto the end of a sentence to be funny. In "Charlie Murphy's True Hollywood Stories" on the *Dave Chappelle Show*, Chappelle dressed up as "Super Freak" singer Rick James and recounted humorous anecdotes from the 1980s. The montage of scenes was peppered with the boastful, "I'm Rick James, bitch!" The sketch was an instant classic. The quote became an obsession for

Chappelle's fans, although he later lost his sense of humor about it all. At a stand-up performance a year later, Chappelle stormed off stage after berating his audience for chanting, "I'm Rick James, bitch!" A few minutes later he returned, complaining, "The show is ruining my life."[14] Also on the *Dave Chappelle Show*, each episode ends with the comedian's catchphrase, "I'm rich, bitch!" (or sometimes "I'm rich, biatch!"). Not to be confused with the rich bitch archetype, this famous line originally came from a sketch about modern Black people being paid millions of dollars in reparations for historical enslavement. The phrase, however, is only funny in a rags-to-riches context, but not when said by someone born into privilege. At the end of a comedy set in San Francisco, entrepreneur Elon Musk joined Chappelle onstage and was introduced with great fanfare as "the richest man in the world." Unpopular with this Bay Area crowd for his business dealings, the audience erupted into aggressive booing. The hissing and jeering only intensified when Musk added, "I'm rich, bitch!"[15]

For women who wield it, this kind of emphatic bitch is often intended to be empowering. In "Bitch, I'm Madonna," the artist tells her detractors that she can do as she pleases, because she's Madonna. Addressing her use of bitch in this song and also in "Unapologetic Bitch" from the same album, Madonna explains, "I'm saying I'm a badass bitch. I'm owning myself. I'm saying I'm strong, I'm tough, and don't mess with me."[16] Madonna was probably inspired by Britney Spears' public performance of "Gimme More." Following controversial struggles with her mental health just months before, Spears returned to the stage triumphantly, announcing her comeback with the inspirational battle cry, "It's Britney, bitch!" This became her signature phrase, which quickly grew into a phenomenon. The tagline has also been mercilessly lampooned in pop culture. In an episode of the US version of *The Office*, bumbling boss Michael is playing music loudly in his red convertible when he announces to the camera, "It's Britney, bitch!" He thinks he's listening to Britney Spears, but it's actually Lady Gaga's "Just Dance." Lady Gaga also uses emphatic bitch in "Bad Romance (I'm a Free Bitch, Baby!)" to say that she won't be pushed around or controlled by others.

Over the years, emphatic bitch has enjoyed immense popularity, but today some think that it has been overplayed. *MAD* magazine once accused Dave Chappelle of letting his comedy material degrade to "placing the word 'bitch' at the end of sentences in the place of a punchline." Pictured was a hypothetical sketch of Chappelle telling a woman, "We're not adding enough fabric softener to our laundry, bitch." Surprisingly, even the staid Richard Dawkins got in on the act, dropping an unexpected bitch at the end of a sentence. During the closing remarks of a debate with a creationist, the biologist justified his confidence in science in these terms, "If you base medicine on science, you cure people. If you base the design of planes on science, they fly. If you base the design of rockets on science, they reach the moon. It works ... bitches."[17]

Life's a Bitch

While a bitch is usually a some*one*, it can also be a some*thing* too. In this sense, a bitch might be a difficult or unpleasant situation. Battling cancer can be a bitch, along with losing a job or navigating an acrimonious divorce. It's often said that *karma's a bitch*. Karma is the principle of cause and effect that's doctrine in Buddhism, Hinduism, and other eastern religions. It concerns the idea that, in life, you get back what you give, both good and bad. Karma is a bitch refers to someone who did something bad, but now it's come back on them. Karma is a harsh mistress who exacts revenge on those who do wrong. In an episode of the teen soap *Riverdale*, Veronica Lodge overhears that an enemy has suffered a car accident. She responds coolly, "Karma's a bitch." The phrase is often said with a touch of glee, because the victim got what they deserved. Curiously, the *Riverdale* scene became the theme of a Chinese selfie fad, in which people appear on camera and lip-sync the line "Karma's a bitch." Then, with a striking slow-motion transformation shot and a makeover that says "look at me now," they radically transform into glamorous models. A related saying is *payback's a bitch*, although payback has darker connotations that imply retribution and revenge. In the movie *Independence Day*, Russell Casse is abducted by aliens who experiment on him, leading to his trauma and belief that they're planning to kill humankind. In retaliation, he destroys an alien attacker, crying out to them, "Payback's a bitch, ain't it?"

Karma and payback can be a bitch, and so can life itself. The idiom *life's a bitch* expresses resigned acceptance of the fact that life is often tough and unfair. For some people, that is. The British royal family, who truly have everything, restrict themselves to exchanging gag-gifts every Christmas Eve. One year, then-Prince Charles was gifted a white leather toilet seat as a joke present. Before he married Meghan Markle, Prince Harry received a "Grow-your-own-girlfriend kit" from sister-in-law Kate Middleton. To great hilarity, Harry once gave his grandmother Queen Elizabeth a shower cap embroidered with the words "Ain't life a bitch?"[18] The extended expression is *life's a bitch and then you die*, lamenting that life is often a cruel struggle and before you know it, it's over, but there's no reward or payoff. It's such a popular phrase it's sometimes abbreviated to LABATYD. The earliest instance of the expression in the English language goes back to Langston Hughes' 1940 autobiography *The Big Sea*, in which the character Bruce says with a tinge of hopefulness, "Life's a bitch, but you can beat it if you try."[19] Similar sayings in other languages go back much farther than the 1940s, suggesting that it's not a native-born Anglicism. The oldest of these seems to be "bitch of a life" that comes from French. An 1845 translation of Eugène Sue's *Latréaumont* reads, "By hell, what have they got to lose? – their bitch of a life?"[20]

The modern pessimistic version of the idiom can be traced back to a 1982 interview in the *Washington Post*, when precocious fifteen-year-old Tony Daniels was asked the meaning of life, to which he replied cynically, "Life's a bitch, then you die."[21] By this time, the adage was probably already in circulation and soon it was a staple on T-shirts, mugs, and bumper stickers. The aphorism is often adapted for comic value in *life's a bitch and then you marry one* and *life's a bitch and so am I*. In the horror movie *Daybreakers*, a plague has transformed numerous humans into vampires when the undead Edward Dalton bemoans to his brother, "Life's a bitch, and then you *don't* die." Calling an inanimate object or thing a "bitch," whether it's an exam, disease, war, or a hard life, suggests it's something that needs to be controlled or dominated. Other mottos of the disaffected complain that life is hard, it's rough, and it sucks. On the other hand, *life's a beach* (and then you catch a wave) is a riff on the phrase, turning it around into a positive with imagery of the sun, sand, water, blue skies, and beautiful people in bathing suits. Similarly, the optimistic *life's a peach*, and *life is peachy* or *peachy keen*, mean that life is wonderful and sweet, just like the sugary fruit itself. These expressions are akin to "life is good."

Like a Bitch

Lots of other "things" can be bitches too. Something that's annoying is often compared to an "annoying" woman; it's *like a bitch*. This expression means "a lot" or "very much" in placeholder pronoun sayings such as "it hurt like a bitch." We've already discussed that a weak or cowardly man might be accused of acting like a bitch or crying like a little bitch. But a less typical use of *like a bitch* emerged from a recording of Donald Trump's locker-room talk with Billy Bush, during which he crowed about forcibly kissing and groping women. As we've mentioned before, Trump bragged that as a celebrity he could do whatever he liked to women, "Grab 'em by the pussy. You can do anything." But then he admitted his failure in trying to seduce one particular woman. Speaking of television personality Nancy O'Dell, he said, "She wanted to get some furniture. I said I'll show you where they have some nice furniture. I moved on her like a bitch. I couldn't get there and she was married."[22] There are many interpretations of this ambiguous use of "like a bitch." At first, it looks like an intensifier to give emphasis to his words, or that Trump meant he hit on O'Dell "like a boss." Upon a closer look, it seems to be a canine simile, that he tried to come on to the woman "as if she were a female dog," or maybe that he attempted to hump her from behind. Comparing people to dogs is one of Trump's favorite ways of dehumanizing those he doesn't like. In numerous social media interactions he gloats about someone being "fired like a dog" or "dumped like a dog."[23]

In other miscellaneous metaphors and similes related to things, decals announce there's a canine in the car with the phrase *dog up in this bitch*, meaning "in this place" or "right here." This is a dog-lover's take on bumper stickers that announce they're transporting precious cargo with "Baby up in this Bitch," a cheeky version of "Baby on Board." Cars and trucks can be bitches too. A vehicle might be branded a "bitch" in frustration if the battery dies, or it runs out of gas. It's often complained that mother nature can be a real bitch too. It can rain like a bitch, while it can be as hot, or as cold, as a bitch. Natural disasters are frequently feminized as bitches, especially earthquakes, floods, and hurricanes. In 1953, the practice of naming hurricanes began. Only female names were used at first, building on the stereotype of women as capricious and "stormy," equating the feminine with destructive and irrational forces that must be subdued by man. This practice ended in the late 1970s with increasing awareness of sexism, and an alternating male–female naming system was adopted. But to this day, hurricanes named after women tend to be characterized as bitches, although those named after men don't tend to be called bastards.

Back in 2005, New Orleans, Louisiana, was nearly destroyed when a hurricane dubbed Katrina hit the city, causing thousands of deaths and billions of dollars in damage. The devastating hurricane was the largest ever recorded to make landfall in the US. In her aftermath, Katrina was cast as a "bitch" because she was uncontrollable and caused widespread destruction. Some victims used dark humor to reassert control over the disaster. One photograph taken a few months after the hurricane showcased the graffiti "Katrina, you BITCH" spraypainted on the side of a damaged house.[24] Souvenir shops in the French Quarter sold T-shirts with slogans like "Katrina, that Bitch!" Katrina was christened not only a bad woman but also a sexually aggressive one; she was a bitch, and a whore. Another T-shirt read, "That Bitch Katrina Blew Me, Stewed Me, Pretty Much Screwed Me! No wonder they name hurricanes after women!" Decades on, Katrina has made a long-lasting impression on pop culture. In the 2022 song,

"Here Comes the Hurricane (Legendary Katrina)" by Kevin JZ Prodigy, the chorus includes an emphatic bitch in its refrain: "Here comes the hurricane, bitch!" With all of this bad publicity, the name Katrina has now become synonymous with the notorious hurricane.

Love Is a Bitch

In terms of metaphor, emotions are often compared to weather; sunshine is associated with happiness, while gray skies are associated with sadness. Bitch is used to describe bad weather, like the saying *it's hot as a bitch outside*, while it's also used to describe negative emotions. Painful feelings can be bitches, especially when it comes to matters of the heart. In songs and literature, it's often lamented that *love is a bitch*. In the novel *The Other Side of Dark*, a mother consoles her lovesick son with the words, "Love is a bitch of a thing. When it's good your head is in the clouds, when it's not, it can be a maddening darkness."[25] Love is personified as a bitch because relationships are hard, love hurts, and breakups are tough, and usually, the partner blamed is the woman. A woman who won't return a man's affections might be branded a heartless bitch, a cruel, or cold-hearted one. In Jet's "Cold Hard Bitch," the singer laments that his feelings were unrequited, "Just a kiss on the lips, And I was on my knees." Numerous pop songs chronicle the trials and tribulations of love, especially spurned male rockers like Rod Stewart in "Ain't Love a Bitch?" and Quiet Riot's "Love's a Bitch."

A bitch of a thing emphasizes that the thing is very difficult to deal with, whether it's being in love or learning a new language. In Frank McCourt's cult memoir *Teacher Man*, he talks about the difficulties of learning to speak English. "If you're hanging out and this foxy white chick comes along the sidewalk, you can look cool as shit, but if you don't got the words or you got some kinda crazy foreign accent, she ain't gonna give you even a look, and you're home, man, playing with yourself and pissed off because English is a bitch of a language that makes no sense and you'll never learn it."[26] It's become a versatile phrase to mean something that's rough. Someone can have a bitch of a day, week, month, or year. They can suffer a bitch of a headache. Or they can have a bitch of a time trying to perform a tricky task, whether it's fixing a leaky faucet or unclogging a blocked toilet. Aspiring Mississippi politician Rick James joked ruefully that he had "a bitch of a time" trying to run for city council because of his famous name, although he was unrelated to the 1980s funk singer. The problem went back to Dave Chappelle's viral catchphrase, "I'm Rick James, Bitch!" Throughout his political campaign, "Vote Rick James" signs were defaced by those who tacked " ..., Bitch" onto the end of the phrase, while many other placards were stolen as trophies by fans of the comedy sketch.[27] James' plans for election were ultimately foiled because the constituents assumed these capers were all just a part of his cutthroat campaign to win at all costs.

On the other hand, there are some positive uses too, in which a bitch is something excellent or awesome, akin to *bitchin'*. In Richard Price's novel *Ladies' Man*, Kenny Becker laments his unsatisfying career as a door-to-door salesman when he says, "If I had any balls I'd quit, go back to school and get a teaching degree. I'd teach English. Books. Books were bitches."[28] A thing that's a bitch in a good way can be stylish or cool. In Faye Kellerman's novel *Stalker*, real estate agent Stacy Mills owns a snazzy red BMW convertible, which is described as "a sassy, smart bitch."[29] It's possible that bitch as a positive descriptor meaning "cool" goes back to jazz argot. As we've seen with Miles Davis' album *Bitches Brew*, bitch was often used – in a good way – with reference to jazz or blues music. A musician who was really hot, a master of their instrument, was traditionally referred to as a "bitch," and Davis often used the word to refer to himself and fellow musicians this way. In his musical memoir about the 1930s jazz scene, Mezz Mezzrow reminisces about a gifted cornet player nicknamed Yellow, "That boy was really a bitch, even though he was never taught to play music. He had more music in him than Heinz has pickles."[30] In an issue of *Crescendo* magazine, an article about jazz musician George Duvivier says, "That's one of the greatest bassists of all time on there. Very underrated – but he is a bitch, believe me."[31] A bitch could be a highly skilled musician and also a talented band too. In 1971, music promoter Bill Graham held a final performance at his San Francisco Fillmore Auditorium with acts featuring Santana, Creedence Clearwater Revival, and jazz fusion band Tower of Power. "This is going to be the greatest mother-fucking evening of our lives," Graham promised as he came onstage to a standing ovation to open the show. "And now, a bitch of a band from the East Bay – Tower of Power!"[32]

Bitch Lasagna

As we know, bitch goes back to Old English and it's at least one thousand years old. Over the centuries, it has evolved into the lively word that it is today. Bitch is so prolific that it has even been adopted into sign languages. American Sign Language (ASL), the sign language used by the Deaf community throughout most of North America, has a rich vocabulary of words, which include profanity like fuck, shit, whore, and bitch. The ASL sign for "bitch" is made by taking the index finger side of the right b-handshape with the palm facing left and strik-ing it against the chin.[33] "Bastard" can be produced by doing the same sign but locating it on the forehead. To the untrained eye, the sign for bitch might be confused with the signs for "be" and "breakfast," which are similar. There are equivalent signs for bitch found across signed languages used in locales where English is the dominant spoken lan-guage, including British Sign Language, New Zealand sign language, and Australian sign language (Auslan).

English is the most widely spoken language in the world, with almost 1.5 billion speakers, including native and non-native speak-ers.[34] And bitch has been borrowed into the languages and dialects of many other countries where English is spoken. English "bitch" is used in countries as diverse as Nigeria, the Philippines, and Denmark, although it is sometimes used a little differently. India is the world's second-largest English-speaking country (after the United States), with 125 million speakers, although most people speak it as a second language. English is one of the country's official languages, along with Hindi. Indian English is a dialect of English spoken there that shows the influence of the languages and cultures of India. And it's from this variety of English that we get the puzzling *bitch lasagna*. The phrase is taken from a social media direct message that became an internet meme. In 2017, a Redditor posted a Facebook Messenger screenshot in which a man named Shah from Bangalore, India, demanded sexually explicit photographs from an unnamed woman. His English is nonstandard, and while he initially petitions her politely as "dear," he grows progressively more angry at being ignored, upon which he abuses her as "you bitch." When his repeated requests for nudies go unanswered, Shah gives up and posts the nonsensical "bitch lasagna." The one-sided conversation went as follows:

> hello dear
> how big is ur pussy
> mm very nice pics
> send me nakde pic snow you bitch
> hello
> bitch lasagna

Without further context, it reads like he's calling her a "bitch lasagna" because she refused to send him any nude pics. Some theorize that this expression was an autocorrection of "hasta lasagna," a parody of the Spanish parting phrases *hasta la vista* ("goodbye") or *hasta mañana* ("until tomorrow"). The accidental term went viral and bitch lasagna became a popular swear word. It's also slang for a woman who won't send sexually explicit photographs when asked to do so. This is a great example of the way that the Internet has encouraged a dramatic expansion in the variety and creativity of language. Such innovations, however, are used to poke fun at so-called "bad English." Bitch lasagna is often invoked to mock "Hinglish," the "corrupt" mix of Hindi and English that's popularly spoken in India. The phrase is also associated with the parody words *Bobs* and *Vegana*, which are "broken English" misspellings of "boobs" and "vagina."

Bitch lasagna became the center of an international controversy. The phrase was adopted as the title of a song by Swedish YouTuber Felix Kjellberg, aka PewDiePie. This was a "diss track" (a song written to attack another artist) in PewDiePie's escalating feud with the

Bollywood YouTube channel T-Series. The song was replete with Indian stereotypes and slurs. As a result, "Bitch Lasagna" became the subject of a defamation lawsuit and was banned in India. But the phrase flourished everywhere else, generating T-shirts, mugs, and other merchandise, and even inspiring recipes for baking a "bitch lasagna." The Hindi and Urdu languages have their own equivalent slang for bitch with the transliteration *kutiya* (and *kutti* in Punjabi).[35] This can also literally refer to a female dog, while a different sense of the word means "hut or cottage." Most South Asians, however, would just use the borrowed English word "bitch" instead, because it's considered to be hip.

Bitch is a trendy word in China too. More than ten million Chinese people speak English, while about 300 million more are learning the language, nearly as many people as there are in the United States. And bitch is widely used in China. In an exchange on social media, Tennessee Senator Marsha Blackburn accused China of having "a 5,000-year history of cheating and stealing." She added, "Some things will never change." Chen Weihua, a top Chinese journalist, replied that Blackburn was "racist" and "ignorant" and then called her a "lifetime bitch."[36] Bitch has been adopted into Chinese culture in some interesting ways. As we know, in the past a *bitch* might be someone who played host at a tea party, the person who bitched the pot or poured the tea. Tea is a British institution and also culturally important in China, where it has been consumed for thousands of years as a beverage with social and spiritual significance. In China today, a popular trope is that of the *green tea bitch* or GTB. The term describes a certain type of woman who's highly ambitious and manipulative but pretends to act sweet, innocent, and pure, that is, like green tea. The Chinese poet Lin Huiyin is seen as the archetype of the green tea bitch. She was described as a ruthless, successful, although plain-looking woman who captured the hearts of rich and talented men.[37] In Western society, the green tea bitch is similar to the Hollywood trope of the *bitch incognito*, a beautiful, charming, sweet as pie girl who is really just a mean girl in disguise.

The green tea bitch is one of several labels categorizing different stereotypes of Chinese women named after popular caffeinated beverages. The *black tea bitch* is a promiscuous woman who smokes, drinks, and wears low-cut tops that display her cleavage. She is the equivalent of the Western "slut." The *milk tea bitch* is the combination of a girly girl and a gold-digger. She presents herself in a traditionally feminine way and tries to attract rich older men in order to obtain gifts and money. The *coffee bitch* is not the person designated to pick up coffee for the entire office, but a fashionista and influencer who enjoys taking photographs of herself in fancy restaurants or on sunny beaches. To show how sophisticated and cultured they are, these women love to code-switch between English and Chinese (that is, to shift between using the two languages). Chinese languages have their own versions of the word bitch too. In Cantonese, *ba po*, *bat po*, and *sai bak po* are all used to mean a nosy, nagging, meddling woman, or a bitch in a stronger sense.[38]

In Mandarin, the dominant language in China with a staggering 1.1 billion speakers, *chāng fù* is used for bitch and whore, while *húli jīng* can mean bitch, slut, or gold-digger. *Sān bā* is slang for bitch, a woman who runs off at the mouth, spouting nonsense.[39] It's a serious insult in China. Another sense of the phrase, however, refers to the numbers three and eight. In Chinese folklore, some numbers are believed to be lucky, like eight, because it sounds similar to the word for "prosper." Other numbers are considered to be unlucky, like four, because it's nearly homophonous with the word for "death." (*Si ba* is a double entendre that can mean the numbers four and eight, but on the flip side, it tells someone to "go die.") In Mandarin, thirty-eight is a double entendre with "bitch" because the number sounds similar to the slur. In China, International Women's Day falls on March 8, and the date is pronounced as "san bah" ("3–8"), leading some to disparage the holiday as "Bitch Day." Some younger Chinese women, however, are now reclaiming the slur as a self-identifying label, much like the attempts at reclaiming bitch in English.

Bitchka

Bitch is a loanword that's been borrowed straight from English into other languages. It's also reimagined in some languages using their phonotactics, that is, the pronunciation that's permissible in those languages. In Polish, for example, *bitchka* is a version that makes bitch sound a bit more Slavic, although *suka* is the most common translation for bitch in Polish, which refers to a female dog, an unpleasant woman, or a submissive man.[40] The Polish language, however, is rich in words that are used in a similar way to bitch: *zdzira, szmata, wywłoka,* and *kurwa* can mean both bitch and whore. The latter can also mean "shit." *Panienka* (*spod latarni*) is yet another Polish phrase for bitch. It literally means "lady under the light post," a reference to prostitutes standing under light posts at night in order to be easily spotted by potential johns. This phrase is similar to older English synonyms of prostitute like *lady of the night, streetwalker,* and to *walk the pavement* in order to solicit clients. In Polish, as in many other languages, there's lots of overlapping between the words bitch, whore, and slut.

The Polish word for bitch, *suka,* is the same in some other Slavic languages too, including Russian and Ukrainian. In 2022, during the Russian invasion of Ukraine, top state television host Vladimir Solovyov wanted to show Kremlin propaganda of Ukrainians attacking Putin's army to counteract the coverage of horrific massacres of Ukrainian cities. He introduced the clip dramatically, saying, "This is how the Ukrainian Nazis, and the Georgian mercenaries who joined their ranks, treat our prisoners of war."[41] Due to a production mishap, however, that wasn't the clip that was shown to the public. In the video that aired, Ukrainian soldiers proclaimed, "Glory to Ukraine," "Glory to the heroes," and "Russia is a bitch." The clip ended with one of the Ukrainian fighters staring straight into the lens as he warned, "Don't come onto our land." The word *suka* is mutually intelligible between the two languages, so the message was clear. Like the positive uses of bitch in English, Slavic languages also have a counterpart to *suka* – *suchka,* which is used as a term of endearment and can also refer to a hot chick.

The existence and use of bad language seems to be a universal, even in the Holy Land. There, the best swearing is uttered in English or Arabic for emphasis; "fuck," "shit," and "bitch" are commonly thrown into Hebrew sentences without any need to translate. As we saw much earlier on, there's a theory that English bitch comes from Hebrew, but it's not true. In fact, they borrowed it from us. *Bitchit* is an Israeli slang term that's obviously adapted from bitch. In Hebrew, the equivalent word *zona* or *zonna* means slut, prostitute, or bitch. *Ben zona* literally means "son of a bitch" or "bastard." In recent years, the phrase has also meant something akin to excellent, like bitchin'. Yiddish is written in the Hebrew alphabet and does use some Hebrew loanwords, although *zona* isn't one of them. Yiddish has its own word, *klafte*, which means both a female dog and a bad person, but as always, it mostly refers to women (Klafte comes from the Hebrew *kelev* for "dog"). In recent years, *klafte* has been reclaimed in Jerusalem street parlance to mean someone who is daring and bold.[42] Yiddish takes some elements from Arabic too, and *klafte* bears a resemblance to Arabic *kalba*, literally meaning "female dog."[43] Unlike English, Arabic has a separate word for a male dog, a *kalb*, which is also used as an insult for an unpleasant man. There's a separate word for bitch as a slur in Arabic, *sharmota*, which also translates to whore and slut, while *qahba* means bitch, whore, and hussy.

The majority of the world's Arabic speakers are not located in the Middle East but instead inhabit Africa and its diasporas.[44] The Arabic language has clearly influenced the use of bitch in these countries, as we can see. *Sharmuta* means whore, slut, and bitch in the Amharic and Tigrinya languages spoken in Ethiopia. In some North African countries, *kalbi* means bitch, while its equivalent is *qahba* in Tunisia and Morocco and *ahba* in Egypt. Indo-European languages such as English and French are also spoken throughout Africa because they were the languages of the colonizers, and this also has shaped the use of bitch. English bitch was borrowed directly into Swahili, a language with some 20 million speakers worldwide, which is used in Kenya, Tanzania, and other East African countries. Swahili has the phrase *mbwa wa kike*, literally meaning "female dog," while its own gloss of bitch as an insult is *malaya*, which is derived from the word for prostitute or outcast. The version borrowed from English, however, is deeply offensive. A few years ago, a fifteen-year-old Kenyan boy murdered his seven-year-old cousin with a hammer for calling him a "bitch."[45]

The Yoruba language has almost 50 million speakers in Nigeria and its neighboring countries, Benin and Togo, where the English-derived *bishi* is the equivalent to bitch. English bitch is also trendy in these countries, where it was picked up through American hip hop culture and co-opted into the fledgling Nigerian rap music scene. Just as bitch has been reclaimed by a number of female rappers in the West, some Nigerian artists have also taken back the word. On her cult album *Savage Bitch Juice*, rapper Sgawd uses the word to mean a woman who's sexy and confident. Many African languages have their own versions of bitch too. In the Zulu language, the equivalent is *unondindwa*, which also means a sexually active girl, loose woman, or prostitute. (In contrast, the Zulu term for sexually active boys is *amasoka*, which means "a man highly favored by girls.")[46] In Afrikaans, the official language of South Africa, *teef* can mean a female dog or a despicable woman. This is the same word that's used for bitch in the Netherlands today, because Afrikaans descended from a seventeenth-century form of Dutch that was used by the early Dutch, German, and French Huguenot colonizers of South Africa.

As we know, English once favored the German word *hund*, but then ditched it for dog. In a back and forth between the two languages, German borrowed dog for a while, respelling it as Dogge (we might remember that in German, all nouns are capitalized). German also borrowed bitch in its literal sense of female dog, but Germanicized it as *Betze, Bätze,* and *Petze*.[47] Modern German has a wealth of words that are a close approximation to the English slur, depending on the situation and required degree of obnoxiousness. *Zicke* refers to a nasty, nagging woman, although it originally meant a she-goat. A *Miststück* is a non-gender-specific insult that's often used like bitch, while it literally means "piece of crap." As you might guess, *Biest* is related to "beast" or "monster," and it's also used to mean a woman who's unpleasant or malicious. A *Schlampe* is a sexually promiscuous woman, comparable to a slut, although it's sometimes translated into English as "bitch." German has an equivalent to son of a bitch too, *Sohn einer Hündin*, in which *Hündin* means a female dog. There are many options for a comparable slur in German, although most younger people prefer to use "bitch" instead, even if they don't speak English.

English "bitch" is fashionable in France too. As already mentioned, the insult closely resembles the name of a small French town. In 2021, Facebook removed the official page for the town of Bitche, without any warning or reason. The social network's algorithm confused the name of the town in Moselle, north-east France, with the English slur. Facebook was immediately alerted to the error, they reinstated the page and apologized for the inconvenience.[48] Anticipating a similar faux pas, another town in the region called Rohrbach-lès-Bitche preemptively renamed its page "Ville de Rohrbach." Bitche gets its name, not from an unpleasant woman, but from an old stronghold standing on a rock above the town. The Romans originally called it *Bytis Castrum*, Latin for "fortified place." Bitche is just a modernized French version of the phrase. Like German, French also has several forms of bitch for speakers to choose from. The words *salaud* and *salope* are equivalent to English "bastard" and "bitch," respectively. *Salope* translates to bitch with the same vulgarity level, but it also has sexual connotations. *Garce* is another word your French teacher probably won't teach you. It's slang for bitch and is the form used in the French version of the sitcom *Don't Trust the B---- in Apartment 23*. Just like English bitch, *garce* is also used to insult a man's masculinity. Hundreds of years ago, *garce* simply meant "girl." *La chienne* translates literally to "female dog," but it's not really used as a slur. French has several all-purpose insults for women that variously imply whore, slut, bimbo, and bitch, including *pouffiasse, putain* (which is also used as a swear word like fuck or shit), and also *pute*.

Variations of *pute* are found across the Romance languages. Portuguese *puta* means whore or slut, but depending on its context it can mean bitch as well. There's a literal word for female dog too, *perra*, although it's rarely used in a metaphorical way. Aside from being an insult, *puta* is also used as a curse to exclaim frustration or surprise, much like damn, shit, and fuck. In the 1800s, the prize-winning British racehorse Filho da Puta was named after "son of a bitch" in Portuguese. Apparently, the owner of the stable where the foal was born named the future champion in a fit of rage upon discovering that his wife had been cheating on him.[49] The Spanish version of the phrase is *hijo de puta*. Unlike English, Spanish has both female and male gendered words for bitch. *Puta* is used toward women, while *puto* is the masculine form, a homophobic slur that's used against gay, effeminate, or "weak" men.

Pute and *puta* are related to Italian *puttana*, meaning "whore." As you might have noticed, the word is also connected to *pasta alla puttanesca*, the tomato-based spaghetti dish. This roughly translates to "prostitute" or "whoreish," which is something they certainly don't spell out on menus in Italian restaurants. The colorful name has inspired many legends about the origins of this Italian meal. Some claim that the recipe was so named because it could be prepared quickly and easily by sex workers between seeing their clients. Others hold that the pungent odors of garlic, onion, anchovies, and chili would waft through the air, attracting customers to the brothel. As titillating as these tales are, there is no evidence that *puttanesca* has anything to do with prostitutes. These are just folk etymologies. Food historian Jeremy Parzen explains that the dish contains "humble" and commonly found ingredients; moreover, the related word *puttanata* means "rubbish" or "crap" in Italian. So "*pasta alla puttanesca* might have originated with someone saying, essentially, 'I just threw a bunch of shit from the cupboard into a pan.'"[50] In this way, *puttanesca* is similar to everything but the kitchen sink, a meal containing a hodgepodge of ingredients.

Bitch is so relevant to the human experience that the word is even found in invented languages. Invented or constructed languages are ones that have not evolved naturally through use, like English, but have been created artificially, like Esperanto. Esperanto is probably the most famous and widely spoken invented language. It was created by Polish ophthalmologist Ludovic Zamenhof in the nineteenth century. Esperanto has the word *hundino* that literally means female dog, while *virinaĉo* and *putino* correspond to bitch and whore respectively.[51] Esperanto was intended to be an international language used for polite intercourse, so these words aren't commonly spoken or written. Another invented language is Interlingua, which is a simplified form of Latin intended for use as an international second language.

Latin is the source of all Romance languages, and much of Interlingua looks and sounds like French, Spanish, and Portuguese. In this language, *puta* means prostitute, slut, or bitch, clearly coming from Spanish *puta* for whore. *Putana* is another word for bitch or whore, which comes from Old Spanish for prostitute or harlot. As we can see, variants of these words are found across the Romance languages, like Italian *puttana* and French *putain*. The origins of these words are uncertain, although they're commonly thought to derive from Latin *puella* for "girl." As we saw, this degradation happened to French *garce* as well. The pejoration of women-related words has happened a lot in English too, with lots of benign ones becoming rude over time. As mentioned before, hussy once meant housewife, a wench was a young woman, and tart was simply short for sweetheart.

Bitch appears in some fictional languages too. In *Game of Thrones*, *aspo* means bitch in the Valyrian language spoken in Braavos, the Iron Islands, and Slaver's Bay. In the High Valyrian language, *ilī bōños* has a wide range of use as an invective, meaning whoreson, bastard, bitch, or slut, while it can be applied toward either gender. In the Na'vi language created for the movie *Avatar*, *kalweyaveng* means "son of a bitch," although it translates literally to "child of a poisonous spider."[52] The Klingon language was invented for the Klingon species in the science fiction series *Star Trek*. Creator Marc Okrand designed the language to sound "alien" by using uncommon linguistic features. Klingon was eventually developed into a fully-fledged language, of which there are a handful of fluent speakers, although its vocabulary excludes profanities. Seeing this lexical gap, loyal fans took this opportunity to invent some swears. These neologisms include *cusašva* for whore, *shlov* for whore or bitch, and *larivan* for pussy or bitch. Some made-up languages have words for a literal bitch. In J.R.R. Tolkien's *Lord of the Rings*, *huil* means a female dog in the Quenya and Gnomish languages. There isn't a lot of profanity in Middle Earth, though, other than tame insults such as "bastard" and "filthy dog," along with some creative curses like "May his beard wither!"

There are over 7,000 languages spoken in the world today.[53] From world languages to indigenous ones, many of these have a word that's comparable to English "bitch," but there are just too many to recount them all here. Some languages, however, don't appear to have an exact equivalent to English bitch in all of its guises. They might have an approximate word meaning an unpleasant person – who's usually a woman – with differing degrees of offensiveness. Other languages have a literal word for "female canine," but without a corresponding metaphorical meaning. In Japanese, the word for a female dog is *meinu*, but it's not an equivalent to the English insult. Calling a woman "meinu" would receive a quizzical look. Instead, *onna* is a common slur hurled at women in Japan. This simply means "woman or female" on the surface, but it's used in a highly disrespectful way in phrases like *baka onna* ("stupid woman"), *hidoi onna* ("cruel woman"), and *ii onna* ("chick"), which often has sexual connotations.[54] With the spread of feminism in Japan, *onna* is becoming less popular. So, there's no exact Japanese equivalent to the English slur. *Bicchi* is a loanword that comes from English bitch, although it usually means slut instead.

In some languages there are words that are even more insulting than bitch. It might be worse to call someone a word for a taboo body part or to abuse them as a name for a terrible disease. It could be more offensive to launch a personal attack on someone's honesty, character, or integrity. Or perhaps there's a different woman-related word that is equally hurtful. It may be even more shocking to call them another animal name like cow, pig, or dog. In the Australian Aboriginal language Warlpiri, there are two different words for dogs. *Maliki* is a polite word for dog without any negative connotations. *Jarntu* is an offensive way of saying dog that is akin to the English insult, which plays on negative stereotypes of dogs as dirty, thieving, or promiscuous creatures.[55] Other languages do have a corresponding word for bitch, but those versions don't always have the weighty history or snarling bite of our English bitch.

Future Bitch

Over the past millennium, bitch has been a busy word. Since it first emerged a lot has changed around the world, and bitch has changed right along with it. To stay alive and relevant, this flexible word has developed many different meanings and uses. Present-day bitch is highly productive, spawning the creation of numerous variations, euphemisms, and new slang terms all the time. Some of these are ephemeral and end up fading away, like bitching the pot, bitch lamp, or Boston's onetime moniker of Bitches' Heaven. Other innovations have some staying power, like bitch for a "bad" woman. Some phrases go viral, like *bitch, please* and *bitch lasagna*. And a few even earn their linguistic immortality in the dictionary, like *biatch* and *resting bitch face*. But the more things change, the more they stay the same. To this day, bitch *still* means a female dog. This original meaning is kept alive by dog breeders and veterinarians, and witty double entendres found in pop culture.

The question is: What will bitch do next? Well, linguists aren't psychics, so it remains to be seen exactly what bitch will do as it moves boldly into the future. But as they say, the best predictor of future behavior is past behavior. With bitch's pattern of branching out into so many different meanings and uses, it's likely that it will continue to stay on this path. Bitch is a popular word. It will probably continue to expand in use and change its shape to fit the needs of the future. And as we know, this language change happens slowly, over the years, decades, and centuries. Of course, there are ongoing attempts to reclaim bitch, to take out its sting. There is also much backlash against this reclamation, which will likely continue too. After all, bitch still carries the baggage of its past – and present – as a gendered slur.

Bitch is a powerful word. One thing we know is that bitch isn't going away in our lifetime.

In fact, bitch could probably stick around for yet another thousand years.

Conclusion

• • • • • • • • • • • • • • • •

A Final Bitch

It's been quite a journey for "bitch." At over one thousand years of age, it's an old word; older by centuries than fuck, cunt, and other popular profanities. Bitch has a long pedigree, from its literal meaning of a female dog to its metaphorical meaning of an unpleasant person, who's usually a woman. It's the perfect insult for any scenario; when people cut you off in traffic, when you hate your boss, or when someone breaks your heart. But it means so much more. Today, bitch is one of the handiest words in the English language. It's used to express a multitude of emotions, like anger, horror, fear, frustration, despair, envy, resentment, shock, surprise, pain, and pity. But on the other hand, it can also express positive emotions like happiness, excitement, and endearment. Bitch is invoked to complain about something, to criticize people, but also to compliment them. It can be used toward your best friend or aimed at your worst enemy.

The subtlety of meaning of bitch, or its not-so-subtle meaning, is achieved by the word's context and intention, which is often conveyed by the tone of the speaker's voice. Bitch is complicated. It can mean so many things at once, and yet, it has still retained its original humble meaning.

Bitch has seen a lot in its time. The word has been around for so long that it witnessed the Norman Conquest of England. In one form or another, bitch survived Old English, Middle English, and Early Modern English, outlasting many other contemporaneous words that fell by the wayside. Originally appearing in the English language as *bicce*, it featured in folk medicine remedies calling for the use of bitch's urine and milk to cure warts and soothe a baby's teething pains. As a word linking dogs with females, bitch didn't waste any time in becoming a slur. But at first, it didn't have the same meaning that it has today. Back then, a bitch was a prostitute, whore, or slut. It compared a woman to a canine bitch in heat, as a metaphor for her horny sexual behavior. Over time, bitch became a generalized bad word for a bad woman; a profanity spat on the streets and shouted over beers in the taverns of London's underbelly. It was there that Shakespeare picked up *son of a bitch*, which he worked into his plays to the delight of his audiences. Almost as long as it's been used against women, bitch has been applied to men too, specifically those considered to be weak, cowardly, or effeminate. In the past, bitch was used in ways it's no longer used. A bitch could be the gracious host of a tea party, or it might even be someone's last name. A bitch could also be a thing, like a makeshift lamp made with a rag dipped into lard then stuffed into a tin can; a crude analogy to sex. And we've discovered how good words can turn bad over time through the process of pejoration, like mistress, hussy, wench, slut, and of course, bitch.

Bitch is one of the oldest words used to insult women in the English language. It could've gone the way of other vintage insults from harlot and harridan to scold and shrew, but it has survived the test of time. For centuries, bitch lurked in the shadows patiently before making a huge comeback, in opposition to feminism. It was a slur that echoed the message of the anti-suffrage movement. As women who didn't conform to traditional feminine stereotypes, suffragists were called Lucy Stoners. They were described as mannish, unsexed, and unnatural, and they were probably branded bitches too (although the newspapers of the time were too polite to publish it). Bitch has always been a weapon wielded against women, but soon it would be picked up and wielded *by* women. In the 1960s, feminists began to reframe the meaning of the word and then rebrand it as their own. Bitch became a poster child for modern feminism. Joreen's *BITCH Manifesto* painted a bitch as a strong and independent woman, inspiring many to wear the label as a badge of honor. Although this empowering, positive use of bitch hasn't stopped others from continuing to use the word in a negative way, pitting it against powerful women, from Bette Davis and Madonna to Yoko Ono and Hillary Clinton. Bitch is still a dangerous weapon used in the mistreatment of women through acts of sexism, racism, harassment, sexual assault, and domestic violence. And oftentimes, bitch is used as a synonym for a woman. But it means so much more.

Bitch is still used toward men and women alike, but it's used somewhat differently. A male bitch isn't powerful and strong, but weak and cowardly. He's a man who's not doing a "good job" of being a man. The way we use bitch for men versus women reflects traditional gender roles. A woman who's labeled a bitch is seen as domineering, assertive, tough, or too sexual, like a "real man" is expected to be. Whereas a man who's called a bitch is judged as submissive, sensitive, or too feminine, like a woman is supposed to be. It's always been an emasculating insult for men. For hundreds of years, bitch was a slur for a "Molly," a man who today might identify as gay, bisexual, or queer. By the early twentieth century, bitch had been reclaimed among the LGBTQ+ community, where it was used for an effeminate or passive gay man. Modern gay culture has embraced the word in many different forms, to describe a "bitchy" gay man through to an insult or a term of endearment. Bitch is often used within the LGBTQ+ in a positive way, although it's also used outside of the group in a negative way, as an instrument of hate speech. Another use that's specific to men is *prison bitch*, which is employed by inmates to mean a subordinate male prisoner who's usually the victim of sexual assault. This phrase also made its way beyond the prison walls to mean anyone who's in a subservient role. And sometimes a man is a *son of a bitch* instead of just a plain old bitch. He might be an objectionable man, although a son of a bitch can also be a tough, badass kind of a guy, like Ernest Hemingway or Harry S. Truman. From scoundrel all the way to asshole, there have been lots of insults for men over the centuries. And many, many more for women. But no matter how bitch is used against men, there is no exact male equivalent for the way it's used against women.

Bitch can be profane, but, as George Carlin observed, it's only a part-time dirty word. Sometimes it just means a female dog. As a slur, we might remember that Francis Grose once called it "the most offensive appellation that can be given to a woman." We may not think that way anymore, but for many people, bitch is still a four-letter word. Thrown into the same basket as expletives like fuck, shit, and cunt, bitch has at times been branded indecent. As a taboo word, it's often been censored in books and newspapers, bleeped on television, radio, and in movies, or simply avoided to protect sensitive eyes and ears. Some have even tried to ban the word altogether, without success. We discovered that we can't abolish a word, because banning often backfires. Nowadays, bitch has been unbleeped, for the most part. In recent decades, rap and hip hop culture has laid claim to bitch, promoting much of the violence and misogyny associated with it today. At the same time, female artists have donned bitch as both a gun and a bulletproof vest. But well before there was Meredith Brooks and her catchy anthem "Bitch," the word had its roots in jazz and the obscene lyrics of the dirty blues with legends like Jelly Roll Morton and Lucille Bogan. Today, whether it's seen as offensive or benign, it's undeniable that bitch is a controversial word. But it's unique in that it's also an everyday word. It's so common nowadays that we take for granted how difficult it was for early writers, actors, and artists to write, speak, or sing the word at all. Little did these iconoclasts know how much the word would eventually be thrust into the spotlight. If anything, some think bitch is so acceptable and overused today that it has lost its bite.

Even though the word is over one thousand years of age, bitch has shown that an old dog *can* be taught new tricks. Over the centuries, the word has undergone an astonishing transformation. Bitch is a linguistic chameleon. Along the way it has developed many different meanings and uses to keep up with the times. Bitch is a shape-shifter too, morphing from Old English *bicce* to its current form and then to creative modern spellings like biatch and biznatch. It's a contortionist of a word that can behave like a noun, an exclamation, or as part of an idiom. When "bitching" is used as a verb it means to complain, but when it's used as an adjective, it means something awesome. In the present day, bitch can be a bitch of a word to understand. Calling someone a bitch once seemed to be a simple insult, but today – after so many reinventions and attempts to repair the word's image – trying to figure out what bitch means can get pretty complicated. As we've seen, there are good bitches and bad bitches; nasty bitches and psycho bitches; sexy bitches and even perfect bitches. Bitch is a label rejected by some but worn proudly by others. It appears in lots of expressions too. You can bitch-slap someone, bitch and moan, wear a resting bitch face, or just stick the word onto the end of a sentence. Like Britney Spears famously said, "It's Britney, bitch!" Difficult things can be bitches too, like going through a bitter divorce or battling cancer. Ultimately, life's a bitch … and then you die.

There's an ongoing debate surrounding the word. Has bitch been – *can* it be – reclaimed? As we've seen, the answer is both yes and no. The feminism movement of the 1960s and 1970s did much to improve the meaning of bitch and to align it to feminist goals, and in doing so laid the foundation for positive uses like boss-ass bitch. We can't forget, however, that bitch has a split personality. While it can be empowering at times, bitch is still a slur. Like other reclaimed words, such as gay, queer, and nigger, bitch continues to be used against people, and especially against women. Bitch has a fluid meaning that takes on the power of the person who wields it. If you intend for bitch to be insulting, it probably will be. Some people will continue to try to reclaim the word. But for others, bitch isn't reclaimed, and can't be, because of its considerable baggage. Today, its core meaning is an insult for women. But perhaps the problem isn't so much what we *call* women, it's how we *treat* women. Bitch has come a long way over the years, but it's possible the reason it hasn't been truly reclaimed is that conditions for women haven't really changed. If there ever comes a time when women aren't made to feel ashamed of their sexuality or judged for their appearance, when there's no sexism in the home or workplace, when women don't constantly fear the possibility of violence, harassment, or sexual assault, and when women feel that they have equality in the society that we live in, then bitch might be able to be reclaimed. Just maybe.

Everyone has an opinion about this iconic word. For some, bitch is deeply hurtful and harmful. It's sexist and offensive. They ask that people stop calling women "bitches" and that their mothers, daughters, grandmothers, wives, aunts, and girlfriends will thank them for it. For others, however, bitch is completely harmless. Then there are those who have turned it into an empowering word for themselves. Our views on bitch are influenced by factors such as gender, sexuality, race, and age. But whether it's considered to be positive, negative, or neutral, it refuses to be ignored. Bitch is a powerful word. Like a slap to the face, or a kiss, it evokes intense emotions in those who hear it. It draws a reaction out of people, either good or bad.

Throughout its journey, bitch has taught us a lot about ourselves, both past and present. A word can be like a time machine. Bitch has always reflected the society of its time, revealing attitudes and beliefs about women, men, relationships, and sex. (And dogs.) Bitch also mirrors our values, morals, and ideals in the way we use the word, or don't use it, as the case may be. It can highlight sexism, homophobia, racism, and other forms of prejudice and discrimination. Bitch also shows us how we view life and its trials and tribulations. And bitch has managed to stay current by reflecting popular culture and changing its shape to fit its surroundings. The story of bitch teaches us that language is not fixed or set in stone. Instead, languages are alive; like living beings they're evolving and changing over time. Language never stands still.

The question remains: Where will bitch go to from here? Well, it's hard to say exactly what will happen to the word as we move forward.

Linguists aren't mind readers. We can make predictions about language, but like a meteorologist trying to predict the weather, those forecasts might end up being terribly wrong. What we do know is that language will continue to evolve, and bitch will likely continue to evolve right along with it. We also know that speakers are the driving forces of language change who will determine the future of bitch. And as a global word, which has been borrowed into numerous other cultures and languages, these variations will also influence the future of the word. Bitch has truly discovered the fountain of youth. It will probably continue to shift and mold itself to fit the needs of modern society, to stay relevant and stay alive. The word isn't going anywhere anytime soon. Bitch is here to stay.

One thing's for sure, bitch is *still* on its journey …

Notes

Introduction:

A Bitchin' Word

1. Charles Panati. 1998. *Sexy Origins and Intimate Things: The Rites and Rituals of Straights, Gays, Bis, Drags, Trans, Virgins, and Others*. Ontario, Canada: Willowbay Books.
2. "bitch, n. 1." *Oxford English Dictionary*. Oxford University Press. Retrieved September 18, 2023.
3. Philip Durkin. 2014. *Borrowed Words: A History of Loanwords in English*. Oxford: Oxford University Press.
4. Sara Pons-Sanz. 2017. *The Language of Early English Literature: From Cædmon to Milton*. London: Bloomsbury.
5. Geoffrey Hughes. 2015. *An Encyclopedia of Swearing: The Social History of Oaths, Profanity, Foul Language, and Ethnic Slurs in the English-speaking World*. London: Taylor & Francis.
6. Francis Grose. 1971 (1785). *A Classical Dictionary of the Vulgar Tongue: A Dictionary of Buckish Slang, University Wit, and Pickpocket Eloquence*. Chicago, IL: Digest Books.

Chapter 1:

A Female Dog

1. *The Simpsons*. 1995. "Two Dozen and One Greyhounds." Season 6, Episode 20.
2. "bitch, n. 1", *Oxford English Dictionary Online*, Oxford University Press. Retrieved November 28, 2022.
3. *Medicina de Quadrupedibus* (Vitell.) x. 264.
4. Peter Goodrich. 2013. "Putting on the Dog: On the Trail of Man's Best Friend as Seen Through the Middle English Dictionary Online and the Middle English Canon." *Enarratio*. 18: 128–150.
5. Samuel Butler. 1759 (1612-1680). *The Genuine Remains in Verse and Prose of Mr. Samuel Butler* (Volume II). London: J and R Tonson.

6. Richard Cleasby and Gudbrand Vigfussen. 1957. *An Icelandic–English Dictionary*. Oxford: Oxford University Press.

7. Titus Maccius Plautus. *Curculio*. John Wright (ed.). 1993. Norman, OK: University of Oklahoma Press.

8. Homer. *The Odyssey*. Robert Fagles (ed.). 1999. (800 BCE). London: Penguin Classics.

9. Homer. *The Iliad*. Robert Fagles (ed.). 1991. (762 BCE). London: Penguin Classics.

10. William Shakespeare. 2008 (1623). *Henry VI: Part One*. Oxford: Oxford University Press.

11. Janet McIntosh and Norma Mendoza-Denton. 2020. *Language in the Trump Era: Scandals and Emergencies*. Cambridge: Cambridge University Press.

12. Douglas Harper. "Etymology of dog." *Online Etymology Dictionary*, www.etymonline.com/word/dog, accessed September 19, 2023.

13. J.A.H. Murray, H. Bradley, W.A. Craigie and C.T. Onions. 1888. *A New English Dictionary on Historical Principles: Founded Mainly on the Materials Collected by the Philological Society*. Oxford: Clarendon Press. p. 577.

14. Emily Bronte. 2002 (1847). *Wuthering Heights*. London: Penguin Classics.

15. John Hall and R. Clark. 2007 (1916). *A Concise Anglo-Saxon Dictionary for the Use of Students*. New York: Macmillan.

16. Samuel Johnson. (1807). *A Dictionary of the English Language*, 12 ed. London:Penguin Classics.

17. Glosses to Homilies of Aelfric. "Sermo ad Populum (Trinity Cambridge B.15 24)." In J.C. Pope, *Homiles of Aelfric*. (1967). I 436.

18. M.S. Rawlinson. 2012. (1610–1620). "The Westminster Whore." *Merry Songs and Ballads, Prior to the Year AD 1800*. B 35. Leaf 36. Ulan Press.

19. S.K. Pal, B. Ghosh and S. Roy. 1999. "Inter- and Intra-Sexual Behaviour of Free-Ranging Dogs (*Canis familiaris*)." *Applied Animal Behaviour Science* 62, 267–278.

20. William Percy, Joseph Haslewood, W.P., Roxburghe Club. 1824 (1601). *The Cuck-Queanes and Cuckolds Errants, or, the Bearing down the Inne : A Comædye; the Faery Pastorall, or, Forrest of Clues*. London: Shakespeare Press by W. Nicol.

21. Jonathon Green. 2017. *Green's Dictionary of Slang*. London: Hodder & Stoughton.

22. Geoffrey Chaucer. 2003 (1392). "The Prologue of the Canon Yeoman's Tale." *The Canterbury Tales*. London: Penguin Classics.

23. Samuel Pepys. 2001 (1662). *The Diary of Samuel Pepys*. New York: Modern Library.

24. Samuel Johnson. 2004 (1755). *Johnson's Dictionary. (A Dictionary of the English Language.)* London: Walker Books.

25. Thomas Harman. 2010 (1567). *A Caveat for Common Cursetors, Vulgarly Called Vagabonds*. Judges, p. 94. Whitefish, MT: Kessinger Publishing.

26. *The Owl*. 1830. New York. September 25.

27. *Green's Dictionary of Slang*. https://greensdictofslang.com/entry/qsee6eq. This sense is listed under 1d.

28. Dave Chappelle. 2003. *Chappelle's Show*. Season 2, Episode 12.

29. *Deuce Bigalow: Male Gigolo*. 1999. Harris Goldberg and Rob Schneider. Happy Madison Productions.

30. William-Alan Landes (ed.) (William Stevenson). 2008 (1533). *Gammer Gurton's Needle: A Medieval Play*. Studio City, CA: Players Press.

31. John Arbuthnot. 2010. (1712). "Law Is a Bottomless-Pit. Exemplified in the Case of the Lord Strutt, John Bull, Nicholas Frog, and Lewis Baboon. Who Spent All They Had in a Law-Suit." Printed from a Manuscript Found in the Cabinet of the Famous Sir Humphry Polesworth. Michigan, Detroit: Gale ECCO.

32. Fidelis Morgan (Mrs. Crackenthorpe). 1992 (1709–10). *The Female Tatler*. London: Everyman Paperbacks.

33. Francis Grose and Pierce Egan (eds.). 1992 (1785). *Classical Dictionary of the Vulgar Tongue*. Dorchester: Dorset Press.

34. Samuel Johnson. 2004 (1755). *Johnson's Dictionary (A Dictionary of the English Language)*. London: Walker Books.

35. M. Morton. 2009. *The Lover's Tongue: A Merry Romp through the Language of Love and Sex*. Toronto: Insomniac Press.

36. A Real Paddy. 1829. *Real Life in Ireland or, the Day and Night Scenes, Rovings, Rambles, and Spress, Bulls, Blunders, Bodderation and Blarney, of Brian Boru, Esq. And His Elegant Friend Sir Shawn O'Dogherty*. London: William Evans.

37. R.M. Lumiansky and D. Mill. 1974 (c.1425). *Slaughter of the Innocents*. Goldsmiths and Masons: Chester Mystery Cycle.

38. J.O. Halliwell (ed.). 1855 (1475). "The Friar and the Boy. Or, the Young Pipers' Pleasant Pastime. Containing his Witty Pranks, in Relation to his Step-mother, Whom he Fitted for her Unkind Treatment. (Also Jack and his Stepdame.)" *Early English Miscellanies in Prose and Verse*. Warton Club Publications.

39. Henry Brinklow. 1884 (1542). *Complaynt of Roderyk Mors*. Early English Text Society, p. 63.

40. William Gilmore Simms. 1840. *Border Beagles: A Tale of Mississippi* (two volumes). Philadelphia: Carey and Hart.

41. Robert Smith Surtees. 2006 (1853). *Mr. Sponge's Sporting Tour*. London: Nonsuch Publishing. p. 202.

42. Thomas Bridge. 1979. *A Burlesque Translation of Homer: In Two Volumes*. London: G.G. and J. Robinson.

43. Anonymous. 1973 (c.1330). "Of Arthour & of Merlin." *The Auchinleck Manuscript*. National Library of Scotland, NLS Adv MS 19.2.1.

44. William Shakespeare. 2015 (1605). *King Lear*. Folger Shakespeare Library. New York: Simon & Schuster.

45. Lord George Gordon Byron. 2006 (1823). *Selected Poems. Don Juan*. Penguin Classics.

46. Hester Lynch Piozzi. 2008 (1786). *Anecdotes of the Late Samuel Johnson*. Charleston, SC: Bibliolife.

47. Anonymous. 2010 (1797). *The Adventures of Jonathan Corn-Cob, Loyal American Refugee Written by Himself*. UK: Gale ECCO. p. 78.

48. The Proceedings of the Old Bailey. London's Central Criminal Court. 1726. 20th April. Thomas Wright. Reference Number: t17260420-67.

49. *Chester Chronicle*. 1829. "Novel Offence – Flabbergasting." October 9. Cheshire, England.

50. *Rockhampton Bulletin*. 1868. October 1. Rockhampton, Queensland, Australia.

51. David N. Klausner (Anonymous). 2010 (1405–25). *The Castle of Perseverance*. Kalamazoo, MI: Medieval Institute Publications.

52. Anonymous. 1882 (1483). *Catholicon Anglicum*. Camden Society. (British Library, Add. 15562) f. 13.

53. Geoffrey Chaucer. 2003 (1392). "The Pardoner's Tale." *The Canterbury Tales*. London: Penguin Classics.

54. Michael Scott. 1998 (1833). *Tom Cringle's Log* (Classics of Naval Fiction Series). Ithaca, NY: McBooks Press.

55. Pierce Egan. 1832. *Book of Sports, and Mirror of Life. Embracing The Turf, The Chase, The Ring, And The Stage: Interspersed With Original Memoirs Of Sporting Men, Etc.* London: T. T. and J. Tegg.

56. Oliver Goldsmith. 2018 (1730–1774). *The Life of Richard Nash, of Bath, Esq; Extracted Principally from His Original Papers*. Farmington Hills, MI: Gale ECCO. p. 157.

57. Edward Ward. 1756. *A Compleat and Humorous Account of All the Remarkable Clubs and Societies in the Cities of London and Westminster, from the Royal-Society down to the Lumber-Troop. Compil'd from the Original Papers of a Gentleman Who Frequented Those Places Upwards of Twenty Years*. London: J. Wren.

58. Francis Grose and Pierce Egan (eds.). 1992 (1785). *Classical Dictionary of the Vulgar Tongue*. Dorchester: Dorset Press.
59. *The Satirist; or, the Censor of the Times*. 1832. London. May 13. p. 159.
60. Anonymous. 1898. *Forest and Stream. A Journal of Outdoor Life, Travel, Nature Study, Shooting, Fishing, Yachting*. December 3. 442/1.
61. Robert Burns. 1842 (1786). (Allan Cunningham, ed.). *Lines on Meeting with Lord Daer. The Works of Robert Burns. Complete in One Volume.* Cheapside, London: Thomas Tegg.
62. David A. Mills. 2011. *A Dictionary of British Place-Names*. Oxford: Oxford University Press.
63. Census of Canada. 1911. Library and Archives Canada. https://central .bac-lac.gc.ca/.item/?app=Census1911&op=img&id=e001929597.
64. Beth Nguyen. 2021. "America Ruined My Name for Me. So I Chose a New One." *The New Yorker*. April 21. www.newyorker.com/culture/ personal-history/america-ruined-my-name-for-me.
65. William Shakespeare. 2016 (1605). *A Midsummer Night's Dream*. Folger Shakespeare Library. London: Simon & Schuster.
66. Geoffrey Chaucer. 2003 (1392). "The Physician's Tale." *The Canterbury Tales*. London: Penguin Classics.
67. Gertrude Block. 2004. *Legal Writing Advice: Questions and Answers*. New York: William S. Hein.
68. Karen Stollznow. 2020. *On the Offensive: Prejudice in Language Past and Present*. Cambridge: Cambridge University Press.
69. Paul Rolly. 2014. "Paul Rolly: Blogger Fired from Language School over 'Homophonia.'" *The Salt Lake Tribune*, July 30. https://archive.sltrib .com/article.php?id=58236366&itype=CMSID.
70. Margaret Carlson. 1995. "The Public Eye: Muzzle the B Word." *Time* 145 (1–8). p. 36. January 16.

Chapter 2:

Feminist Bitch

1. Amy Richards and Jennifer Baumgardner. 2010. *Manifesta: Young Women, Feminism, and the Future*. New York: Farrar, Straus and Giroux.
2. Li Zhou. 2020. "Use of the Word 'Bitch' Surged after Women's Suffrage." *Vox*. August 19. www.vox.com/21365241/19th-amendment-womens-suffrage-backlash.
3. Jane Robinson. 2018. *Hearts and Minds: The Untold Story of the Great Pilgrimage and How Women Won the Vote*. London: Transworld.
4. Laurel Thatcher Ulrich. 1976. "Vertuous Women Found: New England Ministerial Literature, 1668–1735." *American Quarterly*, 28(1), 20–40.

5. Idabel Williams. 1934. *Hell Cat*. New York: Greenberg.
6. Anonymous. 2018 (1895). *The Athenaeum*. Chancery Lane, London: John C. Francis. 533/2.
7. Margaret Walters. 2005. *Feminism: A Very Short Introduction*. Oxford: Oxford University Press.
8. Dolores Barracano Schmidt. 1971. "Great American Bitch." *College English* 32, 8, 900–905. National Council of Teachers of English.
9. Ernest Hemingway. 1999 (1936). *The Short Happy Life of Francis Macomber and Other Stories*. Klett Group.
10. Mark Forsyth. 2014. *The Elements of Eloquence: Secrets of the Perfect Turn of Phrase*. London: Penguin.
11. Jane Mills. 1989. *Woman Words*. New York: The Firm Press.
12. Alice Jardine. 1979. "Interview with Simone de Beauvoir." *Signs* 5 (2), 224–236.
13. Editorial. 1914. "Suffragist or Suffragette?" *The Suffragette*. May 1, p. 56.
14. Joreen (Jo Freeman). 1970. "The BITCH Manifesto." *Atlanta Lesbian Feminist Alliance (ALFA) Archives*. https://idn.duke.edu/ark:/87924/r3hm5j.
15. Amy Herzog, Carol Vernallis and John Richardson. 2015. *The Oxford Handbook of Sound and Image in Digital Media*. Oxford: Oxford University Press.
16. Kate Kastelein. 2012. *Anna Wintour: Vogue Magazine's Editor-In-Chief and Fashion Icon: The Life and Times of Anna Wintour, in One Convenient Little Book*. San Francisco, CA: Hyperink.
17. Andrew Morton. 2001. *Madonna*. United Kingdom: St. Martin's Press.
18. Joanna Coles. 2015. "Gloria Steinem Has Great Advice on What to Do When Someone Calls You a Bitch." *Cosmopolitan*. October 21.
19. *The Sydney Morning Herald*. 2004. "The Dotcom King." August 17. www.smh.com.au/technology/the-dotcom-king-20040817-gdjka3.html.
20. Aubrey Malone. 2015. *Hollywood's Second Sex: The Treatment of Women in the Film Industry, 1900–1999*. United States: McFarland.
21. L. E. Hirsch. 2023. *Can't Stop the Grrrls: Confronting Sexist Labels in Music from Ariana Grande to Yoko Ono*. Lanham, MD: Rowman & Littlefield.
22. Nicki Minaj. 2010. *My Time Now*. MTV documentary.
23. Jane Sherron de Hart. 2020. *Ruth Bader Ginsburg: A Life*. New York: Knopf Doubleday.
24. Karrin Vasby Anderson. 1999. "'Rhymes with Rich': 'Bitch' as a Tool of Containment in Contemporary American Politics." *Rhetoric and Public Affairs* 2(4), 599–623.

25. Mike Kennedy. 1995. "'B-Word' Used in Arsenal of Hate." *Kansas City Star*. January 6.
26. Sophie Wilkinson. 2014. "Men Can Be Bitches Too. And Here's How to Spot Them." *Grazia*. https://graziadaily.co.uk/life/opinion/men-can-bitches-s-spot/. August 11. Retrieved May 20, 2023.
27. Charles Moore. 2013. *Margaret Thatcher: The Authorized Biography*. London: Penguin Books.
28. Denis Muller. 2018. "Sexist Abuse Has a Long History in Australian Politics and Takes Us All to a Dark Place." *The Conversation*. July 3. http://theconversation.com/sexist-abuse-has-a-long-history-in-australian-politics-andtakes-us-all-to-a-dark-place-99222.
29. Susan J. Carroll and Richard L. Fox. 2014. *Gender and Elections: Shaping the Future of American Politics*. Cambridge: Cambridge University Press.
30. Nicholas Schmidle. 2016. "Glenn Beck Tries Out Decency." *The New Yorker*. November 6. www.newyorker.com/magazine/2016/11/14/glenn-beck-tries-out-decency.
31. Leslie Bennetts. 2008. "Go Away? Why Should She?" *Los Angeles Times*. March 9. www.latimes.com/la-op-bennetts9mar09-story.html.
32. Katharine Q. Seelye and Julie Bosman. 2008. "Media Charged with Sexism in Clinton Coverage." *The New York Times*. June 13. www.nytimes.com/2008/06/13/us/politics/13women.html.
33. Lois Beachy Underhill. 1995. *The Woman Who Ran for President: The Many Lives of Victoria Woodhull*. New York: Bridge Works Publishing.
34. Kelly Faircloth. 2016. "Remember When Newt Gingrich's Mama Said He Thought Hillary Clinton Was a Bitch?" *Jezebel*. July 15. https://jezebel.com/remember-when-newt-gingrichs-mama-said-he-thought-hilla-1783546525. Retrieved January 10, 2023.
35. Pamela Kilian. 2003. *Barbara Bush: Matriarch of a Dynasty*. New York: St. Martin's Press.
36. David Freedlander. 2021. *The AOC Generation: How Millennials Are Seizing Power and Rewriting the Rules of American Politics*. United States: Boston, MA: Beacon Press.
37. *Saturday Night Live*. 2008. "Bitches Get Stuff Done." NBC. www.youtube.com/watch?v=Bfpiqm4tuLM.
38. Ian Duncan. 2014. "Woman in Arrest Video Describes Violent Takedown by Police." *Baltimore Sun*. December 9. www.baltimoresun.com/news/crime/bs-md-ci-video-arrest-20141209-story.html. Retrieved January 7, 2023.
39. Margareta Hydén. 1995. "Verbal Aggression as Prehistory of Woman Battering." *Journal of Family Violence* 10, 55–71.

40. Felicia Okeke-Ibezim. 1997. *O. J. Simpson: The Trial of the Century*. United States: Ekwike Publications.
41. Brian E. Walker, Faye. D. Resnick and Mike Walker. 1994. *Nicole Brown Simpson: The Private Diary of a Life Interrupted*. United States: Dove Books.
42. Lauren L. Basson. 2012. *White Enough to Be American? Race Mixing, Indigenous People, and the Boundaries of State and Nation*. Chapel Hill, NC: University of North Carolina Press.
43. Douglas Brinkley. 2000. *Mine Eyes Have Seen the Glory: The Life of Rosa Parks*. London: Weidenfeld & Nicolson.
44. Diana Paton. 2006. "Gender, Language, Violence and Slavery: Insult in Jamaica, 1800–1838". *Gender & History* 18 (2). pp. 246–265.
45. *Saturday Night Live*. 2017. "Girl at a Bar." NBC. www.youtube.com/watch?v=kTMow_7H47Q. Accessed January 19, 2023.
46. OED Online. whore, n. December 2018. www.oed.com
47. Lee Server. 2007. *Ava Gardner: Love Is Nothing*. London: St. Martin's Press.
48. Leora Tanenbaum. 2015. *I Am Not a Slut: Slut-Shaming in the Age of the Internet*. New York: Harper Perennial.
49. *Oxford English Dictionary*, s.v. "cunt, n., sense 4", July 2023. https://doi.org/10.1093/OED/1603534823.
50. Geoffrey Chaucer. 2003 (1392). "The Miller's Tale." *The Canterbury Tales*. London: Penguin Classics.
51. William Shakespeare. 2012 (1603). *Hamlet*. New York: Simon & Schuster.
52. Francis Grose. 1796. *A Classical Dictionary of the Vulgar Tongue*, 3rd ed. London: S. Hooper.
53. David Mack. 2023. "the C-Word Is Everywhere Right Now – and Not in a Bad Way." *Rolling Stone*. May 15 issue.
54. Al Cimino. 2016. *Trump Talking: The Donald, in His Own Words*. United Kingdom: Little, Brown.
55. Philip Rucker and Carol Leonnig. 2021. *I Alone Can Fix It: Donald J. Trump's Catastrophic Final Year*. New York: Penguin Publishing Group.
56. Twitter was rebranded "X" in April 2023. All mentions in this book pre-date that change.
57. Karen Han. 2018. "Roseanne 'Explains' Her Racist Valerie Jarrett Tweet in a Bizarre New Video." *Vox*. July 20. www.vox.com/culture/2018/7/20/17595272/roseanne-barr-racist-valerie-jarrett-tweet-video. Retrieved January 22, 2023.
58. Gabrielle Bluestone. 2016. "Remember When Donald Trump's Wife and Donald Trump's Mistress Got in a Public Brawl in Aspen?" *Gawker*.

January 25. www.gawker.com/remember-when-donald-trumps-wife-and-donald-trumps-mist-1754977102. Retrieved January 27, 2023.

59. Meghan Casserly. 2011. "Science Proves That Women Are Mean (Again). Thanks Science!" *Forbes*. November 29. www.forbes.com/sites/meghancasserly/2011/11/29/science-proves-that-women-are-mean-again/. Retrieved January 23, 2023.

60. Will Taylor. 2022. "Historic 'Black Bitch' Pub Renamed After Owner Fears It's Racist Despite Thousands Opposing 'the Willow Tree' Rebrand." *Leading Britain's Conversation*. November 17. www.lbc.co.uk/news/black-bitch-pub-renamed-racist/. Retrieved January 16, 2023.

61. Andi Zeisler. 2007. "The B-Word? You Betcha." *The Washington Post*. November 18. www.washingtonpost.com/wp-dyn/content/article/2007/11/16/AR2007111601202. Retrieved January 18, 2023.

62. Allison Yarrow. 2018. *90s Bitch: Media, Culture, and the Failed Promise of Gender Equality*. United States: HarperCollins.

63. Dodai Stewart. 2011. "The Catchy New Word for Feminism." *Jezebel*. August 11. https://jezebel.com/the-catchy-new-word-for-feminism-5828798. Retrieved June 1, 2023.

64. Gayle Forman. 2009. *If I Stay*. New York: Penguin.

65. Sherryl Kleinman, Matthew B. Ezzell and A. Corey Frost. 2009. "Reclaiming Critical Analysis: The Social Harms of 'Bitch.'" *Sociological Analysis* 3 (1), 46–68. www.jmu.edu/socanth/sociology/wm_library/ezzell.reclaiming_critical_analysis.pdf.

66. Geoff Herbert. 2016. "Meredith Brooks on Taylor Swift–Kanye Feud: 'No Woman Wants to Be Called a Bitch.'" *Syracuse*. www.syracuse.com/celebrity-news/2016/07/meredith_brooks_bitch_taylor_swift_kanye_west_feud.html. Retrieved January 24, 2023.

Chapter 3:

Son of a Bitch

1. Francis Beaumont and John Fletcher. 2010 (1625). *The Coxcomb: A Comedy*. Farmington Hills, MI. Gale Ecco.

2. Thomas Shadwell. 2011 (1671). *The Humorists: A Comedy*. British Library, Historical Print Editions.

3. Hugh Rawson. 1995. *Rawson's Dictionary of Euphemisms and Other Doubletalk: Being a Compilation of Linguistic Fig Leaves and Verbal Flourishes for Artful Users of the English Language*. London: Crown.

4. John Neal. 2009 (1840). *Seventy-Six, Or, Love and Battle*. London: J. Cunningham. p. 52.

5. Lyle Larsen. 2011. *Stein and Hemingway: The Story of a Turbulent Friendship*. United States: McFarland.
6. Russell Crandall. 2023. *Forging Latin America: Profiles in Power and Ideas, 1492 to Today*. Lanham, MD: Rowman & Littlefield.
7. John A. Farrell. 2018. *Richard Nixon: The Life*. New York: Vintage Books.
8. Rob Roy and Chris Lawson. 2015. *The Navy SEAL Art of War: Leadership Lessons from the World's Most Elite Fighting Force*. United States: Crown.
9. David McCullough. 2003. *Truman*. London: Simon & Schuster.
10. Jon Hunner. 2012. *J. Robert Oppenheimer, the Cold War, and the Atomic West*. Norman, OK: University of Oklahoma Press.
11. Robert D. Hare. 2011. *Without Conscience: The Disturbing World of the Psychopaths Among Us*. New York: Guilford Press.
12. Michael Haas. 2023. *Beyond Polarized American Democracy: From Mass Society to Coups and Civil War*. New York: Taylor & Francis.
13. Henry Louis Mencken. 2011 (1911). *The American Language*. United States: Waking Lion Press. pp. 317–318.
14. Eric Partridge. 2002. *A Dictionary of Slang and Unconventional English: Colloquialisms and Catch Phrases, Fossilised Jokes and Puns, General Nicknames, Vulgarisms and Such Americanisms as Have Been Naturalised*. Kiribati: Routledge.
15. Ethan Sears. 2021. "Martellus Bennett: Patriots Lost Game Due to Jimmy Garoppolo 'Being a B—H.'" *New York Post*. October 22. https://nypost.com/2021/10/22/martellus-bennett-patriots-lost-due-to-bitch-jimmy-garoppolo/. Retrieved February 22, 2023.
16. James Joyce. 2017 (1916). *A Portrait of the Artist as a Young Man*. United Kingdom: Pan Macmillan.
17. Lou Schuler. 2018. "How Arnold Became Arnold: The Men's Health Legends Interview with Arnold Schwarzenegger." *Men's Health*. October 10. www.menshealth.com/entertainment/a23621596/arnold-schwarzenegger-bodybuilding-interview/. Retrieved February 20, 2023.
18. Gary L. Heyward. 2015. *Corruption Officer: From Jail Guard to Perpetrator Inside Rikers Island*. United Kingdom: Atria Books.
19. Dennis Wepman, Ronald B. Newman and Murray B. Binderman. 1986. "Death Row." In *The Life: The Lore and Folk Poetry of the Black Hustler*. Los Angeles, CA: Holloway House. p. 1702.
20. S.A. Cosby. 2021. *Razorblade Tears: A Novel*. United States: Flatiron Books.
21. Rebecca Trammell. 2011. "Symbolic Violence and Prison Wives: Gender Roles and Protective Pairing in Men's Prisons." *The Prison Journal* 91(3), 305–324.

22. Michael Christopher. 2021. *Van Halen: The Eruption and the Aftershock*. United States: Backbeat.
23. Gennifer Hutchinson. 2010. "I See You." *Breaking Bad*. Series 3, Episode 8.
24. Rodney Carrington. "Prison Bitch." www.lyricsbox.com/rodney-carrington-prison-bitch-complete-version-lyrics-bpmqsct.html. Retrieved February 6, 2023.
25. LaDonna Childress. 2005. "To Fulfill a Promise: Using Canons 3B(5) and 3B(6) of the Judicial Code of Conduct to Combat Sexual Orientation Bias against Gay and Lesbian Criminal Defendants." 34. Southwestern. *University Law Review* 607.
26. Francis Grose. 1788. *A Classical Dictionary of the Vulgar Tongue*. London: S. Hooper.
27. Paul Baker. 2004. *Fantabulosa: A Dictionary of Polari and Gay Slang*. London: Bloomsbury Academic.
28. Chas Hodges. 2008. *Gertcha! Chas and Dave Our Story*. United Kingdom: John Blake Publishing.
29. Robert McAlmon. 1923. *A Companion Volume*. Norwich, VT: Elysium Books.
30. Howard Baer. 1949. *O, Huge Angel*. United States: Roy Publishers. p. 103.
31. Mike Usinger. 2022. "Will Smith Apologizes to Chris Rock for the Oscars Broadcast Bitchslap Seen and Heard around the World." *The Georgia Straight*. March 28. www.straight.com/movies/will-smith-apologizes-to-chris-rock-for-oscars-bitchslap-heard-around-world. Retrieved February 10, 2023.
32. Charlotte Heathcote. 2009. "Why Boy George Can't Wait to Go Back to Prison." *Express*. July 26. www.express.co.uk/celebrity-news/116487/Why-Boy-George-can-t-wait-to-go-back-to-prison. Retrieved February 8, 2023.
33. David M. Halperin. 2012. *How to Be Gay*. New York: Harvard University Press.
34. *Yank*. 1945. United States: Headquarters Detachment, Special Service, War Department. April 6, p. 17.
35. Jim Buzinski. 2015. "Panthers Players Publicly Called Odell Beckham Jr. a 'Bitch,' 'Ballerina' and 'Female.'" *Out Sports*. December 22. www.outsports.com/2015/12/22/10643980/carolina-panthers-josh-norman-giants-odell-beckham-gay-slurs. Retrieved February 9, 2023.
36. Doug Meyer. 2015. *Violence Against Queer People: Race, Class, Gender, and the Persistence of Anti-LGBT Discrimination*. New Brunswick, NJ: Rutgers University Press.

37. Victoria A. Brownworth. 2016. "Lesbians and Rape: Another Coming Out Story." *Huffington Post*. February 2. www.huffpost.com/entry/lesbians-and-rape-another-coming-out-story_b_3616916. Retrieved June 3, 2023.

38. D. Harper (n.d.). Etymology of villain. *Online Etymology Dictionary*. www.etymonline.com/word/villain. Retrieved February 14, 2023.

39. OED Online. *"blackguard, n."* December 2018. Oxford University Press. www.oed.com.

40. John Algeo and Carmen A. Butcher. 2013. *The Origins and Development of the English Language*. United States: Cengage Learning.

41. William Shakespeare. 2020 (1623). *All's Well That Ends Well*. New York: Simon & Schuster.

42. *Oxford English Dictionary*, s.v. "bastard, v." July 2023. https://doi.org/10.1093/OED/1004110282.

43. Alison Weir. 2002. *Henry VIII: The King and His Court*. New York: Ballantine Books. p. 220.

44. James Boswell. 2009 (1783). *Life of Samuel Johnson*. London: Penguin Classics. p. 48.

45. Lorenzo Sabine. 2007 (1854). *Notes on Duels and Duelling*. Whitefish, MT: Kessinger Publishing. p. 68.

46. David Andrew Schultz. 2010. *Encyclopedia of the United States Constitution*. Ukraine: Facts on File, Incorporated.

47. *Oxford English Dictionary*, s.v. "asshole, n." July 2023. https://doi.org/10.1093/OED/7895053168.

48. Sarah Ogilvie. 2023. "When the Word 'Prick' Was a Compliment." *Prospect*. January 25. www.prospectmagazine.co.uk/columns/when-the-word-prick-was-a-compliment-etymology. Retrieved February 18, 2023.

49. Evan Thomas. 1987. "George Bush: Fighting the 'Wimp Factor.'" *Newsweek*. October 19.

50. *OED Online*. s.v. faggot, n. and adj. December 2018. Oxford University Press. www.oed.com. Retrieved February 19, 2023.

51. Karen Stollznow. 2020. *On the Offensive: Prejudice in Language Past and Present*. Cambridge: Cambridge University Press.

52. Hanna Yusuf. 2019. "Is It OK to Tell Someone to 'Man Up'?" *BBC News*. June 24. www.bbc.com/news/uk-48743113. Retrieved February 20, 2023.

53. Anna Mikhailova. 2019. "Brexit Latest News: Boris Johnson Tells Jeremy Corbyn to 'Man Up' as Labour Look Set to Vote down Election." *The Telegraph*. October 25. www.telegraph.co.uk/politics/2019/10/25/brexit-latest-news-general-election-extension-boris-johnson/. Retrieved February 20, 2023.

54. Dani Di Placido. 2022. "Greta Thunberg Humiliates Andrew Tate After 'Enormous Emissions' Boast." *Forbes*. December 28. www.forbes.com/sites/danidiplacido/2022/12/28/greta-thunberg-humiliates-andrew-tate-after-enormous-emissions-boast/. Retrieved February 14, 2023.

Chapter 4:

The B Word

1. Laura Gowing. 1993. "Gender and the Language of Insult in Early Modern London." *History Workshop*. Spring Issue, No. 35, 1–21. Oxford: Oxford University Press.

2. Peter Harrington. 2013. *The Original Slang Dictionary: Francis Grose's Own Copy of His "Classical Dictionary of the Vulgar Tongue."* London: Peter Harrington. www.peterharrington.co.uk/blog/the-original-slang-dictionary-francis-groses-own-copy-of-his-classical-dictionary-of-the-vulgar-tongue/. Retrieved September 13, 2023.

3. Anonymous. 1759. *Low Life above Stairs: A Farce. As It Is Acted in Most Families of Distinction Throughout the Kingdom*. United Kingdom: J. Williams.

4. Winchester, Hants. 1851. *Hampshire Chronicle*. November 22. pp. 4–5.

5. Jim Beckerman. 2023. "Everyone Else Uses Four-Letter Words. Should Newspapers?" *North Jersey*. January 25. www.northjersey.com/story/opinion/columnists/2023/01/25/should-newspapers-print-four-letter-words-everyone-else-does/. Retrieved March 3, 2023.

6. *Dogdom: Monthly*. 1907. March issue. Battle Creek, MI: Dogdom Publishing Company. Classified. p. 923.

7. A. Scott Berg (ed.). 1978. *Max Perkins: Editor of Genius*. United States: Thomas Congdon Books. pp. 93–95.

8. Michael Reynolds. 1998. *The Young Hemingway*. United States: W. W. Norton.

9. Lynn Harris. 2005. "L.A. Press to the Gray Lady: Start Your Bitching!" *Salon*. December 7. www.salon.com/2005/12/07/no_bitch_at_times/. Retrieved March 3, 2023.

10. Michael M. Grynbaum. 2007. "It's a Female Dog, or Worse. Or Endearing and Illegal." *The New York Times*. August 7. www.nytimes.com/2007/08/07/nyregion/07bword.html. Retrieved March 3, 2023.

11. Christian Britschgi. 2019. "Massachusetts Bill Would Impose $200 Fines, 6 Months in Jail for Using the Word 'Bitch.'" *Reason*. August 10. https://reason.com/2019/10/22/massachusetts-legislator-proposes-200-fines-6-months-in-jail-for-using-the-word-bitch/. Retrieved June 3, 2023.

12. Alison Flood. 2015. "Authors: End to Censored Versions of Books Is 'Victory for the World of Dirt.'" *The Guardian*. www.theguardian.com/ books/2015/mar/27/clean-reader-books-app-censorship-victory-authors-celebrate. Retrieved March 5, 2023.

13. Wenbo Wang, Lu Chen, Krishnaprasad Thirunarayan and Amit P. Sheth. 2014. "Cursing in English on Twitter." *Proceedings of the 17th ACM Conference on Computer Supported Cooperative Work & Social Computing*, pp. 415–424.

14. Bess Levin. 2023. "Yes, the Trump White House Demanded Twitter Remove Chrissy Teigen's Tweet Calling Trump a 'Pussy Ass Bitch.'" *Vanity Fair*. February 8. www.vanityfair.com/news/2023/02/chrissy-teigen-donald-trump-tweet-removed. Retrieved March 18, 2023.

15. Change.org. 2019. Petition "Change Oxford Dictionary's Sexist Definition of Woman." www.change.org/p/change-oxford-dictionary-s-sexist-definition-of-woman. Retrieved March 3, 2023.

16. Oxford University Press. 2021. "Excluding Offensive or Derogatory Terms in the Dictionary Would Be 'Akin to Censorship.'" *News*. March 10. https://global.oup.com/news-items/archive/iwd_language_panel? cc=us. Retrieved March 3, 2023.

17. Aaron Walawalkar. 2020. "Oxford Dictionaries Amends 'Sexist' Definitions of the Word 'Woman.'" *The Guardian*. November 7. www .theguardian.com/books/2020/nov/07/oxford-university-press-up-dates-definitions-word-woman. Retrieved March 5, 2023.

18. Netflix. 2021. "'Bitch.' History of Swear Words." Season 1, Episode 3.

19. Kory Stamper. 2018. *Word by Word: The Secret Life of Dictionaries*. New York: Knopf Doubleday.

20. Sonia Elks and Umberto Bacchi. 2021. "Whore No More: Italian Dictionary Scraps 'Sexist' Definitions of a Woman." *Reuters*. May 14. www.reuters.com/article/us-italy-women-dictionary/whore-no-more-italian-dictionary-scraps-sexist-definitions-of-a-woman-idUSKB-N2CV1W6

21. Thomas P. Doherty. 1999. *Pre-Code Hollywood: Sex, Immorality, and Insurrection in American Cinema, 1930–1934*. United States: Columbia University Press.

22. Allan Hunter. 1985. *James Stewart*. United Kingdom: Spellmount.

23. George Carlin. 1972. "Seven Words You Can Never Say on Television." *Class Clown. Santa Monica Civic Auditorium*. Little David/ Atlantic.

24. James Sullivan. 2010. *Seven Dirty Words: The Life and Crimes of George Carlin*. Philadelphia, PA: Da Capo Press.

25. Federal Communications Commission. 2022. *Broadcast of Obscenity, Indecency, and Profanity.* www.fcc.gov/enforcement/areas/broadcast-obscenity-indecency-profanity.

26. Bob Colleary. 1979. "Guerilla My Dreams." *M*A*S*H.* Season 8, Episode 3. Aired October 1, 1979.

27. Norman Lear. 1974. "Walter's Heart Attack." *Maude.* Season 3, Episode 3. Aired September 23, 1974.

28. Morrie Gelman. 1998. *Norman Lear Interview.* Television Academy Foundation. https://interviews.televisionacademy.com/interviews/norman-lear. Retrieved March 10, 2023.

29. Geoffrey Nunberg. 2012. *Ascent of the A-Word: Assholism, the First Sixty Years.* New York: Hachette Books.

30. Robert L. Mott. 2003. *Radio Live! Television Live! Those Golden Days When Horses Were Coconuts.* United States: McFarland.

31. Federal Communications Commission. 2005. *Memorandum Opinion and Order.* https://docs.fcc.gov/public/attachments/FCC-04-280A1.pdf. Retrieved March 13, 2023.

32. Jon Brodkin. 2015. "Comcast Customer Says She Got a Bill Addressed to 'Super Bitch.'" *Ars Technica.* February 5. https://arstechnica.com/information-technology/2015/02/comcast-customer-says-she-got-a-bill-addressed-to-super-bitch/. Retrieved March 13, 2023.

33. Michael Adams. 2018. "How I Met Your Mother: The Bitch Chronicles, Part 5 – All the Bitches." *Strong Language.* December 31. https://stronglang.wordpress.com/2018/12/31/how-i-met-your-mother-the-bitch-chronicles-part-5-all-the-bitches/. Retrieved March 15, 2023.

34. Ben Barry. 2008. www.carmagazine.co.uk/car-news/pontiac/pontiac-trans-am---smokey-and-the-bandit/.

35. Edward Wyatt. 2009. "More Than Ever, You Can Say that on Television." *The New York Times.* November 13. www.nytimes.com/2009/11/14/business/media/14vulgar. Retrieved 15 March, 2023.

36. William Seaton. 2021. "Jelly Roll Morton's 'the Murder Ballad' and the Artful Use of Vulgarity." *Poetry on the Loose.* July 1. http://williamseaton.blogspot.com/2021/07/jelly-roll-mortons-murder-ballad.html. Retrieved March 20, 2023.

37. Angela Y. Davis. 2011. *Blues Legacies and Black Feminism: Gertrude Ma Rainey, Bessie Smith, and Billie Holiday.* New York: Knopf Doubleday.

38. Paul Tingen. 2003. *Miles Beyond: The Electric Explorations of Miles Davis, 1967–1991.* New York: Billboard Books.

39. Carlos Santana. 1998. "Remembering Miles and *Bitches Brew.*" *The Complete Bitches Brew Sessions.* Columbia/Legacy, pp. 7–8.

40. Elizabeth J. Rosenthal. 2001. *His Song: The Musical Journey of Elton John.* New York: Billboard Books.

41. Paul Elliott. 1998. "Their Year: The Prodigy." *Q.* 137, 95.

42. Jody Pennington and Sharon Packer (eds.). 2014. *A History of Evil in Popular Culture: What Hannibal Lecter, Stephen King, and Vampires Reveal about America.* New York: Bloomsbury.

43. T. Ice and Heidi Siegmund. 1995. *The Ice Opinion: Who Gives a Fuck?* New York: St. Martin's Press.

44. The Jelly Roll House Blog. 2010. "The Professor's Lyrics." March 17. http://jellyrollhouse.blogspot.com/2010/03/professors-lyrics.html. Retrieved March 20, 2023.

45. Cherryl Aldave. 2003. "Forgotten Elements: A Bitch Iz a Bitch." *Hip Hop DX.* January 28. https://hiphopdx.com/interviews/id.198/title .forgotten-elements-a-bitch-iz-a-bitch.

46. Robin D. G. Kelley. 1996. *Race Rebels: Culture, Politics, and the Black Working Class.* New York: The Free Press.

47. Martin James. 2002. *Prodigy.* London: Sanctuary.

48. Sherryl Kleinman, Matthew B. Ezzell and A. Corey Frost. 2009. "Reclaiming Critical Analysis: The Social Harms of 'Bitch.'" *Sociological Analysis* 3 (1), 46–68. www.jmu.edu/socanth/sociology/wm_library/ ezzell.reclaiming_critical_analysis.pdf.

49. Felicia A. Viator. 2020. *To Live and Defy in LA: How Gangsta Rap Changed America.* Cambridge, MA: Harvard University Press.

50. Elijah Wald. 2012. *The Dozens: A History of Rap's Mama.* New York: Oxford University Press.

51. Rolling Stone. 2012. "Jay-Z Never Said He Would Stop Using 'Bitch' in Lyrics." www.yahoo.com/entertainment/news/jay-z-never-said-stop-using-bitch-lyrics-213549923.html. Retrieved December 21, 2023.

52. Tricia Rose. 2008. *The Hip Hop Wars: What We Talk About When We Talk About Hip Hop–and Why It Matters.* New York: Basic Books.

53. Nadeska Alexis. 2012. "Kim Kardashian Flattered by Kanye West's 'Perfect B—ch.'" *MTV.* August 8. www.mtv.com/news/i65wo7/kim-kardashian-happy-kanye-west-perfect-bitch-song. Retrieved March 25, 2023.

54. Connor Simpson. 2012. "Discussing Linguistics with Kanye West." *The Atlantic.* September 2. www.theatlantic.com/culture/archive/2012/09/ discussing-linguistics-kanye-west/324033/. Retrieved March 23, 2023.

55. Geoff Nunberg. 2012. "Swearing: A Long and #%@&$ History." *NPR.* July 11. www.npr.org/2012/07/24/156623763/swearing-a-long-and-history. Retrieved March 25, 2023.

56. Charles Baron De Montesquieu. 2011 (1748). *The Spirit of Laws.* New York: Cosimo.

Chapter 5:

Basic Bitch

1. Michael Adams. 2009. *Slang: The People's Poetry*. Oxford: Oxford University Press.
2. Hannah Seligson. 2013. "Laughing All the Way to the Bank." *The New York Times*. June 26. www.nytimes.com/2013/06/27/fashion/laughing-all-the-way-to-the-bank.html.
3. CNN Com Wire Service. 2021. "'Biatch' Is a Term of Endearment, Says Lawyer for Rioter in Pelosi's Office." *The Mercury News*. April 26. www.mercurynews.com/2021/04/26/biatch-is-a-term-of-endearment-says-lawyer-for-rioter-in-pelosi-office/. Retrieved April 4, 2023.
4. Hannah Gadsby. 2020. *Douglas*. Netflix. www.netflix.com/title/81054700.
5. Soraya Nadia McDonald. 2015. "'Happy Kanye' Makes an Appearance at the Grammys. Sort of." *The Washington Post*. www.washingtonpost.com/news/morning-mix/wp/2015/02/09/is-this-what-happy-kanye-looks-like/. Retrieved April 6, 2023.
6. C. Fabian Benitez-Quiroz, Ronnie B. Wilbur and Aleix Martinez. 2016. "The Not Face: A Grammaticalization of Facial Expressions of Emotion." *Cognition* 150, 77–84.
7. ABC News. 2014. "Why Kim Kardashian Says She Doesn't Smile 'Too Often.'" December 30. https://abcnews.go.com/Entertainment/kim-kardashian-smile/story?id=27902456.
8. Jess Cartner-Morley. 2015. "'Basic': The Biggest Insult of 2015." *The Guardian*. December 23. www.theguardian.com/fashion/2015/dec/23/basic-insult-kate-moss-lil-wayne-sylvia-plath. Retrieved April 6, 2023.
9. Sylvia Plath. 2007. *The Unabridged Journals of Sylvia Plath 1950–1962*. New York: Anchor Books.
10. Jon Fine. 2016. *Your Band Sucks: What I Saw at Indie Rock's Failed Revolution (But Can No Longer Hear)*. New York: Penguin.
11. *Urban Dictionary*. www.urbandictionary.com/define.php?term=Bitch+Please.
12. NewsRadio. 1996. "Physical Graffiti." Season 2, Episode 17. Aired March 24.
13. Eric Partridge. 2015 (1949). *A Dictionary of the Underworld: British and American*. New York: Allen & Unwin.
14. Jesse David Fox. 2014. "The Bittersweet Legacy of Dave Chappelle's 'I'm Rick James, Bitch.'" *Vulture*. February 11. www.vulture.com/2014/02/10th-anniversary-of-im-rick-james-bitch-chappelle.html. Retrieved April 15, 2023.

15. Kylie Cheung. 2022. "Elon Musk Yells 'I'm Rich, Bitch,' Is Booed into Oblivion at Dave Chappelle Show." *Jezebel.* December 12. https://jezebel.com/elon-musk-yells-im-rich-bitch-is-booed-into-oblivion-1849882626. Retrieved April 6, 2023.

16. Vanessa Grigoriadis. 2015. "Madonna Talks 'Fifty Shades of Grey' ('Not Very Sexy'), the Pope and Why the 'Word Police Can F— Off'". *Billboard.* February 13. www.billboard.com/music/music-news/madonna-interview-rebel-heart-50-shades-of-grey-pope-word-police-6472671/. Retrieved April 9, 2023.

17. Mahmood Fazal. 2018. "Talking to the Guy Who Invented the Word 'Meme': Richard Dawkins". *Vice.* May 8. www.vice.com/en/article/d35ana/talking-to-the-guy-who-invented-the-word-meme-richard-dawkins. Retrieved October 2, 2023.

18. Marcia Moody. 2014. *Harry: A Biography.* London: Michael O'Mara.

19. Langston Hughes. 2015 (1940). *The Big Sea: An Autobiography.* New York: Farrar, Straus and Giroux.

20. Eugène Sue. 1845. *De Rohan; Or, the Court Conspirator: From the French of "Latréaumont."* London: W. Dugdale.

21. Sara Rimer. 1982. "Brainchild." *The Washington Post.* October 10. p. 17.

22. BBC News. 2016. "US Election: Full Transcript of Donald Trump's Obscene Videotape." October 16. www.bbc.com/news/election-us-2016-37595321. Retrieved April 9, 2023.

23. Nick Wing. 2016. "Donald Trump Clearly Doesn't Understand How Dogs Work: The Donald's Simile Game Is Weak 'Like a Dog.'" *Huffington Post.* February 9. https://www.huffingtonpost.co.uk/entry/donald-trump-dogs_n_56b99a5ee4b04f9b57dafa54. Retrieved April 9, 2023.

24. Kris Macomber, Christine Mallinson and Elizabeth Seale. 2011. "'Katrina That Bitch!' Hegemonic Representations of Women's Sexuality on Hurricane Katrina Souvenir T-Shirts." *Journal of Popular Culture* 44 (3), 525–544.

25. Joan L. Nixon. 2011. *The Other Side of Dark.* New York: Delacorte Press.

26. Frank McCourt. 2005. *Teacher Man: A Memoir.* New York: Scribner.

27. Brandee J. Tecson. 2005. "Rick James Has a Bitch of a Time Running for City Council. 'Chappelle Show' Fans Pilfer Signs from Mississippi Candidate." *MTV.* April 13. www.mtv.com/news/9n96pw/rick-james-has-a-bitch-of-a-time-running-for-city-council. Retrieved April 18, 2023.

28. Richard Price. 2011. *Ladies' Man: A Novel.* New York: Picador.

29. Faye Kellerman. 2019. *Stalker* (Peter Decker and Rina Lazarus Series, Book 12). New York: HarperCollins.

30. Bernard Wolfe and Mezz Mezzrow. 2016. *Really the Blues.* New York: New York Review Books.
31. Les Tomkins. 1966. "Disc Discussion." *Crescendo. The Musician's Viewpoint.* December issue, p. 27.
32. John Glatt. 2014. *Live at the Fillmore East and West: Getting Backstage and Personal with Rock's Greatest Legends.* Essex, CT: Lyons Press.
33. Elaine Costello. 2008. *Random House Webster's Compact American Sign Language Dictionary.* United Kingdom: Diversified Publishing.
34. Peter Sundkvist, Gunnel Melchers and Philip Shaw. 2019. *World Englishes.* Oxford: Taylor & Francis.
35. Tej K. Bhatia. 2015. *Colloquial Hindi.* London: Taylor & Francis.
36. Nania Bhardwaj. 2020. "Tennessee senator slurs China for cheating and stealing, and top Chinese journalist calls her a 'lifetime b----'." *Business Insider.* December 4. www.businessinsider.com/tennessee-senator-called-lifetime-bitch-by-top-chinese-journalist-2020-12. Retrieved April 22, 2023.
37. Manya Koetse. 2013. "The 'Green Tea Bitch' – Stereotyping Chinese Women." *What's on Weibo.* April 10. www.whatsonweibo.com/dangerous-women-the-green-tea-bitch/. Retrieved April 22, 2023.
38. *The Alternative Cantonese Dictionary.* 2004. https://www.yumpu.com/en/document/view/11504859/the-alternative-cantonese-dictionary.
39. Massoud Hayoun. 2012. "What's China Talking About Today? Mocking Women's Day." *The Atlantic.* March 8. www.theatlantic.com/international/archive/2012/03/what-chinas-talking-about-today-mocking-womens-day/254133/. Retrieved October 9, 2023.
40. Angielsko-Polski Słownik. 2011. *Cambridge Learner's Dictionary English–Polish.* Cambridge: Cambridge University Press.
41. Julia Dabis. 2022. "Putin Crony Melts Down After Airing Wrong Clip of Soldiers Calling Russia 'a Bitch.'" *The Daily Beast.* https://www.thedailybeast.com/state-tv-host-vladimir-solovyov-melts-down-after-airing-wrong-clip-of-ukrainians-calling-russia-a-bitch. Retrieved April 24, 2023.
42. Yael Brygel. 2015. "Klafte Brightens up Downtown." *Jerusalem Post.* July 30. www.jpost.com/in-jerusalem/klafte-brightens-up-downtown-410604. Retrieved October 18, 2023.
43. Myriam Dali and Eric Mathieu. 2021. *A Theory of Distributed Number.* Netherlands: John Benjamins.
44. Bernd Heine and Derek Nurse. 2000. *African Languages: An Introduction.* Cambridge: Cambridge University Press.

45. Peter Mwaura. 2015. "Kenyans Not Ready to Be Compared to Dogs; Forget Idioms, It's Still an Insult!" *Nation.* February 26. https://nation.africa/kenya/blogs-opinion/opinion/kenyans-not-ready-to-be-compared-to-dogs-forget-idioms-it-s-still-an-insult-1071560. Retrieved April 28, 2023.

46. Jane Sunderland, Lia Litosseliti, Lilian Lem Atanga and Sibonile Ellece. 2013. *Gender and Language in Sub-Saharan Africa: Tradition, Struggle and Change.* Netherlands: John Benjamins.

47. Friedrich Kluge. 2015 (1883). "Petze." In *John Francis Davis, translation of the Etymological Dictionary of the German Language.* Andesite Press.

48. BBC. 2021. "Ville De Bitche: Facebook Mistakenly Removes French Town's Page." *BBC News.* April 13. www.bbc.com/news/world-europe-56731027. Retrieved April 29, 2023.

49. Eduardo Garcia. 2014. "The Unusual Name of a Champion Horse." *GGN.* February 6.

50. L.V. Anderson. 2014. "You're Doing It Wrong: Puttanesca Sauce." *Slate.* October 23.

51. John C. Wells. 2010. *English–Esperanto–English Dictionary.* New York: Mondial.

52. *Na'vi Dictionary.* https://dict-navi.com/en/.

53. Cristina Suárez-Gómez and Elena Seoane. 2016. *World Englishes: New Theoretical and Methodological Considerations.* Netherlands: John Benjamins.

54. Janet S. Shibamoto Smith and Shigeko Okamoto. 2004. *Japanese Language, Gender, and Ideology: Cultural Models and Real People.* New York: Oxford University Press.

55. Harry Hayes. 2017. "In the Remote Aboriginal Community of Yuendumu, Dogs Are Not Just Pets." *ABC News.* October 7. www.abc.net.au/news/2017-10-08/dogs-not-just-pets-in-remote-aboriginal-community-of-yuendumu/8998016. Retrieved April 29, 2023.

Index